IDENTITY AND THE SECOND GENERATION

IDENTITY AND THE SECOND GENERATION

HOW CHILDREN OF IMMIGRANTS FIND THEIR SPACE

EDITED BY

FAITH G. NIBBS
AND
CAROLINE B. BRETTELL

VANDERBILT UNIVERSITY PRESS
NASHVILLE

© 2016 by Vanderbilt University Press
Nashville, Tennessee 37235
All rights reserved
First printing 2016
This book is printed on acid-free paper.

Library of Congress Cataloging-in-Publication Data on file
LC control number 2015001075
LC classification number JV6344.I34 2015
Dewey class number 305.23—dc23

ISBN 978-0-8265-2068-5 (hardcover)
ISBN 978-0-8265-2069-2 (paperback)
ISBN 978-0-8265-2070-8 (ebook)

CONTENTS

Acknowledgments

This book had its beginnings as a panel on the second-generation children of immigrants at the 2012 annual meeting of the American Anthropological Association. We want to thank the many contributors, some of whom participated in the original panel and others who later volunteered chapters for the volume as it developed. All the authors brought their academic expertise and ethnographic knowledge to bear on the production of a unified and focused volume. We would like to acknowledge in particular Louise Lamphere for agreeing to write an afterword. We are grateful to the anonymous reviewers who offered insightful comments that helped to improve the quality and coherence of the volume and to Eli Bortz, editor at Vanderbilt University Press, for his careful and patient stewardship of this project. We would also like to thank the many children of immigrants across the United States, Canada, and Europe who shared their time and experiences with us in order to generate a greater understanding of the spaces of identity they occupy. We are also grateful to Faith Nibbs's research assistant and graduate student at Southern Methodist University, Carrie Perkins, who helped in compiling the final material for publication. Finally, we would like to thank SMU and colleagues in the Department of Anthropology for providing a stimulating and supportive work environment.

IDENTITY AND THE SECOND GENERATION

INTRODUCTION

Faith G. Nibbs and Caroline B. Brettell

By the end of the first decade of the twenty-first century, there were close to seventeen million children of immigrants (defined as children under eighteen living with one foreign-born parent) in the United States (Batalova and Fix 2011). These children represented almost a quarter of all children in the United States. A German survey of similar date indicated that a third of all children in that country belonged to immigrant families, while in France it is estimated that the children of immigrants represent close to one-fifth of all children (Cebolla-Boado and Gonzalez-Ferrer 2008; Clauss and Nauck 2009).

On both sides of the Atlantic, there has been a growing interest in studies of this population, the so-called second generation (Portes and MacLeod 1996, 1999; Portes and Rumbaut 2001; Rumbaut and Portes 2001; Andall 2002; Hall 2002; Súarez-Orozco and Súarez-Orozco 2002; Súarez-Orozco and Todorova 2003; Kasinitz, Mollenkopf, and Waters 2004; Kim 2004; Alba 2005; Kim 2006; Thomson and Crul 2007; Heath et al. 2008; Kasinitz, Mollenkopf, Waters, and Holdaway 2008; Foner 2009; Alba and Waters 2011; Kasinitz, Matsumoto, and Zeltzer-Zubida 2011; Ziolek-Skrzypczak 2013; Ali and Gidley 2014; Heath 2014). Much of this work draws on aggregate data sets from large metropolitan areas and focuses on achievements against desired outcomes: rates of education, rates of employment, rates of intermarriage, and levels of language acquisition (Sakamoto and Woo 2007; Cruz 2008; Barban and White 2011; Capps and Fix 2012; Ludemann and Schwerdt 2013; Alba and Holdway 2013). Suárez-Orozco et al. (2008), for example, explore the impact of school on immigrant and second-generation youth, looking in particular at academic engagement and performance and searching for explanations for why many immigrant youth fall through the cracks while others outperform their native-born peers (see also Deaux et al. 2007; Portes and Fernández-Kelly 2008; and Kao et al. 2013). Perlmann (2005) compares the outcomes for the Italian second generation of a century ago with the Mexican second generation of today. On schooling, he concludes that Mexican youth of today lag further behind native whites than did their counterparts of a century ago—something that is then aggravated by their alarmingly high drop-out rate. Nevertheless, he is still seeing progress by comparison with the immigrant generation, and by comparison with the Italian youth of the past he identifies growing wage inequality as the most serious challenge to the progress of the children of

Mexican immigrants today. This, he concludes, may mean that economic assimilation happens more slowly—"four or five generations rather than three or four" (p. 124). However, a more recent study (Hao and Woo 2012), based on a sample of eleven thousand children from diverse backgrounds who were tracked from age thirteen into their early thirties, concludes that the children of immigrants are doing better than those with more deeply rooted family lineages in the United States. These advantages applied to both Asian and Hispanic children.

The second-generation literature also explores issues of ethnic self-identification, of how race in America is negotiated, of generational and cultural dissonance both in the United States and abroad, and of processes of change. Acculturation, assimilation, segmented assimilation, integration, incorporation, convergence, reactive ethnicity, lived hybridity, and immigrant youth culture are all analytical concepts that have been used (Portes and Zhou 1993; Maira 2002; Min 2002; Butterfield 2004; Lee 2004; Alba 2005; Aparicio 2007, 2008; Dhingra 2007; van Niekerk 2007; Rumbaut 2008; Shankhar 2008; Brettell and Nibbs 2009; Maira 2009; Heath 2014). Often change, particularly in relation to assimilation, is theorized dichotomously—the children of immigrants are either assimilated into the social life of the host society or they resist absorption.

The essays in this collection explore in greater depth the social worlds or spaces of identity for the children of immigrants, thereby linking this volume to the broader spatial turn in the social sciences. This spatial approach emphasizes the relationship between space, social relationships, and social identities, hence formulating spaces as fields of interaction, human experience, and belonging (Low 1996; Olwig and Hastrup 1997; Nibbs 2014). Some of these spaces are structural contexts where the identities (including the right to belong) of the children of immigrants are to some extent shaped for them; others are arenas where the children of immigrants have more agency to construct their own identities. For example, Abu El-Haj (2009) describes community arts as an alternative space for citizenship education among Arab American youth. Several of the authors in this volume are particularly attentive to the dimensions of discourse that characterize the spaces of identity for immigrant youth.

The approach in this volume is cross-national and includes studies of the children of immigrants in the United States, Canada, and several European contexts. This cross-national approach poses a methodological problem, as Portes (1994) and more recently Andall (2002) have argued. Methods of data collection and definitions of whom to count and include when referring to the second generation are not consistent between countries. In the United States, early definitions of the second generation were loosely defined as immigrant children "either born here [USA] or brought from the mother country at an early age" (Child 1943: 3). Later definitions defined them as "native-born children with at least one foreign-born parent or children born aboard who came to the United States before age 12" (Portes and Zhou 1993: 75). In the European context, British scholar

Modood (1997) lumps both native-born and fifteen-year-old foreign-born children together in the same analysis.

A more precise definition was offered by Rumbaut (1997) based on research on the children of immigrants to the United States. He distinguished between those persons born in a country with one or both parents born outside the United States including its territories of Puerto Rico, Guam, the Virgin Island, and American Samoa (second generation), and a "1.5 generation," defined as persons born abroad who came to the United States as children. More recently, Karthick Ramakrishnan (2004) has introduced an additional category, the "2.5 generation," which he defines as children with only one parent born in a foreign country. He argues that the experiences of these children are significantly different from those with two native-born parents or two foreign-born parents and suggests they should therefore be distinguished from the so-called second generation.

Beyond the myriad categorizations of children of immigrants, varying policy distinctions can also pose a problem for comparative research derived from statistical sampling from census records. In Canada, for example, the census asks for the birthplace of parents and children to distinguish among generation groups (Boyd and Grieco 1998). However, in Italy, migrants' children assume their parents nationality until they reach adulthood. "This means that a recently-arrived 16 year old from Sierra Leone is statistically indistinguishable from a 16 year old of Sierra Leonean origin who was born in Italy" (Andall 2002: 390). Likewise in France, the statistical "immigrant" category includes only the foreign born regardless of whether they arrived in France as adults or children (Simon 2003). Moreover, the sociopolitical significance of these labels may have profound effects on the identity of the children of immigrants, adding to the conceptual complexity of these categories. While the essays in this volume consider the experiences of the children of immigrants, broadly but not necessarily exclusively defined as "second generation," in a range of host societies, each contributor outlines exactly who they are referring to in their particular analysis in relation to their research location and data. We think that this expansive approach to the children of immigrants is necessary given the diversity of definitions and policies directed toward young people of "foreign" ancestry.

In addition to drawing broadly on the burgeoning literature on the children of immigrants, this collection also draws theoretically on work that links social spaces or sites to the politics of identity (Keith and Pile 1993). In his analysis of modern anxieties in the Pacific, Besnier (2011: 17) writes about sites that animate the "structures of power and the ideological scaffolding propping these structures." He continues, "a site is thus not just the location where social action takes place but also the context whose ideological and structural configuration authorizes specific forms of social action, and the latter in turn reinforces the ideological scaffolding of the site." From this perspective, spaces or sites are formulated as territories of meaning, empowerment, and negotiation. In broader terms this approach is inspired by Homi Bhabha's formulation of the third space as a site where new signs of identity and innovative forms of collaboration and contestation can be initiated (Bhabha 1994: 1).

Immigration scholars of both the first and the second generation have also explored issues of belonging, often thought of in migration literature as a singular movement of the immigrant from being deterritorialized to becoming reterritorialized, or from being detached from a host community to becoming attached (see Probyn1996; Fortier 2000; Mandel 2008; Reed-Danahay and Brettell 2008; Getrich 2008; Crul and Schneider 2010). However, Nibbs (2014: 223–24) in her work on Hmong refugees, has demonstrated how belonging is "a multifaceted phenomenon that overlaps, intersects, and often conflicts with other social arenas where perceived togetherness is also desired." Her approach advances our thinking to consider how the social dynamics of fitting in are simultaneously represented in immigrant experiences that go beyond the immigrant/host dichotomy. Organized around a range of spaces of experience for the children of immigrants, this collection of essays continues to unpack how identities and senses of belonging are constructed and/or contested within the spaces of experience and how they can serve as sites of empowerment as well as sites of social control. Each chapter addresses in some way the barriers and/or bridges to belonging. This can range from the ways in which the identities of the children of immigrants may be selectively managed through policy or social networking, to the negotiation, translation, and physical realization of belonging at the individual level.

OUTLINE OF CHAPTERS

The book opens with an essay that takes a comparative and cross-generational approach to the study of second-generation experience, thereby emphasizing connections between time and space. Takeyuki Tsuda explores differences between cohorts of Japanese Americans. First are the second generation (*nisei*) who grew up prior to World War II. These children of immigrants were descended largely from agricultural immigrants from poor, rural Japan and grew up in an America that became increasingly hostile to their homeland and hence who, together with their parents, faced discrimination and eventually internment during the war. They had few transnational connections, and indeed many distanced themselves from their homeland as a result of their experiences as youth. By contrast, the postwar second generation (*shin-nisei*) are the offspring of much wealthier Japanese immigrants who have come to the United States as professionals or elite business expatriates. They have grown up in a globalized America and an America much more favorably disposed to their ancestral homeland than it was a generation earlier. Their associations with and attitudes toward their homeland are decidedly different and hence powerfully illustrate the significance of historical and generational space to the experience and identities of immigrant youth.

The Japanese have deep immigrant roots in America. Clearly so do the Chinese, and there were also smaller numbers of South Asians in the United States in the early twentieth century (Leonard 1997). In the 2010 census, the largest foreign-born populations in the United States, after Mexicans, were Filipinos and Indians. Immigrants from China, Vietnam, and Korea are also present in substantial numbers. In Chapter 2, Caroline Brettell focuses on Asian immigrant youth within the educational space of the American university. However, rather than addressing dimensions of achievement that have captured much of the scholarly attention so far, her emphasis is on programs and organizations that foster not only explorations of identity but also opportunities for learning leadership skills for the children of Asian immigrants. Drawing on a "community of practice" model and methods of participant observation on one university campus, Brettell offers first an analysis of ethnic student organizations as spaces of identity as well as places of civic engagement and sociality. This is followed by a case study of an annual conference, sponsored by the same university, that exposes the second generation to models of leadership that nudge participants to think about and become more aware of who they are and of the categories and stereotypes with which they might have to wrestle in the public spaces of American society.

While Brettell emphasizes how organizations and organizational activities provide social contexts that encourage the children of immigrants to think about dimensions of their own identity, she acknowledges that these are also spaces of sociality and places where connections and friendships can be formed. Indeed, it is perhaps more common among young people to rely on the intimacies of friendships—that is, personal spaces—to help them define who they are. The anthropology of friendship is a relatively new field of inquiry within the broader literature on social organization, and while it has a close association with research on social networks, immigration scholars have not fully interrogated friendship networks as spaces for the construction of identities. This is the research question that Lisa Haayen tackles in Chapter 3, drawing on her study of Mexican American youth who live in a highly diverse neighborhood (Pleasant Park) in the city of Dallas.

Haayen begins by drawing a conceptual distinction between ethnic identities and personal identities—the latter defined as developing an understanding of a unique self and best encapsulated by the comment of one of her research participants who stated, "My friends make me who I am." In Haayen's formulation, friendship relationships are social fields within which personal identity is being shaped and sanctioned by others who share a similar point of view. Her data show that despite the diversity of the neighborhood, the friendship networks of Mexican youth who live there are based on commonalities of age, geography, social class, and ethnicity. Living in friendship spaces where others understand who they are, "the real me," is empowering to these youth. It provides them, Haayen observes, with social validation.

Haayen accords her Mexican youth a good deal of agency in navigating their neighborhood and their friendships, and hence in the formation of their personal identities. Such agency is also reflected in Bruno Riccio's analysis of second-generation associational spaces in Chapter 5. But his attention is focused on associations founded within the public sphere for political purposes, including making claims of citizenship and the right to belong. His data is drawn from research in Italy in general, and the city of Bologna more specifically. Not only does he demonstrate that the organizational spaces of the second generation are quite different in mission from those of the first generation, but he also argues that they provide a platform for challenging racism and discrimination, and changing public attitudes toward immigrants. Riccio explores not only the physical dimensions of these organizations, but also their virtual dimensions. Some of the activities of these associations take place in the space of the Internet, and it is here, in these new political spaces, that members of this second generation find empowerment and the means to renegotiate their identities. However, members of the second generation also realize that in the on-the-ground physical associational spaces they can carry out more targeted political projects of belonging. Both are necessary to the larger project of reterritorialization and belonging within Italian social and cultural space.

Clearly the Internet has become a powerful virtual space for identity formation in general (Gibb 2002; Graham and Khosravi 2002; Clarke 2004) and for the children of immigrants in particular. Parker and Song (2007), for example, in research on British-born Chinese, explore the way in which use of the Internet facilitates the production of collective identity, the development of a sense of belonging in Britain, and political and social action. These authors observe that "in facilitating self-expression, the [web]sites have made British Chinese social identity an object of public deliberation to an unprecedented degree. . . . [These] discussion boards . . . are significant sites for the exploration of life as a minority in a multicultural society" (p. 1049). They go on to conclude that not only have these websites "become part of a networked infrastructure for friendships, relationships, social activities, charitable donations, and political interventions," they are also "helping to define an embryonic second-generation civil society" (p. 1059). In Chapter 4, Faith Nibbs continues this discussion by investigating how boundaries are maintained and negotiated among second-generation Hmong in the United States and Germany within the new kinds of social spaces created in cyberspace. Prior to ubiquitous Internet use, these youth could segregate their identities in different spheres, the public and private. However, as the Internet is bringing the private into the public, it melds these worlds in a way that limits their agency to create group boundaries between insiders and outsiders. In this way, she finds the World Wide Web an important emerging sphere where different diasporic subjectivities are being communicated and contested under new rules of engagement. She examines how these messages between members of the second generation are carried across broader diasporic societies and with what consequences, increasing our understanding of how the myriad social positions and cultural boundaries that exist across diasporas are shaped and reshaped through computer-mediated spaces.

The children of immigrants live in and negotiate not only the various personal, public, institutional, political, and virtual spaces of the society and culture in which they grow up but also the broader transnational social fields that link their homeland to their parents' homeland. Transnationalism has become a central analytical concept in studies of migration across a range of disciplines. For the most part, the transnational perspective facilitates an understanding of the extent to which as well as how first-generation immigrants have remained tied to their country of origin. Eventually, however, scholars began to explore whether or not the children of immigrants would retain the same attachments (Levitt and Waters 2002; Haller and Landolt 2005; Wessendorf 2007; Haikkola 2011; Levitt et al. 2011; Soehl and Waldinger 2012) and hence whether transnationalism "had a life" beyond the first generation. Do members of the second generation live and act within transnational spaces as their parents have?

In Chapter 6, Josiane Le Gall and Ana Gherghel present evidence from Portuguese Azorean children and grandchildren of immigrants living in Montreal that transnationalism exists beyond the first generation, albeit in different forms. Their exploration of the transnational spaces occupied by these youth uncovers the lived experiences of new cultural forms of transnationalism, explaining how and why they have replaced the political and economic ties of their parents. Operating in these transnational spaces, they argue, fosters a "transnational habitus" among second- and third-generation immigrants that is rooted in an attachment to their heritage. The homeland of their parents and grandparents serves as a symbolic resource for cultural practices and identity. Le Gall and Gherghel offer additional data to support the argument recently made by Levitt et al. (2011: 480) that some children of immigrants "remain connected to people and places around the world, albeit with varying degrees of frequency and strength. They draw upon cultural elements available at the various sites and levels of the transnational social fields they inhabit, accessing them through travel, technology and popular media and by participating in a variety of ethnic and religious organizations."

While Le Gall and Gherghel demonstrate how transnational ties are formed, mediated, and perpetuated through active social relationships, Linda Ho Peché, in Chapter 7, examines a form of emotional and spiritual transnationalism that fosters ties in the absence of active relationships in the homeland. Her research fits into a broader investigation of "roots migrants," for whom the homeland becomes a third space for articulating identity (Basu 2004, 2007; Potter 2005; Christou 2006; Wessendorf 2007). Through the firsthand account of a heritage tour in Pulau Galang, she demonstrates how the children of Vietnamese immigrants without direct and immediate knowledge of their parent's homeland are led through a carefully orchestrated heritage tour to figuratively and spiritually connect to ancestral spirits and, by extension, a collective past. Several of the individuals taking these tours fulfilled burial rites for relatives who had died in the camps, thus making these journeys a form of religious pilgrimage and the space of identity a religious space. While these trips are particularly important for families with filial obligations to fulfill, Ho Peché argues that they are also narrated to the participants and the broader Vietnamese diasporic community in the discursive rhetoric of "sacrifice and freedom." For example, in addition to organizing visits to refugee camps, the organizations that sponsor these trips also engage in active fund-raising to restore the many grave sites across Southeast Asia, and to erect memorials that commemorate the "boat people" experience. Ho Peché's work highlights an important link between the multiple identities of children of migrants and connections with an ancestral homeland that they forge for themselves as they go in search of roots and hence shape their own identities in a borderless spiritual space.

Chapters 1 through 7 emphasize in varying degrees the agency of the children of immigrants in shaping their own identities and senses of belonging in a variety of social and political spaces, both national and transnational. However, in many cases, various institutional and legal contexts are instrumental in influencing who these children are, even how they are "categorized." States have a responsibility to protect children but also to regulate them. While Brettell writes about an educational space that is meant to be empowering, educational spaces (and especially schools) have often been historically imagined by scholars as sites where migrants are "taught" to be citizens, but often in profoundly classed and racist ways (Bourdieu and Passerson 1990; Levinson et al. 1996; Hall 2002; Lukose 2009). In Chapter 8, Stéphanie Larchanché sheds light on how the categorization of children as "immigrant youth" problematizes the issue of legal status and cultural belonging for migrant children in France. Unlike Brettell, who emphasizes organizational contexts within university educational spaces, Larchanché draws on the cases studies of three schoolchildren to highlight the language of referrals to mental health care centers that is used in the institutional spaces of French schools. She demonstrates how cultural difference is perceived in these spaces, which in turn produce pathological situations for the children of immigrants who are often stigmatized as "difficult" or from difficult backgrounds. Schools, she argues, are sites of social control and ultimately therefore barriers to belonging. Further, cultural difference is used as a proxy for social inequality and class difference, and vice versa, depending on the particular case and context.

In the final chapter, Erin Moran, drawing on research in Ireland, tackles the treatment of migrant children seeking political asylum. In places, such as Ireland, where dramatic demographic shifts are challenging deeply held beliefs about national identity, social conflicts are expressed through debates over the role of the state, the purpose of government, and modes of governance, and how legal spaces operate and impact immigrant youth. The children of immigrants, particularly those of the 1.5 generation who may be in the host country without authorization, arriving with an adult, or those arriving without an adult, must reckon with legal definitions of who they are and of their right to belong and their claims to legal status and citizenship. Gonzales and Chavez (2012) draw on the concept of abjectivity (see Willen 2007) to explore the experiential dimensions of young people who have been raised as Americans but who come of age to confront the fact that they are undocumented and hence that their opportunities are limited and their status "wretched" and undeserving. They must, as these authors note, learn to live as illegals. However, as Erin Moran's analysis of Dublin asylum seeker Eluhanla shows, legal status is not static, and changes in status affect the way in which children understand and choose to perform their identity, which presents moral and political challenges in how the state relates to them. Moran illuminates the conflicts between issues that are driven by law and those that are driven by the welfare of a child. Ireland offers a particularly interesting case because in 2004 it repealed birthright citizenship—that is, citizenship accorded automatically by being born within a country no matter where one's parents were born. New laws stipulated that for a baby born in Ireland to be accorded Irish citizenship, at least one parent had to be an Irish citizen or both parents had to have been resident in Ireland for at least three years prior to the birth. In some sense this has limited the number of children who can be considered second generation with the full rights of citizens and hence impacts issues of belonging.

Collectively, the chapters in this book draw greater attention to a wide variety of sites or spaces of second-generation experience. In these sites, the children of immigrants may find that who they are is sometimes constructed by others; but they may equally operate in spaces where they find room to construct their own sense of who they are and how they belong. This book moves the research on the children of immigrants into a host of new or emerging areas of investigation: friendship, the participation in various organizations and associations, involvement in the public sphere, and the engagement with both virtual and transnational spaces. In her Afterword to the volume, Louise Lamphere not only teases out some themes that are common across groups of papers but also draws our attention to dimensions of the second-generation experience that require further attention. She also builds on the comments of some of the authors by offering her own assessment of the policy implications of the research presented in this volume.

REFERENCES

Abu El-Haj, Thea Renda. 2009. Imagining Postnationalism: Arts, Citizenship Education, and Arab American Youth. *Anthropology and Education Quarterly* 40 (1): 1–19.

Alba, Richard. 2005. Bright vs. Blurred Boundaries: Second-Generation Assimilation and Exclusion in France, Germany, and the United States. *Ethnic and Racial Studies* 28 (1): 20–49.

Alba, Richard, and Jennifer Holdway (eds.). 2013. *The Children of Immigrants at School.* New York: New York University Press.

Alba, Richard, and Mary C. Waters (eds.). 2011. *The Next Generation: Immigrant Youth in a Comparative Perspective*. New York: New York University Press.

Ali, Sundar, and Ben Gidley. 2014. Advancing Outcomes for All Minorities: Experiences of Mainstreaming Immigrant Integration Policy in the UK. *Migration Policy Institute Reports*, July. *www.migrationpolicy.org/research/advancing-outcomes-all-minorities-experiences-mainstreaming-united-kingdom*.

Andall, Jacqueline. 2002. Second-Generation Attitude? African-Italians in Milan. *Journal of Ethnic and Migration Studies* 28 (3): 389–407.

Aparicio, Ana. 2007. The Integration of the Second and 1.5 Generations of Moroccan, Dominican and Peruvian Origin in Madrid and Barcelona. *Journal of Ethnic and Migration Studies* 33 (7): 1169–93.

———. 2008. Contesting Race and Power: Second-Generation Dominican Youth in the New Gotham. *City and Society* 19 (2): 179–201.

Barban, Nicola, and Michael J. White. 2011. Immigrants' Children's Transition to Secondary School in Italy. *International Migration Review* 45 (3): 702–26.

Basu, Paul. 2004. Route Metaphors of "Roots-Tourism" in the Scottish Highland Diaspora. In *Reframing Pilgrimage: Cultures in Motion*, Simon Coleman and John Eade, eds., pp. 150–74. London: Routledge.

———. 2007. *Highland Homecomings*. London: Routledge.

Batalova, Jeanne, and Michael Fix. 2011. *Up for Grabs: The Gains and Prospects of First- and Second-Generation Young Adults*. Washington, DC: Migration Policy Institute.

Besnier, Niko. 2011. *On the Edge of the Global: Modern Anxieties in a Pacific Island Nation*. Stanford, CA: Stanford University Press.

Bhabha, Homi K. 1994. *The Location of Culture*. London, Routledge.

Bourdieu, Pierre. 1991. *Language and Symbolic Power*. Edited by John Thompson. Translated by Gino Raymond and Matthew Adamson. Cambridge, MA: Harvard University Press.

Bourdieu, Pierre, and Jean-Claude Passeron. 1990. *Reproduction in Education, Society and Culture*. Vol. 2. Translated by Richard Nice. London: Sage.

Boyd, Monica, and Elizabeth Grieco. 1998. Triumphant Transitions: Socioeconomic Achievements of the Second Generation in Canada. *International Migration Review* 32 (4): 853–76.

Brettell, Caroline B., and Faith G. Nibbs. 2009. Lived Hybridity: Second-Generation Identity Construction through College Festival. *Identities: Global Studies in Culture and Power* 16 (6): 678–99.

Butterfield, Sherri-Ann. 2004. "We're Just Black": The Racial and Ethnic Identities of Second-Generation West Indians in New York. In *Becoming New Yorkers: Ethnographies of the New Second Generation*, Philip Kasinitz, John H. Mollenkopf, and Mary C. Waters, eds., pp. 288–312. New York: Russell Sage Foundation.

Capps, Randy, and Michael Fix. 2012. *Young Children of Black Immigrants in America: Changing Flows, Changing Faces*. Washington, DC: Migration Policy Institute.

Cebolla-Boado, H., and A. Gonzalez-Ferrer. 2008. *La inmigración en España (2000–2007): De la gestión de flujos a la integración de los inmigrantes*. Madrid: Centro de Políticos y Constitucionales.

Child, Irvin. 1943. *Italian or American? The Second Generation in Conflict*. New Haven, CT: Yale University Press.

Christou, Anastasia. 2006. American Dreams and European Nightmares: Experiences and Polemics of Second-Generation Greek-American Returning Migrants. *Journal of Ethnic and Migration Studies* 32 (5): 831–45.

Clarke, Kamari. 2004. *Mapping Yoruba Networks: Power and Agency in the Making of Transnational Communities*. Durham, NC: Duke University Press.

Clauss, Susanne, and Bernhard Nauck. 2009. The Situation among Children of Migrant Origin in Germany. *Innocenti Working Paper*, no. 2009–14, Florence, UNICEF Innocenti Research.

Crul, Maurice, and Jens Schneider. 2010. Comparative Integration Context Theory: Participation and Belonging in New Diverse European Cities. *Ethnic and Racial Studies* 33 (7): 1249–68.

Cruz, Vanessa. *Educational Attainment of First and Second Generation Immigrant Youth*. 2008. Washington, DC: Urban Institute.

Deaux, Kay, Nida Bikmen, Alwyn Gilkes, Ana Ventuneac, Yvanne Joseph, Yasser A. Payne, and Claude M. Steele. 2007. Becoming American: Stereotype Threat Effects in Afro-Caribbean Immigrant Groups. *Social Psychology Quarterly* 70 (4): 384–404.

Dhingra, Pawan. 2007. *Managing Multicultural Lives: Asian American Professionals and the Challenge of Multiple Identities*. Stanford, CA: Stanford University Press.

Foner, Nancy. 2009. *Across Generations: Immigrant Families in America*. New York: New York University Press.

Fortier, Anne-Marie. 2000. *Migrant Belongings: Memory, Space, Identity*. Oxford: Berg.

Getrich, Cristina M. 2008. Negotiating Boundaries of Social Belonging: Second-Generation Mexican Youth and the Immigration Rights Protests of 2006. *American Behavioral Scientist* 52 (4): 533–56.

Gibb, Camilla. 2002. Deterritorialized People in Hyperspace: Creating and Debating Harari Identity over the Internet. *Anthropologica* 44 (1): 55–67.

Gonzales, Roberto G., and Leo R. Chavez. 2012. "Awakening to a Nightmare": Abjectivity and Illegality in the Lives of Undocumented 1.5 Generation Latino Immigrants in the United States. *Current Anthropology* 53 (3): 255–81.

Graham, Mark, and Shahram Khosravi. 2002. Reordering Public and Private in Iranian Cyberspace: Identity, Politics and Mobilization. *Identities: Global Studies in Culture and Power* 9 (2): 219–46.

Haikkola, Lotta. 2011. Making Connections: Second-Generation Children and the Transnational Field of Relations. *Journal of Ethnic and Migration Studies* 37 (8): 1201–17.

Hall, Kathleen D. 1995. "There's a Time to Act English and a Time to Act Indian": The Politics of Identity among British-Sikh Teenagers. In *Children and the Politics of Culture*, Sharon Stephens, ed., pp. 243–64. Princeton, NJ: Princeton University Press.

———. 2002. *Lives in Translation: Sikh Youth as British Citizens*. Philadelphia: University of Pennsylvania Press.

Haller, William, and Patricia Landolt. 2005. The Transnational Dimensions of Identity Formation: Adult Children of Immigrants in Miami. *Ethnic and Racial Studies* 28 (6): 1182–214.

Hao, Lingxin, and Han S. Woo. 2012. Distinct Trajectories in the Transition to Adulthood: Are Children of Immigrants Advantaged? *Child Development* 83 (5): 1623–39.

Heath, Anthony. 2014. Introduction: Patterns of Generational Change: Convergent, Reactive or Emergent? *Ethnic and Racial Studies* 37 (1): 1–9.

Heath, Anthony F., Catherine Rothon, and Elina Kilpi. 2008. The Second Generation in Western Europe: Education, Unemployment, and Occupational Attainment. *Annual Review of Sociology* 34: 211–35.

Kao, Grace, Elizabeth Vaquera, and Kimberly Goyette. 2013. *Education and Immigration*. Cambridge, UK: Polity Press.

Kasinitz, Philip, Noriko Matsumoto, and Aviva Zeltzer-Zubida. 2011. "I Will Never Deliver Chinese Food": The Children of Immigrants in the New York Metropolitan Labor Force. In *The Next Generation: Immigrant Youth in a Comparative Perspective*, Richard Alba and Mary C. Waters, eds., pp. 229–48. New York: New York University Press.

Kasinitz, Philip, John H. Mollenkopf, and Mary C. Waters (eds.). 2004. *Becoming New Yorkers: Ethnographies of the New Second Generation*. New York: Russell Sage Foundation.

Kasinitz, Philip, John H. Mollenkopf, Mary C. Waters, and Jennifer Holdaway. 2008. *Inheriting the City: The Children of Immigrants Come of Age*. New York: Russell Sage Foundation.

Keith, Michael, and Steve Pile (eds.). 1993. *Place and the Politics of Identity*. New York: Routledge.

Kim, Dae Young. 2004. Leaving the Ethnic Economy: The Rapid Integration of Second-Generation Korean Americans in New York. In *Becoming New Yorkers: Ethnographies of the New Second Generation*, Philip Kasinitz, John H. Mollenkopf, and Mary C. Waters, eds., pp. 154–88. New York: Russell Sage Foundation.

———. 2006. Stepping-Stone to Intergenerational Mobility? The Springboard, Safety Net, or Mobility Trap Functions of Korean Immigrant Entrepreneurship for the Second Generation. *International Migration Review* 40 (4): 927–62.

Lee, Sara S. 2004. Class Matters: Racial and Ethnic Identities of Working and Middle-Class Second-Generation Korean Americans in New York City. In *Becoming New Yorkers: Ethnographies of the New Second Generation*, Philip Kasinitz, John H. Mollenkopf, and Mary C. Waters, eds., pp. 313–38. New York: Russell Sage Foundation.

Leonard, Karen I. 1997. *The South Asian Americans*. Westport, CT: Greenwood.

Levinson, Bradley A. U., Douglas E. Foley, and Dorothy C. Holland, ed. 1996. *The Cultural Production of the Educated Person: Critical Ethnographies of Schooling and Local Practice.* New York: State University of New York Press.

Levitt, Peggy, and Mary C. Waters. 2002. *The Changing Face of Home: The Transnational Lives of the Second Generation.* New York: Russell Sage Foundation.

Levitt, Peggy, Kristen Lucken, and Melissa Barnett. 2011. Beyond Home and Return: Negotiating Religious Identity across Time and Space through the Prism of the American Experience. *Mobilities* 6 (4): 467–82.

Louie, Vivian. 2004. "Being Practical" or "Doing What I Want": The Role of Parents in the Academic Choices of Chinese Americans." In *Becoming New Yorkers: Ethnographies of the New Second Generation*, Philip Kasinitz, John H. Mollenkopf, and Mary C. Waters, eds., pp. 79–114. New York: Russell Sage Foundation.

Low, Setha. 1996. Spatializing Culture: The Social Production and Social Construction of Public Space. *American Ethnologist* 23 (4): 861–79.

Ludemann, Elke, and Guido Schwerdt. 2013. Migration Background and Educational Tracking: Is There a Double Disadvantage for Second-Generation Immigrants? *Journal of Population Economics* 26 (4): 455–81.

Lukose, Ritty A. 2009, *Liberalization's Children: Gender, Youth, and Consumer Citizenship in Globalizing India.* Durham, NC: Duke University Press.

Maira, Sunaina Marr. 2002. *Desis in the House: Indian American Youth Culture in New York City.* Philadelphia: Temple University Press.

———. 2009. *Missing: Youth, Citizenship and Empire after 9/11.* Durham, NC: Duke University Press.

Mandel, Ruth. 2008. *Cosmopolitan Anxieties: Turkish Challenges to Citizenship and Belonging in Germany.* Durham, NC: Duke University Press.

Min, Pyong Gap (ed.). 2002. *The Second Generation: Ethnic Identity among Asian Americans.* Walnut Creek, CA: AltaMira.

Modood, T. 1997. Qualifications and English Language. In *Ethnic Minorities in Britain*, T. Modood, R. Berthoud, J. Lakey, J. Nazroo, P. Smith, S. Virdee, and S. Beishon, eds., pp. 60–82. London: Policy Studies Institute.

Nibbs, Faith G. 2014. *Belonging: The Social Dynamics of Fitting In as Experienced by Hmong Refugees in Texas and Germany.* European Monograph Series. Durham, NC: Carolina Academics Press.

Olwig, Karen Fog, and Kirsten Hastrup (eds.). 1997. *Siting Culture: The Shifting Anthropological Object.* New York: Routledge.

Papastergiadis, N. 1997. Tracing Hybridity in Theory. In *Debating Cultural Hybridity: Multi-cultural Identities and the Politics of Anti-racism.* P. Werbner and T. Modood, eds., pp. 257–81. London: Zed Books.

Parker, David, and Miri Song. 2007. Inclusion, Participation and the Emergence of British Chinese Websites. *Journal of Ethnic and Migration Studies* 32 (7) 1043–61.

Perlmann, Joel. 2005. *Italians Then, Mexicans Now: Immigrant Origins and Second-Generation Progress, 1890–2000.* New York: Russell Sage Foundation.

Portes, Alejandro. 1994. Introduction: Immigration and Its Aftermath. *International Migration Review* 28 (4): 632–39.

Portes, Alejandro, and Patricia Fernández-Kelly. 2008. No Margin for Error: Educational and Occupational Achievement among Disadvantaged Children of Immigrants. *Annals of the American Academy of Political and Social Science* 620: 12–36.

Portes, Alejandro, and Dag MacLeod. 1996. Educational Progress of the Children of Immigrants: The Roles of Class, Ethnicity, and School Context. *Sociology of Education* 69 (4): 255–75.

———. 1999. Educating the Second Generation: Determinants of Academic Achievement among the Children of Immigrants in the United States. *Journal of Ethnic and Migration Studies* 25 (3): 373–96.

Portes, Alejandro, and Rubén G. Rumbaut. 2001. *Legacies: The Story of the Immigrant Second Generation.* Berkeley: University of California Press; New York: Russell Sage Foundation.

Portes, Alejandro, and Min Zhou. 1993. The New Second Generation: Segmented Assimilation and Its Variants among Post-1965 Immigrant Youth. *Annals of the American Academy of Political and Social Sciences* 530 (1): 74–98.

Potter, Robert B. 2005. Young, Gifted and Black: Second-Generation Transnational Return Migrants to the Caribbean. *Progress in Development Studies* 5 (3): 213–36.

Probyn, Elspeth. 1996. *Outside Belongings.* New York: Routledge.

Ramakrishnan, Karthick. 2004. Second-Generation Immigrants? The "2.5 Generation" in the United States. *Social Science Quarterly* 85 (2): 380–99.

Reed Danahay, Deborah and Caroline B. Brettell (eds.). 2008. *Citizenship, Political Engagement, and Belonging: Immigrants in Europe and the United States.* New Brunswick, NJ: Rutgers University Press.

Rumbaut, Rubén G. 1997. Ties That Bind: Immigration and Immigrant Families in the United States. In *Immigration and the Family*, Alan Booth, Ann Crouter, and Nancy Landale, eds., pp. 3–45. Mahwah, NJ: Lawrence Erlbaum Associates.

———. 2008. Reaping What You Sow: Immigration, Youth, and Reactive Ethnicity. *Applied Developmental Science* 12 (2): 108–11.

Rumbaut, Rubén G., and Alejandro Portes (eds.). 2001. *Ethnicities: Children of Immigrants in America.* Berkeley: University of California Press; New York: Russell Sage Foundation.

Sakamoto, Arthur, and Hyeyoung Woo. 2007. The Socioeconomic Attainments of Second-Generation Cambodian, Hmong, Laotian, and Vietnamese Americans. *Sociological Inquiry* 77 (1): 44–75.

Shah, Bindi. 2008. The Politics of Race and Education: Second-Generation Laotian Women Campaign for Improved Educational Services. *Social Justice* 35 (2): 100–18.

Shah, Svati P. 2009. Making Sense of the Second Generation. *Economic and Political Weekly* 44 (30): 14–17.

Shankar, Shalini. 2008. *Desi Land: Teen Culture, Class, and Success in Silicon Valley.* Durham, NC: Duke University Press.

Simon, Patrick. 2003. "France and the Unknown Second Generation: Preliminary Results on Social Mobility. *International Migration Review* 37 (4): 1091–119.

Soehl, Thomas, and Roger Waldinger. 2012. Inheriting the Homeland? Intergenerational Transmission of Cross-Border Ties in Migrant Families. *American Journal of Sociology* 118 (3): 778–813.

Suárez-Orozco, Carola, and Marcelo M. Suárez-Orozco. 2002. *Children of Immigration*. Cambridge, MA: Harvard University Press.

Suárez Orozco, Carola, Marcelo M. Suárez Orozco, and Irina Todorova. 2008. *Learning in a New Land: Immigrant Students in American Society*. Cambridge, MA: Belknap Press of Harvard University Press.

Suárez-Orozco, Carola, and Irina L.G. Todorova. 2003. Understanding the Social Worlds of Immigrant Youth. Special issue of *New Directions for Youth Development* 100 (Winter).

Thomson, Mark, and Maurice Crul. 2007. The Second Generation in Europe and the United States: How Is the Transatlantic Debate Relevant for Further Research on the European Second Generation? *Journal of Ethnic and Migration Studies* 33 (7): 1025–41.

van Niekerk, Mies. 2007. Second-Generation Caribbeans in the Netherlands: Different Migration Histories, Diverging Trajectories. *Journal of Ethnic and Migration Studies* 37 (7): 1063–81.

Vermeulen, Hans, and Joel Perlmann (eds.). *Immigrants, Schooling and Social Mobility: Does Culture Make a Difference?* Basingstoke: MacMillan.

Wessendorf, Susanne. 2007. Roots Migration: Transnationalism and Return among Second-Generation Italians in Switzerland. *Journal of Ethnic and Migration Studies* 37 (7): 1083–102.

Willen, Sarah. 2007. Toward a Critical Phenomenology of "Illegality," State Power, Criminality and Abjectivity among Undocumented Migrant Workers in Tel Aviv, Israel. *International Migration* 45 (3): 8–38.

Wilpert, Czarina. 1988. From One Generation to Another: Occupational Position and Social Reproduction—Immigrant and Ethnic Minorities in Europe. In *Entering the Working World*, Czarina Wilpert, ed., pp. 1–23. Aldershot: Gower.

Ziolek-Skrzypczak, Magdalena. 2013. Integrating Immigrant Youth: Transatlantic Perspectives. *Migration Information Source*, September.

1 HISTORY AND THE SECOND GENERATION

Differences between Prewar and Postwar Japanese American Nisei

Takeyuki (Gaku) Tsuda

INTRODUCTION: GENERATIONAL SPACES

For quite some time, the leaders of the Japanese American community have been concerned about the steady decline in participation among youth in Japanese American organizations such as the Japanese American Citizens League and various Japanese American historical societies.[1] This is especially a concern with the Japanese American Historical Society of San Diego. Started by a group of elderly second-generation Japanese Americans (*nisei*) who had been interned in concentration camps during World War II, the JAHSSD has a large membership and is more active than JACL in San Diego. Its annual meeting would draw close to two hundred members. However, the JAHSSD focuses primarily on historical events surrounding World War II and has struggled to attract Japanese American youth, who are either *yonsei* (fourth generation) or *shin-nisei* (the "new nisei" descendants of post–World War II Japanese immigrants in the United States). As a result, the members who attended JAHSSD events were almost exclusively elderly and middle aged.

In order to address the lack of youth participation, the JAHSSD and JACL decided to hold its 2006 annual Day of Remembrance event on the University of California at San Diego campus in collaboration with the university's Japanese American student organization, called the Nikkei Student Union. The Day of Remembrance is the annual commemoration of the internment of Japanese Americans during World War II and is held on February 19, the date on which President Franklin D. Roosevelt signed Executive Order 9066.

Unfortunately, the 2006 event was poorly organized. It was held in the central courtyard plaza of UCSD's student center. The speakers were mainly elderly nisei from JAHSSD who spoke at length about their experiences of being interned during World War II. They sat at a makeshift table on a stage in front of the student theater under a sign that advertised an upcoming performance of *The Vagina Monologues*. The event was constantly disrupted by the hustle and bustle of UCSD students, who were either walking through the plaza on their way to class or having lunch and conversations at nearby tables and paid no attention to what the speakers were saying. To make matters worse, music and announcements were blaring through the courtyard from another student organization trying to recruit new members, constantly threatening to drown out the Day of Remembrance speakers.

Although there were plenty of students in the courtyard, it was distressing to see how few Japanese American students had bothered to show up. Most of the audience members who had come specifically to attend the event were elderly nisei and older third-generation *sansei* mainly from JAHSSD and JACL. They listened intently to the speakers and reacted a number of times to what they were saying. Most of the handful of Japanese American students who were present were fourth-generation yonsei who were Nikkei Student Union board members. Partly because of the noise and distractions in the plaza, they were not paying attention to the speakers and mainly chatted among themselves. The general impression one received was of an older generation attempting to pass on their experiences and historical legacy to a younger generation, who had moved beyond the past and were too preoccupied with their daily lives to even notice.

However, most conspicuous in their absence were any shin-nisei students from the postwar second generation. Although the yonsei NSU board members were not listening to the speakers, at least they had come, perhaps out of respect for their elders. In contrast, the shin-nisei from NSU did not even bother to show up. "I've never attended Day of Remembrance events," one of them once told me. "In fact, I didn't even know what that was until I joined NSU. I feel no real connection to the internment of Japanese Americans, since my family didn't go through it. My family was in Japan during World War II. They were running away from American air raids over Tokyo."

Since the Japanese Americans are one of the oldest Asian American ethnic groups in the United States, there are some pronounced generational divisions within the community. Most notable is the division between the elderly, prewar nisei, whose Japanese parents immigrated to the United States during the 1910s and 1920s, and the younger, postwar shin-nisei generation, who are mainly a product of Japanese immigration after the 1960s. Although they are technically of the same second generation, the prewar nisei were shaped by their internment during World War II, a life-changing tragedy that continues to define who they are. It remains relevant to their current lives, especially through their participation in community events, their efforts at establishing memorials to commemorate it, and their attendance at periodic reunion events with others who were interned in the same concentration camp.

In contrast, the shin-nisei came of age mainly after the 1980s and are far removed from the prewar discrimination and struggles of the elderly nisei. Although they are definitely aware of the internment experience and its importance, having studied about it in school or visited remnants of the internment camps, they felt little personal connection to it since it was not part of their family's history. During a discussion about the Japanese American internment experience in the "Culture Forums" held by the Nikkei Student Union, one of the former shin-nisei board members was rather blunt about his different historical consciousness. "All of this focus about internment in the Japanese American community kind of alienates shin-nisei like me," he stated in front of the others. "I'm also Japanese American, but I have a different history. If other Japanese Americans don't see me as Japanese American because of this, that's OK. My family wasn't in the camps. They were in Japan and suffered during World War II. I feel much more connected to the Japanese war experience than I do to the internment [of Japanese Americans]."

Although the prewar nisei and shin-nisei are both second generation in terms of immigration, they are clearly from completely different generations in terms of history. In other words, they occupy different generational spaces of social belonging and identity because they are a product of different historical eras. The prewar generation of nisei are primarily the descendants of agricultural immigrants from poor, rural Japan who arrived in the United States after the turn of the twentieth century. They grew up during a period of increasing American hostility toward their ethnic homeland and discrimination against Japanese Americans, which led to their internment in concentration camps during World War II. They also had fewer opportunities to maintain transnational connections to their ethnic homeland. As a result, many of them eventually distanced themselves from their Japanese heritage, culturally assimilated to American society, and emphasized their national identity and loyalty as Americans.

In contrast, the postwar second generation are children of wealthier Japanese immigrants who came to the United States as professionals and elite business expatriates starting in the 1960s. The shin-nisei came of age in a multiethnic and increasingly globalized America after Japan's image in the United States had improved considerably because of its postwar economic prosperity and the popularity of Japanese commodities and popular culture. They therefore suffered much less discrimination and had many more opportunities to become transnationally engaged with their ethnic homeland. Unlike the prewar nisei, they maintain strong ties to their ethnic heritage and to Japan, have become fully bicultural, and have developed transnational identities. Therefore, because of their different formative historical experiences, the prewar nisei inhabit an exclusively assimilationist and nationalist space, whereas the postwar nisei construct their ethnicities and identities in a much more transnational space.

CONCEPTUALIZING IMMIGRANT AND HISTORICAL GENERATIONS

The concept of generations can be understood from both an immigrant and historical perspective. The immigration studies literature on the second generation uses the concept of generation in two ways. First, generations can refer to genealogical birth order within an immigrant family. Therefore, the first generation are the immigrant parents, and the second generation are their children. Many studies of the second generation classify generations only according to family birth order, so that all children of immigrants are members of the second generation regardless of whether they were born in the country of origin or the host country (e.g., Rumbaut and Portes 2001; Portes and Rumbaut 2001; Levitt and Waters 2002; Smith 2006; Kasinitz, Waters, Mollenkopf, and Holdaway 2008). However, immigrant generations also refer to distance from the country of origin (see also Kasinitz, Waters, Mollenkopf, and Holdaway 2008: 400; Foner 2009: 3). In this sense, the second generation includes only the children of immigrants who were born in the host country, who are further removed from the country of origin than their first-generation parents. The children of immigrants who were born in the country of origin but immigrated as youth and raised in the host country are therefore called the 1.5 generation, since they are in between the first-generation immigrant parents and the second generation in terms of distance from the origin country. This chapter adopts the latter definition of immigrant generation so that "second-generation Japanese Americans" refers only to those born in the United States to Japanese immigrant parents.

However, generation can also refer to a specific age group that is a product of a certain historical period. Such "historical generations" were born and grew up around the same time and have similar historical experiences. Therefore, generation can also refer to historical age cohorts, such as the prewar or postwar generation, the Baby Boomer generation, or Generation X. According to Karl Mannheim's seminal theoretical work on the subject (1952: chap. 7), generations are not based solely on biology or genealogy but are ultimately cohorts defined by common historical location. However, it is not simply shared historical experiences that define the members of a generation, but historical events that they experienced *during a young age*, which have a determining influence on the rest of their lives. Therefore, Mannheim pointed out that older and younger people who experience the same historical processes together are not members of the same generation. In this sense, historical generations are age cohorts who had similar formative historical experiences in childhood or youth. Mannheim is strongly implying that subsequent historical events do not have as decisive an impact on a generation's consciousness and identity as those it experienced when it first came of age.

A historically grounded conception of generation may be just as important as an immigration-based conception of generations in explaining similarities and differences within immigrant-origin ethnic groups (Eckstein 2002). There is no doubt that there are significant differences between the first and second immigrant generations in terms of educational achievement, cultural assimilation, socio-economic mobility, identity, and transnational engagement (e.g., see Perlmann and Waldinger 1997; Boyd and Grieco 1998; Levitt and Waters 2002; Rumbaut 2005; van Niekerk 2007). However, certain differences within an immigrant-origin ethnic group are the product of historical cohort differences and cannot be explained simply by an immigrant generation perspective based on family birth order or distance from the country of origin.

Of course, immigration studies about the second generation are not completely oblivious to historical generational differences. A number of researchers have noted the significant differences between the current second generation, whose immigrant parents arrived in the United States after the 1960s, and the second-generation descendants of the last great wave of immigrants in the late nineteenth and early twentieth centuries (Gans 1992; Portes and Zhou 1993; Perlmann and Waldinger 1997; Eckstein 2002; Levitt and Waters 2002: 13–14; Perlmann 2005; Portes et al. 2005: 1001–3; Rumbaut 2005: 1041–43). Although these studies appear to be purely historical comparisons and give the impression that the prewar second generation is no longer around, a good number of individuals from this earlier historical cohort are still alive today as elderly people and coexist with the postwar second generation. However, research on the contemporary second generation focuses exclusively on the descendants of post 1960s immigrants, and the author is not aware of any studies of the elderly prewar second generation.

There are a number of immigrant groups like the Japanese with a long history of immigration that spans both the pre- and postwar period such as the Chinese, Filipinos, Mexicans, Russians, and other eastern and southern Europeans. The contemporary second-generation descendants of these immigrant groups therefore have substantial members from both the pre- and postwar period so that the second immigrant generation consists of two different historical generations and age groups whose formative childhood experiences occurred during different time periods.[2] As a result, they continue to live in different historically constituted spaces of interaction and belonging today. I argue that such differences based on historical generation can be just as significant as the differences between the first and second immigrant generations. Therefore, for such ethnic groups, it is highly problematic to ignore such historical differences among members of the second generation simply because they share the same immigrant family birth order or distance from the ethnic homeland.

THE PREWAR NISEI: AMERICANIZATION AND NATIONALIST BELONGING

As members of the prewar historical generation, today's elderly Japanese American second generation was shaped by historical events pertaining to World War II, which placed them on an ethnic trajectory that led to very different assimilation and identity outcomes compared to the postwar shin-nisei. Because they grew up in an era of increasing anti-Japanese hostility leading up to World War II and were interned in concentration camps during the war as enemy aliens, they had to demonstrate their loyalty as Americans in order to avoid discrimination. As a result, they emphasized cultural assimilation over the retention of their ethnic heritage or transnational ties to Japan. Because of such formative historical experiences, the generational space that is the basis for their sense of ethnic identity and belonging remains an exclusively nationalist field of interaction.

JAPANESE AMERICAN INTERNMENT AND POSTWAR DISCRIMINATION

My prewar nisei interviewees were interned in concentration camps as children and teenagers and continue to have very strong recollections of their experience. The great irony of the internment experience, however, is that it was extremely difficult for the first-generation immigrant parents, but much less so for their second generation children. The parents often lost their homes, businesses, and jobs, and their families were uprooted, relocated, and locked up in concentration camps for years in desolate locations in California or Arizona with extreme temperatures. Not only were they forced to live in miserable and crowded barracks with no privacy, they often lost their former authority over their children in the camps and faced constant anxiety about their futures, causing some of them to suffer from psychological problems such as depression.

In contrast to the parents, the second-generation children were relatively shielded from the trauma and emotional suffering of the internment experience (often by the parents themselves). In fact, they enjoyed the activities for children in the camps and often spent their days playing with other Japanese American children. They were relatively free from parental control, and instead of spending much time with their parents, they often ate, played, and went to school with the other children (see also O'Brien and Fugita 1991: 76).

During the Day of Remembrance at UC San Diego, I was repeatedly struck by how none of the prewar nisei speakers had any traumatic, heart-wrenching stories to tell. Instead, they emphasized that the internment experience was "fun" and "like a hell of a long summer camp." Others spoke about how "we had a good time" and "didn't have the worries of our parents." Their stories were filled with accounts of playing with the other kids, sports and games, social groups and cliques, going to (or ditching) school, and sometimes with amusing anecdotes about daily camp life. There was little anger, indignation, and resentment, and the general attitude was that they made the best of a bad situation since there was not much they could do about it.

Such themes were also reflected in my interviews with the prewar second generation. "It was actually a safe environment," Ruth Mori, an elderly lady, recounted.

"All the kids were together, and we could play and study and didn't really have to listen to our parents. It was actually fun like a summer camp. We didn't find it that harsh of an environment, because we were too young to be really fully aware of what was going on. It didn't mean much to us at that time, you know. We were just like, OK, so here we are. So be it." Others emphasized the intense camaraderie among youth in the camps. "All my friends were Japanese [American] for the first time in my life, and I hung out with them all the time instead of my family," another nisei recalled. "I enjoyed it. We played every sport you could think of—basketball, softball, judo. I made lifelong friends that I still meet during reunions—it's a strong bond."

Although my other interviewees did not necessarily enjoy their camp experience, they did not characterize it as a true hardship. According to Kiyoshi Sakamura:

> It was a relatively easy life. It wasn't a hardship for me. Some would say the living conditions were really harsh. But so what? It was not true suffering. We always had three meals a day on time, a cot, and army blankets. It was an American-style concentration camp, not in the true sense of a concentration camp. We were just concentrated in one camp. It was really cold in the winter, but when you're fifteen years old, you don't really get cold because you are moving around all the time. The only real hardship was that we lost our freedom and couldn't leave the camp. But who was really thinking about the loss of our Constitutional rights at that time? Later, some got special permission to leave the camp.

However, even though the internment experience was not necessarily a traumatic hardship for the prewar second generation, it still had a major impact on their ethnic consciousness after the war. Kiyoshi expressed a common sentiment probably shared by others of his historical cohort:

> The experience wasn't that harsh, but you still realize, especially as you get older, that we were locked up during World War II because we were seen as enemy aliens. It didn't happen to the Germans or Italians, only to the Japanese Americans. Despite the fact that we were American citizens born and raised here, Americans saw us as the enemy, just because of the way we look. That stays with you your entire life, even to this day.

Other prewar nisei spoke about the discrimination they continued to face in American society after they were released from the internment camps. At the Day of Remembrance at UC San Diego, a couple of speakers implied that it was harder for Japanese American kids after they left camp because they reentered American schools, only to endure harassment, hostility, and constant teasing. According to one of the women speakers, "some of the kids called me names and threw rocks at me and yelled 'your people killed my father during the war!' They didn't seem to realize my family had nothing to do with the Japanese soldiers who fought against the Americans in the Pacific."

In my interviews, elderly nisei spoke about incidents where continued anti-Japanese sentiment after the war had a personal effect on them. One of the most poignant examples was recounted by Bob Nakamura:

> I was on active service for the air force [in the early 1950s] and had come back from overseas and was stationed in a little town by Buffalo, New York. We were part of the military police patrolling the town, and we took a break to have coffee. So the guy serves us coffee, and then he asks me, "Where are you from?" I said, "I'm from California." "Where were you born?" "California." "Where were your parents born?" I didn't say anything. He then says, "Are they from China? Korea?" I said, "No. My parents are from Japan." Then he suddenly goes, "I don't serve Japs!" and pulls the coffee away. I was stunned. Here I am wearing an American military uniform and had just been serving overseas, and I get treated like this!

Because internment and anti-Japanese sentiment right after the war had such a formative impact on the nisei, I often noticed that they remained more sensitive to lingering prejudice about Japanese and Japanese Americans even to this day compared to other Japanese Americans, although some of them mentioned they have not experienced discrimination recently. One elderly nisei woman clearly was uncomfortable talking about this when I broached the subject. "I stay away from deep conversations about such things," she said. "If they want to talk about such things, they can go to places where they can express it. That's not my thing. I'm sorry, I just stay away from those things."

Although much of the prejudice against people of Japanese descent is currently expressed in a jocular manner, it still impacts the prewar nisei in a very personal way, perhaps stirring up old memories. "Some people still use the Jap word," one of my interviewees noted. "I don't know if they do it jokingly or what, but it bothers me a lot. You don't want to hear it, even if it's in fun or jest and not directed at me specifically. It can get upsetting."

The prewar second generation are especially aware of continued prejudice connected to World War II, especially among American veterans who fought the Japanese in the Pacific. Even John Kusumoto, who claimed he was no longer concerned about prejudice against Japanese Americans and did not attribute the negative treatment he receives to his ethnicity, continued to be bothered by the behavior of one of his acquaintances, who served in the US Navy during World War II:

> He would always make these little remarks about the Japanese. It's done in a friendly fashion, but he makes jokes about two-man Japanese submarines [that attacked Pearl Harbor] or kamikazes and things like that. He seems to do it specifically to Japanese Americans. He's always kidding my Japanese American

friend from Hawaii too. And for a long time, every year on December 7, we'd get this nice, big fax or e-mail from him that says, "Remember Pearl Harbor!"

"WE EARNED THE RIGHT TO BE CALLED AMERICANS": NISEI REACTIONS TO DISCRIMINATION

The prewar nisei's experience of internment and anti-Japanese discrimination during and after World War II had a formative impact on their ethnic consciousness and national identities. When faced with marginalization and discrimination, ethnic minorities can respond in two ways (see Tsuda 2001). They can react against a discriminatory majority society by asserting their ethnic minority identity or national origins as an oppositional "counter-identity" (Tsuda 2003: chap. 3) or what Portes and Rumbaut call "reactive ethnicity" (2001: chap. 7). On the other hand, they can also react to negative majority treatment with a more accommodating, assimilation-oriented strategy in which they attempt to avoid discrimination by better incorporation and acceptance into majority society.

Second-generation Japanese Americans clearly adopted the second option by asserting their American national identities and claiming membership in the nation-state instead of strengthening their Japanese ethnic consciousness in opposition to American society. Since they are American-born citizens who had already been subject to the assimilation process, it was natural for them to respond to severe ethnic discrimination and incarceration by demonstrating to other Americans that they are just as loyal and patriotic to their country of birth, despite their Japanese descent. For a number of my prewar nisei informants, this was a deliberate act of strategic intentionality in an effort to overcome discrimination and prejudice and gain full recognition as Americans. "They really had a history of proving that they are American," a shin-nisei who grew up in the 1990s observed when reflecting on generational differences among Japanese Americans. "These people had to prove they were patriotic. Prove that they are white. So they had to leave their Japanese heritage behind."

Mike Oshima was also quite explicit about how the internment experience had affected his sense of ethnicity. "Internment made it quite clear to all of us that we weren't considered real Americans because of our Japanese ancestry, even if we are US-born citizens. In that sense, we had no choice but to become fully Americanized, to show that we *are* Americans. It was forced on us to think that way, and so I was like, 'by golly, I'm going to be that way!'"

After they were released from the internment camps, the prewar nisei had to assert their national identities as Americans in order to counter the racial discrimination they continued to face. For instance, when Bob was called a "Jap" and denied service at the coffee shop during his service in the US Air Force (described above), he responded by demanding that his status as an American be recognized: "I confronted this guy and told him, 'I don't care what you think of me, but I want you to respect the uniform I wear. Regardless of my ancestry, I am serving this country as an American.'" "The racial epithet, 'Jap,' became a rallying cry for nisei," Larry Honkawa recalled. "Because of racial discrimination, designating ourselves as Americans became necessary. Even before the internment, when the war clouds over the Pacific formed in the 1930s, some of us were already identifying ourselves as *Americans* of Japanese ancestry (AJAs for short), especially in Hawaii."

One of the very important ways in which Japanese Americans earned recognition as patriotic Americans was through their service in the US military both during and after World War II. They were initially categorized as enemy aliens after the Japanese attack on Pearl Harbor and were excluded from the draft. In addition, all soldiers of Japanese ancestry were removed from active service. However, the American government eventually reversed its decision and approved the formation of a segregated Japanese American combat unit because of the exemplary service of Japanese Americans in military intelligence as well as those who were discharged ROTC cadets assisting in the war effort. The government administered a controversial loyalty questionnaire to interned Japanese Americans asking whether they would be willing to serve in the US armed forces whenever ordered, and whether they would swear unqualified and sole allegiance to the United States and faithfully defend the country. Despite being interned as enemy aliens and having their fundamental rights as American citizens violated, many nisei men answered both questions in the affirmative.[3]

As a result, the 442nd Japanese American Regimental Combat Team was formed and sent to Europe, where the nisei soldiers fought heroically in order to prove their loyalty as Americans. Initially, the 442nd was an all-volunteer force, consisting mainly of Japanese Americans from Hawaii who were not interned (ten thousand enthusiastically volunteered and close to three thousand were inducted) along with fifteen hundred volunteers from the mainland United States who came from the internment camps. Eventually, the draft was instated for Japanese Americans, and a total of thirteen thousand served in the regiment. They quickly became known for fighting bravely at all costs (their motto was "Go for Broke") and saw some of the heaviest combat in both Italy and France, liberating a number of towns.

The 442nd's most famous battle was the rescue of the Texas "Lost Battalion," which was cut off and surrounded by German forces in eastern France near the German border. The battle is considered one of the most ferocious in the history of the US Army and ended in a mass suicide charge by the Japanese Americans in a final desperate attempt to rescue the Lost Battalion. Overall, the 442nd suffered over eight hundred casualties, including two hundred deaths, just to liberate 211 members of the Texas battalion. Even after the battle, they were not relieved and were ordered to advance further for eight more days. The 442nd eventually became the most decorated military unit in American history for its size and length of service and also had one of the highest casualty rates, earning 9,486 Purple Hearts (awarded to those wounded or killed in action).

The exploits of the 442nd helped Japanese Americans gain greater acceptance in American society after World War II. Jim Sakura, one of my interviewees who served in the 442nd, reflected on this as follows:

> I am proud of my service in the 442nd, although I don't talk about it much. After the war, people would come up to me and say, "Did you belong to that famous regiment during World War II?" and I'd say, "Yes, I was part of that." Then they'd say, "Oh, you boys were so wonderful!" People realized the Greatest Generation wasn't just whites. Japanese Americans sacrificed a lot for our country as well. I think it really changed perceptions of us.

Even those prewar nisei who were too young to serve in the 442nd shared similar sentiments. "Being a Japanese American is a matter of pride for me," Mike, a board member of the JAHSSD, stated during our interview. He continued as follows:

> It's because of what our generation was able to accomplish during the war years, especially the veterans. You know what they did, the sacrifices they made, and it was a matter of great pride for all of us. What they did made it so much easier for the rest of us to assimilate to American society. We earned our Americanness. Like our veterans memorial says, "Dedicated to all Japanese American veterans who defended their country for the right to be called Americans." Those are my words.

Because of their racialization as enemy aliens during World War II and the ethnic discrimination they experienced during this period, second-generation Japanese Americans therefore demanded inclusion in the nation-state by demonstrating their loyalty and patriotism as Americans. By emphasizing their national identity as Americans of Japanese ancestry, they were among the first Asian Americans to challenge racially exclusionary notions of national belonging where being American is associated with being racially white. When Bob, the former president of the JAHSSD, speaks about the internment of Japanese Americans to current high school students, he told me that he ends his talk by asking them: "What's an American supposed to look like? Tell me, what's an American supposed to look like? An American is what is in your head and your heart, not what you look like or the color of your skin. Look around you—there are other types of Americans than just white ones."

AMERICANIZATION AND THE WEAKENING OF ETHNIC HERITAGE

In addition to their desire to demonstrate their Americanness in a discriminatory environment, most second-generation Japanese Americans who grew up during the World War II period also did not have many opportunities to maintain their

Japanese cultural background. The postwar nisei generally felt that their parents did not put much pressure on them to maintain the Japanese language and culture. "I don't recall a whole lot of that in our family," John said. "There were a few displays in our home regarding Japan and things like that. But my family did not have any real reference to Japanese culture or anything. This is why I used to think we were more of an American family than a Japanese one." Most interviewees mentioned that their parents did not even insist that they attend Japanese school in the local community. "It was more something I did because the other nisei kids were doing it," Sally Sakumura noted. "My friends were going to go to Japanese school, so I went too."

Most of the prewar nisei grew up speaking some Japanese with their immigrant parents, but they did not retain their Japanese language abilities into adulthood. Although they went to a weekend Japanese school or took language classes in the Japanese American community, they did so only for one or two years in most cases. As a result, most of them reported that they could speak only a little Japanese or could hold only a very basic conversation in the language at best. In addition, they had forgotten how to read and write in Japanese.

The relative lack of cultural heritage and language retention among prewar second-generation Japanese Americans seems to be a product of both the history of Japanese immigration to the United States and the World War II era in particular. Although most prewar Japanese immigrants initially intended to be temporary sojourners and return to Japan after amassing wealth, they ended up remaining in America permanently. By the time their nisei children were coming of age, it was quite apparent that they would probably never return to Japan, which became even clearer as their social connections to Japan were cut off by World War II and their imprisonment in internment camps. The devastation Japan suffered as a result of the war also made the prospects of any possible future return to the homeland unlikely and undesirable.[4]

As a result, the prewar nisei assimilated to mainstream culture and became quite Americanized. In contrast to the current emphasis on multiculturalism and the maintenance of ethnic diversity, assimilation was the dominant ideology at the time and the expected and proper way for the second generation to become incorporated into American society. In fact, the parents of the prewar nisei often acknowledged and even encouraged the cultural assimilation of their children to American society, instead of pressuring them to retain the Japanese language and culture. "There was no real conflict with our parents because I think they were encouraging and pushing us to become more American," Mike observed. "They were like, 'This is your country.'"

"Without mentioning it, I think the message was already there about assimilating," Bob recalled. "Our parents had eight kids, and their names are George, Harry, Fred, Tom, Marion, Bob, Elsie, and Mary. All Americans names! And they came up with these names back in the 1920s and '30s when they couldn't even speak

English. It gives you the strong message they intended everyone to be American, whether they admitted it directly or not."

It is therefore quite apparent that the prewar lives of the nisei were mainly confined to a national space as Americans. In addition, they did not have many opportunities to develop transnational connections to Japan or construct transnational identities in which they simultaneously identify with both the United States and Japan. Like other members of the prewar immigrant second generation, it was harder for them to develop relations with their ethnic homelands because of the greater difficulty of international travel at the time and the lack of contemporary telecommunication networks, global mass media, and the Internet. In addition, the Japanese American nisei faced additional constraints that were a product of their historical situation that further reduced any possible transnational attachments to Japan. Although there is some evidence that the nisei during the interwar years (between World War I and II) did develop dual transnational identifications with both the United States and Japan (Ueda 2002),[5] the prewar nisei who are alive today came of age around World War II. Not only did rising anti-Japanese sentiment at the time and their internment as enemy aliens discourage them from affiliating transnationally with Japan, the Japanese American community also lost its transnational ties to Japan because of the war and their imprisonment in concentration camps.

THE LEGACY OF WORLD WAR II: CONTINUED NATIONALIST IDENTITIES

As members of the prewar historical generation, the formative experiences that the nisei had when they were young continue to inform their ethnic consciousness today. Therefore, they still conceive of their ethnic identity and sense of belonging in nationalist terms, and relatively few identified with their Japanese cultural heritage. Mike spoke about how the prewar period when he came of age had a formative impact that has lasted his entire life:

> I still feel more loyal as an American than others. It's because of the internment and all we went through in World War II. Like I go to a ball game, and I always stand up and put my hand over my heart and sing the national anthem, whereas other people are running around waving their hats and not taking it seriously. I don't take my Americanness for granted like them. It's something that I earned.

Despite the contemporary multicultural environment in the United States that cherishes ethnic diversity and cultural heritage, the prewar nisei unequivocally stated that they are fully or mostly American and do not consider themselves very Japanese. "Everything about me is strictly American," Bob declared. "I don't speak Japanese; I've never been to Japan. Number one, I'm American. I can't say I'm Japanese. I just look Japanese with a Japanese last name, but that's about it."

Only a couple of prewar nisei felt that there were aspects of themselves that may be a product of their Japanese cultural heritage. One was John, a retired manager at a local firm, who felt he was probably "100 percent American," but not as outgoing or as friendly as others. He also attributed his effective managerial skills possibly to his Japanese heritage but was ultimately not sure. "Maybe that is some of my Japaneseness coming out, but I'm really converting it to American business practices," he observed. "I've read some books on Japanese management style. Not that I'm following any particular one, but I may have incorporated some of that in my own management. But an American manager might do that as well." In fact, it was quite interesting that more *third-generation* Japanese Americans spoke about what they felt was the lingering impact of Japanese culture on their personalities.

I also noticed a common tendency among almost all the prewar nisei to deemphasize or not even mention their ethnicity or Japanese heritage to others, and simply live as "ordinary Americans." This is a product of their lingering ambivalence about their ethnic heritage from their prewar and immediate postwar experiences as well as the fact that they did not retain much of their parents' Japanese cultural background when they were growing up as youth. "I don't advertise that I'm Japanese," Ruth stated. "If they ask me, I'll tell them, but otherwise, I don't volunteer anything." Later in our conversation, she elaborated further: "It depends on who I'm talking with. If he's Caucasian, I say I'm an American. I make a strong point that I'm an American. I don't mention being Japanese descent. If I'm talking to another Asian, and they ask me, I say, yes, I'm Japanese descent, which I'm proud of. But I'd still tell him, I'm American. I never stress the Japanese part."

In this manner, the current identities and social interactions of the prewar nisei are still confined to a national space. In fact, they have not expanded their identities and interactions in transitional ways that would encompass both the United States and Japan despite postwar social transformations that would encourage them to do so. Prejudice and discrimination against Japanese Americans has largely subsided since World War II, and American attitudes toward Japan have dramatically improved because of the country's economic and political rise in the global hierarchy of nations and its continuing status as a longtime and staunch ally of the United States. In addition, there has been a shift from a previous assimilationist to an ethnic pluralism ideology that encourages immigrant-descent minorities to remain connected to and even recover their ethnic roots.

Nonetheless, the elderly Japanese American nisei I interviewed continue to be influenced by their formative youth experiences as part of the prewar historical generation, and they have not developed transnational ties or a stronger affiliation with Japan later in their lives. In general, they have not started studying Japanese, reconnected with their ancestral heritage, or pursued careers related to Japan. Nor have they adopted a more transnational ethnic consciousness that goes beyond a simple nationalist identification.

Although most of the prewar nisei have visited Japan in the last several decades, they went as tourists and not to explore their ethnic roots per se or to become more transnationally engaged with their ethnic homeland. "It was just like being a tourist in a foreign country," Jim explained. "I just went to see another country, how other people live. I didn't feel like I was connecting to my roots or anything. No, nothing of that sort." In general, the prewar nisei enjoyed their vacations in Japan, had a wonderful time touring different parts of the country, and were treated well by the Japanese with whom they interacted. Most of them did meet briefly with their relatives in Japan, who showed them photos of their family, took them to the ancestral village or grave, and shared memories from long ago. However, because these trips to Japan were brief, onetime visits and their experiences in the country were rather superficial as tourists, they did not establish any long-term and sustained transnational relationship with the country. Nor did the nisei develop a greater transnational consciousness in which their identity as Americans was simultaneously accompanied by a greater identification with Japan. Instead, they experienced their ethnic homeland as essentially a foreign country. "It was great to reconnect with my relatives and see photos of my grandparents. I felt like I went back to my roots," Mike recalled. "But it didn't make me feel more Japanese or anything. I'm really a clueless foreigner in Japan. It actually reinforced in my mind that I'm an American of Japanese descent."

In addition, few postwar second-generation Japanese Americans had any social relationships with current immigrants from Japan living in the United States, which would allow them to maintain or reactivate ties to their ethnic homeland and heritage (see also Okamura 1998: 22–23). Other Asian American communities have large numbers of recent immigrants from Asia who not only have an important social and cultural impact, but constantly provide a cultural and social link back to the ethnic homeland. As Tomás Jiménez (2010) notes, such new immigrants are a source of "ethnic replenishment" for later generation immigrant descendants of the same national origins.[6] In the case of the Japanese Americans, however, there has not been a large influx of Japanese immigrants since the 1960s who could revitalize their ethnic culture because Japan's increasing postwar economic prosperity reduced the incentive to immigrate to the United States (Okamura 2008: 144). In addition, there is also little contact between the relatively small number of Japanese immigrants and the older Japanese American community for a number of reasons (see also Spickard 1996: 151–52). In addition to the language barrier, a large historical and social class divide exists between these two communities, since the Japanese Americans are generally descendants of unskilled agricultural immigrants who arrived in the United States before the 1930s. In contrast, current Japanese immigrants came to the United States after the 1960s as relatively elite, high-skilled immigrants (mainly students, professionals, and businessmen). Many of them have a temporary, sojourner mentality and live in their own separate expatriate communities, giving them little incentive to associate with Japanese Americans.

THE POSTWAR NISEI: BICULTURALISM AND TRANSNATIONAL IDENTITIES

As descendants of Japanese immigrants who arrived in the United States after the 1960s, the shin-nisei were raised during a completely different historical era than the prewar nisei and therefore have a quite different ethnic consciousness. Because they came of age primarily after the 1980s and 1990s in a much more pro-Japanese, multicultural, and globalized environment, they have retained their Japanese cultural heritage to a much greater extent, and their ethnicity and identities are bicultural and binational in scope. Therefore, although they are also second-generation immigrants as are the prewar nisei, they are members of a completely different historical generation whose lives take place in a much more transnational ethnic space.

BEING JAPANESE AMERICAN IN POSTWAR AMERICA

There have been a number of obvious but significant changes since World War II that have caused the postwar shin-nisei to remain much more strongly connected to their ethnic heritage and homeland compared to their prewar counterparts (see also Kitano 1993: 202–3; Takahashi 1997: 211). In contrast to the mainly white, assimilationist world in which the prewar nisei came of age, the postwar nisei are a product of a much more ethnically diverse and multicultural America that tolerates and even encourages the second generation to maintain their native cultures and languages and live in transnational spaces (see Foner 2002; Levitt 2001: 203). A couple of my shin-nisei interviewees spoke of how the current ethnic diversity in the United States allowed them to become bicultural instead of adopting a singular American nationalist identity. Takehiro Watanabe, a university faculty member, spoke about his past experiences in this respect as follows:

> I grew up in a really diverse community: there were blacks, Mexican people, and Japanese Americans. So I just blended into the local community and tried to fit in. There wasn't that much pressure to show that you're really American. For me, Japanese American identity was more hybrid, a mixture of cultures. It wasn't just defensively asserting your Americanness. I like the notion of fluid, flexible, transnational identities.

Meanwhile, American attitudes toward Japan have been completely transformed as a formerly despised, enemy nation has become an economically prosperous and respected First World country that is the United States' oldest and closest East Asian ally (see also O'Brien and Fugita 1991: 127). Because of the generally positive images about Japan, there is considerable fascination among some Americans about Japan, including its culture, history, food, global commodities, technology, and popular culture. This has encouraged second-generation Japanese Americans to identify with Japan to a much greater extent than the prewar nisei.

The shin-nisei I spoke with generally felt that American images of Japan were quite positive, and they could not think of many negative images. They noted how the country is regarded as a modern, highly advanced, and rich nation that is a pro-American ally. They also mentioned favorable perceptions of the country's technology, electronics, cars, computer games, and anime as well as the American fascination with historic images of Japan based on samurais, ninjas, geishas, and Japanese art. A few of them also spoke of perceptions of Japan as an orderly and harmonious society based on social obligations and hierarchical respect. The postwar nisei seemed to feel that any negative American reactions toward Japan were mainly a thing of the past. A number of them mentioned prejudice against Japanese based on Pearl Harbor and World War II but felt it was mainly confined to elderly people and old war movies and not really relevant today.

As noted earlier, levels of discrimination also have a strong impact on the ethnic culture and consciousness of the second generation. In contrast to the ethnic hostility and incarceration that the prewar nisei suffered, the postwar nisei felt that they are no longer subject to much prejudice or discrimination. Most of them could not remember an instance when they were directly mistreated or personally discriminated against because of their ethnicity, except when they were children and were teased by other kids. "You hear instances of discrimination against other people, like blacks, or Muslims after 9/11," Steve Okura noted. "That gets me upset. And I definitely have this awareness of institutionalized discrimination against Japanese in the past. But personally, I've never experienced anything that I consider discrimination."

In contrast to the prewar era, most discrimination against Asian Americans today seems to be structural or relatively hidden (such as the glass ceiling) and is rarely overt or direct. In fact, even my most socially aware shin-nisei interviewees, such as Takehiro, found it difficult to attribute possible unequal treatment directly to racial discrimination:

> Professionally, I can't say there was an incident that was blatantly racist or discriminatory. It's very hard to say. If I don't get an academic job that I felt I was qualified for, is that because I wasn't white? Or because I didn't have a PhD from Harvard? When I started new faculty positions, I felt the staff weren't treating me well, or they gave me a really terrible office until I made a big fuss about it. Is that because of my race, or because I was still a junior faculty member? I don't know.

As a result of these postwar changes, the shin-nisei feel that Japanese Americans are generally well regarded today. When asked about American perceptions of Japanese Americans, the shin-nisei referred to positive stereotypes about Asian Americans in general. Almost all of them mentioned that they are seen as model minorities who are smart and hardworking academic overachievers and are good at math, science, and computers.[7] Some felt they are regarded as socioeconomically well-to-do, as well as quiet, good citizens.

Finally, second-generation Japanese Americans today have had significant opportunities to maintain active transnational ties to their ethnic homeland of Japan compared to the prewar nisei. As a number of researchers have noted, today's second generation live in a much more globalized world characterized by the greater ease of international travel, global mass media, and the Internet, which enable them to stay connected with their parents' country of origin to a much greater extent (Kasinitz et al. 2004: 5–6; 2008: 4). In addition, because of the postwar economic prosperity of Japan, the parents of the shin-nisei immigrated to the United States as generally well-to-do businessmen and professional expatriates who often travel back and forth between the United States and Japan as part of their careers. They also have the economic means to live transnational lives.[8] Most shin-nisei have therefore visited Japan numerous times during their lives with their parents, and some of them have actually lived there by themselves in order to work or go to school. As a result, they grew up in a much more transnational ethnic spaces compared to the prewar nisei.

ETHNIC HERITAGE AND BICULTURALISM

Therefore, since World War II, being ethnically Japanese in the United States has become a much more positive experience in a multicultural and transnational world, and prewar prejudice and discrimination directed against those of Japanese descent has subsided. Because postwar second-generation Japanese Americans grew up in this transformed ethnic landscape, they have a much stronger attachment to Japan and their cultural heritage than the prewar nisei, and most of them have become fully bicultural. It is important to remember that members of the second generation do not always strengthen their ethnic minority identity or affiliation with their national origins as a "reactive ethnicity" against increased majority discrimination and socioeconomic marginalization (cf. Espiritu and Wolf 2001; Portes and Rumbaut 2001: chap. 7). They may also do so as an affirmative reaction to the positive meanings that can be associated with their heritage and homeland.

A couple of my interviewees explicitly mentioned that they felt a certain pride in their Japanese cultural background. "I wouldn't say it's a nationalistic pride, or anything," Matt Honkawa remarked. "But I do take a bit of pride in being Japanese, or maybe satisfaction is a better word. I enjoy being Japanese, like the food, culture, and being able to speak the language. I don't proudly assert it, but it is part of who I am."

It was rather remarkable that all the shin-nisei I spoke with were fully bilingual and bicultural.[9] They generally rated their Japanese as quite fluent. They could also read and write with some facility. Again, the contrast is quite stark with the prewar nisei, who were generally monolingual English speakers with only basic or minimal ability in the Japanese language. Takehiro gave a typical assessment of his Japanese: "I'd say I'm pretty fluent. I can more or less speak like a Japanese and don't stand out as a foreigner in Japan. I don't really have an accent in Japanese. But I don't write very well and don't like to write in Japanese. If I read a [Japanese] book, it would take me at least twice as long as a book in English."

Most of the shin-nisei explicitly spoke about how their parents pressured them to study the Japanese language, in contrast to the rather laissez-faire attitude of the parents of the prewar nisei generation. "There was a lot of pressure in my family about the language thing," Takehiro recalled. "My parents really wanted me to study the language. They were pretty proud Japanese nationalists, especially my dad." It is not clear why postwar Japanese immigrants have insisted on native language retention among their children much more than their prewar counterparts and I did not explicitly ask about this in my interviews. However, it is clear that most of the Japanese professionals and businessmen in the United States are temporary sojourners and plan to return to Japan with their children. Although some of them end up remaining permanently in the United States (as was the case with the parents of my interviewees), they often continue to entertain the notion of eventual repatriation. In addition, even those Japanese immigrants who become permanent settlers often retain strong transnational ties with their homeland, which may be a reason why they want their children to maintain their cultural heritage.

In general, it seems that the shin-nisei complied with their parents' wishes. Most of them attended Japanese Saturday schools, which were created for the children of Japanese businessmen and other professionals in large American cities with significant Japanese expatriate communities. Since most of these expatriates intend to repatriate in a matter of years, these schools can be quite rigorous and attempt to keep up with the curriculum in Japan. The shin-nisei I interviewed generally attended these schools for many years (sometimes from first grade to the end of junior high school or even high school) and therefore took classes mainly with students from Japan, although there were other Japanese Americans in their classes. In this sense, although recent Japanese immigrants and their expatriate communities have not provided any ethnic replenishment for the prewar second generation Japanese Americans, they have certainly done so for the shin-nisei. In fact, without the ready availability of expatriate Japanese Saturday schools, it is unlikely they would have become so fluent in Japanese.

The shin-nisei attended Japanese Saturday school not simply because of parental pressure, but also because it was something they wanted to do. This may be related to the positive meanings and experiences attached to their Japanese heritage and ethnic homeland as well as the current multicultural climate. A couple of them also mentioned that being bilingual may help them for their professional careers later in life. "I had very strict parents, so quitting [Japanese school] was not an option," Steve said. "But I didn't really complain. Actually, I didn't want to quit myself. The thought never really crossed my mind. I had a lot of Japanese friends [from Japan] in Japanese school and enjoyed going." In fact, Steve even contemplated applying to Japanese universities.

The shin-nisei also felt pretty culturally Japanese when compared with the pre-war nisei and spoke about aspects of themselves which they positively attributed to their cultural heritage and upbringing. Yuki Sumimoto felt he was more group-oriented like the Japanese in Japan and had a communal attitude compared to other Americans:

> I think more about the good of the community and about forgoing individual gains for the group. I think that stems for my going to Japan and the schools there. Students there have to do everything themselves, like clean the school and serve themselves. Here, I think people tend to be more selfish and take it for granted that other people will do things for them and they don't have to give back. Sometimes that annoys me. Because of my experience in Japan, I realize the importance of conforming and doing things for the benefit of others.

Even Donald Ishii, who was only half Japanese descent, felt that he had inherited positive aspects of Japanese culture through his upbringing:

> I'm pretty darn whitewashed [assimilated]. But when it comes to the work ethic and heritage, I'm Japanese. I have a Japanese work ethic. The Japanese are far, far superior to any other people in terms of work ethic culture that I've ever seen. I also have a Japanese business mind. I have a Japanese respect for people. And I have a Japanese loyalty and trustworthiness.

Because they are fully bilingual and bicultural, the shin-nisei I spoke with reported that their cultural adaptation to Japan is quite smooth and they feel quite comfortable living there. For them, Japan was never truly a foreign country, and they are able to sufficiently speak and "act Japanese" to the point where they have no trouble being socially accepted in Japan (Tsuda 2009b: 240–41). Consider the experiences of Matt, who had worked in Japan:

> My experiences in Japan are quite positive. I can easily switch to a Japanese identity. Otherwise, if you stick out, you make things difficult for yourself there. I know how to be Japanese because growing up, my mom taught me Japanese manners, customs, and spoke both languages to me. I had plenty of Japanese friends growing up and related well to my teachers and peers at Japanese school, so knew what

Japanese culture was like. Interacting with Japanese in general is pretty natural for me. So in terms of living in Japan, it was very easy and comfortable for me. . . . It was sort of a reproduction of my Japanese school experiences in the US.

"I can be totally accepted as Japanese in Japan if I want," Steve remarked. "I used to be really sensitive about acting Japanese in Japan. It used to bother me when the Japanese saw me as different. So I felt I had to be more Japanese than other Japanese people."

In fact, because of their strong Japanese cultural backgrounds, a good number of my shin-nisei interviewees did not identify much with the broader Japanese American community. Because they grew up in the postwar Japanese expatriate community and are much more connected to Japan and Japanese culture, they felt quite different from prewar nisei, sansei, and fourth-generation yonsei. The only exception was Takehiro, an older shin-nisei who grew up in a Japanese American community after World War II. Only a couple of shin-nisei had ever been a member of any Japanese American organizations.

For instance, according to Matt: "When I say I'm Japanese American, I'm not identifying with Japanese American history or anything like that. I'm identifying mainly with Japan. It's not that I don't relate to Japanese Americans. I have sansei and yonsei buddies. But I feel different from them because my understanding of Japanese culture is greater." Although he was a student at UC San Diego, he never bothered to show up to Nikkei Student Union events on campus (the Japanese American student organization). "They're yonsei. They don't speak any Japanese," he noted. "The purpose of the club isn't to continue Japanese culture. For me, it's just not important that I surround myself with other Japanese Americans."

TRANSNATIONAL ETHNIC CONSCIOUSNESS

Because of their biculturalism and their experiences in Japan, postwar second-generation Japanese Americans have ethnic identities that are more transnational in orientation in contrast to the exclusively nationalist consciousness of their prewar predecessors. In the immigration literature, one of the key variables that determine the level of transnational engagement is again seen as immigrant generation since the first generation undoubtedly is more actively connected to their country of origin than their second-generation descendants. As a result, there has been considerable debate about the extent to which the second generation maintains transnational ties to the parental homeland (see Levitt and Waters 2002), with some scholars arguing that transnationalism declines considerably among the second generation and is quite limited in scope (e.g., Portes and Rumbaut 2001: chap. 6; Kasinitz, Waters, Mollenkopf, and Anil 2002; Rumbaut 2002) while others argue that it persists and continues to be quite significant (e.g., Levitt 2002; Smith 2006).

I argue that we need to reorient the discussion of transnationalism across the generations. First, as the case of the Japanese Americans demonstrates, differences in historical generation can be just as important as differences in immigrant generations in determining the level of transnational activity and consciousness. The postwar shin-nisei live in transnationalized social fields while the lives of their pre-war nisei counterparts are limited to a predominantly nationalist space. Therefore, the amount of transnational engagement between two historical cohorts of the same immigrant generation may vary more than the difference in transnationalism between immigrant parents and their second-generation descendants.

In addition, it is important to distinguish between the transnational social connections of the second generation and their ethnic *identities*. While it is quite apparent that transnational social relations with the ethnic homeland considerably attenuate among those of the second generation compared to their parents, they are more likely to construct transnational identities based on a simultaneous, dual identification with the host and origin countries (Tsuda 2012: 642–43). First-generation immigrant parents often do not identify in transnational ways since they continue to maintain a strong nationalist identification with their home countries and do not develop as much attachment to the host society. In contrast, their second-generation children naturally come to identify with their country of birth, while at the same time, they may simultaneously develop a significant affinity to their ancestral homeland because of the influence of their parents and trips they take to their parents' country of origin. In addition, increased access to information about their ethnic homeland through the mass media and the Internet has given them new opportunities to develop a more expansive transnational ethnic consciousness.

In terms of cross border social relations, the shin-nisei are not as transnationally engaged with Japan as their parents. They have traveled to Japan a number of times, a few have lived there briefly, and a number of them continue to maintain both actual and virtual connections to their ethnic homeland. However, unlike their parents, they do not travel as often to Japan, and most do not have transnational business or professional connections to the country. Nor do they stay in constant touch with their relatives in Japan or vote in Japanese elections.

Nonetheless, the shin-nisei have developed quite prominent transnational identities that simultaneously encompass both the United States and Japan. This is quite a contrast to their parents, whom some of them described as "Japanese nationalists," "gung ho Japanese," or "patriotic toward Japan." Michiko Kawamura reflected on this generational difference as follows:

> My mother never really assimilated in America and doesn't speak much English. She's forever Japanese in her thinking. The thought of becoming an American citizen has never even crossed her mind although she's been here for decades and will never go back to Japan. In fact, it bothers her because I've recently started

to call myself Japanese American. When I grew up, she kept saying I'm "pure Japanese." Of course, I have both cultures inside of me and am connected to both countries. I don't think of myself as just one or the other. I'm actually a dual national.

Although the shin-nisei generally felt that their American and Japanese cultural identities were incompatible, they saw them as coexisting simultaneously as multiple, transnational affiliations that were appropriately deployed on different occasions and countries. Michiko described her experiences in this regard:

> I'm fully bicultural, but that doesn't mean I act American and Japanese at the same time. That's not possible. My identity is a very situational thing. When I'm with white Americans here [in the United States], I consider myself fully American. I feel like I'm accepted as an American and I can act and speak like one and I have no trouble. When I go back to Japan or I hang out with Japanese from Japan here in the US, I feel very Japanese. I can speak like a native. I can bow. I can mix in with Japanese well enough that I don't stick out. So I can use both sides of my identity completely proficiently.

Likewise, Matt also spoke about how he "switches identities" from American to Japanese when he goes to Japan, which he found is quite easy to do. Although he initially reinforced his American identity as a partial reaction to those aspects of Japan he did not like when he was younger, he eventually came to adopt a more accommodating, transnational ethnic consciousness. "Depending on which country I'm in, I can feel pretty Japanese or feel quite American," he remarked. "I can totally fit in and embrace Japan. When I'm in Japan, I feel great, like I could live there for a long time. But when I get back to the US, I feel great being back home. I can operate fine in both cultures."

Finally, there were a few shin-nisei who conceived of themselves in even more flexible and cosmopolitan ways that went beyond simply a dual transnational identification. For instance, Takehiro, a university faculty member, was not comfortable thinking of himself simply in nationalist terms as American and said he "like[s] the notion of fluid, flexible, transnational identities." However, what he was thinking of was an even more radical, multiple subjectivity. Consider the following exchange I had with him during our interview:

> *Takehiro:* I think when I was much younger I used to be more on those terms, kind of a binary, like American, Japanese. But as we know from people who work on identity, identity is a much more complicated matter than that. So what is an American? What is a Japanese? So I like the idea of not being stuck in some kind of category.
>
> *Author:* So you no longer think of yourself in those kinds of binary terms?

> *Takehiro:* No, no. As I said, I probably used to, but I don't think that way any-more at all. I think of myself as having these real complicated relationships with a lot of different communities. There was a time when I identified a lot with black culture. I liked black culture.
>
> *Author:* So you see yourself as a true cosmopolitan.
>
> *Takehiro:* I don't know if I'm a true cosmopolitan, but I feel like I have these mul-tiple affiliations and I'm kind of a composite at the intersection of all these dif-ferent kinds of identities. And not just one identity to the exclusion of the other ones. I don't even think in terms of like "Oh, I'm one third this, and one third that . . ." Or whatever.

CONCLUSION: DIFFERENT HISTORIES, DIFFERENT ETHNICITIES

This chapter has argued for the importance of examining historical cohort differ-ences between members of the second immigrant generation. The immigration literature has been rather oblivious to history and often assumes that that immi-grant generation is the most important factor that explains internal differences in assimilation and identity among immigrant-origin ethnic groups. Although it is undeniable that the second immigrant generation will have fundamentally different experiences from their first-generation immigrant parents, there can be consider-able diversity among members of the second generation depending on the historical period in which they came of age, which has led to considerably different contem-porary ethnic outcomes.

In the case of second-generation Japanese Americans, there are significant his-torical generational differences between those who grew up before and after World War II. As a result, they currently inhabit completely different ethnic spaces in terms of assimilation/biculturalism, ethnonational belonging, and transnational engagement. The prewar nisei came of age during a period of intense discrimina-tion against Japanese descendants and were interned as enemy aliens, forcing them to fight (literally and figuratively) in order to have their American identities and loyalties recognized. Because of the historical constraints of interment and war dur-ing a preglobal era, they had relatively few opportunities to develop transnational connections to their ethnic homeland and therefore became quite assimilated and Americanized. As members of the prewar historical generation, such formative experiences during their youth continue to inform their lives today, as most elderly nisei still inhabit exclusively nationalist spaces of belonging and identity.

In contrast, the shin-nisei, as members of the postwar historical generation, are descendants of transnational Japanese professionals and grew up in an increasingly multicultural and globalized America where their ethnic homeland is now regarded in favorable terms. As a result, they are much more engaged with their ethnic heri-tage, and their bicultural lives and identities are based on transnational spaces of belonging that simultaneously encompass both the United States and Japan. Theirs is not a reactive ethnicity asserted against a discriminatory mainstream society, but an affirmative identification with a heritage and homeland that are now positively construed.

Therefore, although the pre- and postwar nisei are members of the second immigrant generation, they are generations apart in terms of history. Such historical cohort differences may be just as significant as immigrant generational differences between nisei, sansei, and yonsei when explaining the ethnic experiences of various groups of Japanese Americans. Japanese Americans are, of course, not the only ethnic group that has significant historical generational differences among those of the second immigrant generation. There are plenty of other ethnic groups that have had a long history of immigration to the United States, such as Mexican Americans, Chinese Americans, and Filipino Americans, as well as various white ethnic groups. For all these groups, members of the same immigrant generation may be from completely different historical generations.

When examining the impact of different histories on the second generation, however, we must not neglect the important influence of age. After all, second-generation members from different historical periods are usually of quite different age groups. For instance, shin-nisei are more bilingual and engaged with their ethnic heritage and homeland, not only because they are members of the postwar multicultural and transnational historical generation, but also because most of those in my sample were still young. Much of the learning of cultural heritage and native languages as well as visits to the ethnic homeland occur under the auspices of parents when the second generation are still children or youth. In addition, college is when a number of Asian American youth explore and fully discover their ethnicity (Espiritu 1994; Kibria 2002; see also Levitt 2002: 140), partly because of the tolerant, multiethnic social environment that prevails on university campuses, the presence of large numbers of other Asian American students, and opportunities to study abroad in the ethnic homeland. In fact, when the prewar nisei were young, a number of them had spoken and studied some Japanese while growing up in immigrant families and communities. However, they have long since forgotten the language as their parents passed away and they grew older. As Peggy Levitt points out (2002), transnational (and I would also say ethnic heritage) activity does not remain constant throughout the life cycle but ebbs and flows at different stages.

This issue of age is also relevant to the ethnic future of the second generation. Although the shin-nisei youth are currently bicultural and transnationally engaged, will they eventually become more detached from their ethnic heritage as they grow older, like the prewar nisei? It is quite evident that second-generation ties to heritage and homeland are very much dependent on transnational immigrant parents, who foster, if not insist, on the maintenance of the native language and culture and take their children with them for their return visits to their country of origin. Therefore, it is possible that the second-generation youth of today will become less ethnic and transnational as their first-generation parents pass away and they become busy adults preoccupied with their professional careers (see, e.g., Smith 2006: chap. 8) and their own children, who will be another generation removed from the ethnic homeland.

Although the lives of current second-generation Japanese American youth may indeed unfold in this manner as they grow older, I would argue that they will continue to remain connected to their heritage and homeland to a notable extent. Two of my older, middle-aged shin-nisei informants were still fluent in Japanese, and one continued to conduct research in Japan. The other had become more detached from Japan over time and did not travel there as often as in her youth but mentioned a continued desire to visit or even live there in the future. We have seen that the lives of prewar nisei were forever shaped by the historical period of World War II when they came of age. Despite the postwar turn toward multiethnicity and the rise of East Asia, they remain culturally nationalized and have shown little interest in recovering their ethnic heritage or developing ties to Japan. Likewise, the shin-nisei will continue to be influenced by their multicultural and transnational upbringing as they grow older. Because they are members of different historical generations who occupy different generational spaces, the early formative experiences of the pre- and postwar nisei have placed them on different ethnic trajectories that will continue to determine their future ethnic spaces of identity and belonging. In this sense, history is indeed destiny.

NOTES

1. For instance, in San Diego and Phoenix, the JACL youth group went defunct many years ago.
2. In such cases, the contrast between the elderly prewar and young postwar second generation is therefore not simply a matter of age; that is, it reflects more than commonplace differences between old people and youth that are found everywhere.
3. Nearly 25 percent answered "no" to both questions, wrote qualified answers, or refused to answer the questions and left them blank. When the draft was instated for Japanese Americans, some of these individuals became draft resistors. This became a source of conflict in the Japanese American community that continued after World War II.
4. It is interesting to note that a very small number of nisei returned to Japan with their parents after they were released from the internment camps at the end of World War II because they saw no future for themselves in the United States.
5. However, Ueda (2002: 35) does note that nisei of this period also had few opportunities to visit Japan.
6. Although Jiménez examines the impact of Mexican immigrants on later-generation Mexican Americans, new immigrants can also provide ethnic replenishment for older second-generation groups like the prewar Japanese Americans who have lost touch with their ethnic homeland and heritage.

7. Most of my informants spoke of this perception as an ethnic stereotype, but only two were directly ambivalent or critical of it.

8. The increase in high-skilled, middle-class immigrants in recent decades may be another factor that has enabled the second generation to remain transnationally connected to their ethnic homelands compared to earlier historical cohorts (Levitt and Waters 2002: 18).

9. The only exceptions were those who were biracial (and thus Japanese descent on only one side of the family) and Doug, who was 2.5 generation.

REFERENCES

Alba, Richard, and Mary C. Waters (eds.). 2011. *The Next Generation: Immigrant Youth in Comparative Perspective*. New York: New York University Press.

Boyd, Monica, and Elizabeth Grieco. 1998. Triumphant Transitions: Socioeconomic Achievements of the Second Generation in Canada. *International Migration Review* 32 (4): 853–76.

Brettell, Caroline B., and Faith G. Nibbs. 2009. Lived Hybridity: Second-Generation Identity Construction through College Festival. *Identities: Global Studies in Culture and Power* 16 (6): 678–99.

Eckstein, Susan. 2002. On Deconstructing and Reconstructing the Meaning of Immigrant Generations. In *The Changing Face of Home: The Transnational Lives of the Second Generation*, Peggy Levitt and Mary C. Waters, eds., 211–15. New York: Russell Sage Foundation.

Espiritu, Yen Le. 1994. The Intersection of Race, Ethnicity, and Class: The Multiple Identities of Second-Generation Filipinos. *Identities* 1 (2–3): 249–73.

Espiritu, Yen Le, and Diane Wolf. 2001. The Paradox of Assimilation: Children of Filipino Immigrants in San Diego. In *Ethnicities: Children of Immigrants in America*, Rubén G. Rumbaut and Alejandro Portes, eds., pp. 157–86. Berkeley: University of California Press.

Feliciano, Cynthia, and Rubén G. Rumbaut. 2005. Gendered Paths: Educational and Occupational Expectations and Outcomes among Adult Children of Immigrants. *Ethnic and Racial Studies* 28 (6): 1087–118.

Foner, Nancy. 2002. Second-Generation Transnationalism, Then and Now. In *The Changing Face of Home: The Transnational Lives of the Second Generation*, Peggy Levitt and Mary C. Waters, eds., pp. 242–52. New York: Russell Sage Foundation.

———. 2009. Introduction: Intergenerational Relations in Immigrant Families. In *Across Generations: Immigrant Families in America*, Nancy Foner, ed., pp. 1–20. New York: New York University Press.

Gans, Herbert. 1992. Second-Generation Decline: Scenarios for the Economic and Ethnic Futures of the Post-1965 American Immigrants. *Ethnic and Racial Studies* 15 (2): 173–92.

Haller, William, and Patricia Landolt. 2005. The Transnational Dimensions of Identity Formation: Adult Children of Immigrants in Miami. *Ethnic and Racial Studies* 28 (6): 1182–214.

Hickman, Mary, Sarah Morgan, Bronwell Walter, and Joseph Bradley. 2005. The Limitations of Whiteness and the Boundaries of Englishness: Second-Generation Irish Identifications and Positionings in Multiethnic Britain. *Ethnicities* 5 (2): 160–82.

Jiménez, Tomás. 2010. *Replenished Ethnicity: Mexican Americans, Immigration, and Identity.* Berkeley: University of California Press.

Kasinitz, Philip, John H. Mollenkopf, and Mary C. Waters. 2004. Worlds of the Second Generation. In *Becoming New Yorkers: Ethnographies of the New Second Generation,* Philip Kasinitz, John H. Mollenkopf, and Mary C. Waters, eds., pp. 1–19. New York: Russell Sage Foundation.

Kasinitz, Philip, John H. Mollenkopf, Mary C. Waters, and Jennifer Holdaway. 2004. Children of Immigrants, Children of America. In *Becoming New Yorkers: Ethnographies of the New Second Generation,* Philip Kasinitz, John H. Mollenkopf, and Mary C. Waters, eds., pp. 393–403. New York: Russell Sage Foundation.

———. 2008. *Inheriting the City: The Children of Immigrants Come of Age.* New York: Russell Sage Foundation.

Kasinitz, Philip, Mary C. Waters, John H, Mollenkopf, and Merih Anil. 2002. Transnationalism and the Children of Immigrants in Contemporary New York. In *The Changing Face of Home: The Transnational Lives of the Second Generation,* Peggy Levitt and Mary C. Waters, eds., pp. 96–122. New York: Russell Sage Foundation.

Kibria, Nazli. 2002. *Becoming Asian American: Second-Generation Chinese and Korean American Identities.* Baltimore: Johns Hopkins University Press.

Kitano, Harry. 1993. *Generations and Identity: The Japanese American.* Needham Heights, MA: Ginn.

Levitt, Peggy. 2001. Transnational Migration: Taking Stock and Future Directions. *Global Networks* 1 (3): 195–216.

———. 2002. The Ties That Change: Relations to the Ancestral Home over the Life Cycle. In *The Changing Face of Home: The Transnational Lives of the Second Generation,* Peggy Levitt and Mary C. Waters, eds., pp. 123–44. New York: Russell Sage Foundation.

Levitt, Peggy, and Mary C. Waters (eds.). 2002. *The Changing Face of Home: The Transnational Lives of the Second Generation.* New York: Russell Sage Foundation.

———. 2002. Introduction. In *The Changing Face of Home: The Transnational Lives of the Second Generation,* Peggy Levitt and Mary C. Waters, eds., pp. 1–30. New York: Russell Sage Foundation.

López, David, and Ricardo Stanton-Salazar. 2001. Mexican Americans: A Second Generation at Risk. In *Ethnicities: Children of Immigrants in America,* Rubén G. Rumbaut and Alejandro Portes, eds., pp. 57–90. Berkeley: University of California Press.

Mannheim, Karl. 1952. *Essays on the Sociology of Knowledge.* New York: Oxford University Press.

Min, Pyong Gap (ed.). 2002. *Second Generation: Ethnic Identity among Asian Americans.* Walnut Creek, CA: AltaMira.

Min, Pyong Gap, and Joann Hong. 2002. Ethnic Attachment among Second-Generation Korean Americans. In *Second Generation: Ethnic Identity among Asian Americans*, Pyong Gap Min, ed., pp. 113–27. Walnut Creek, CA: AltaMira.

O'Brien, David, and Stephen Fugita. 1991. *The Japanese American Experience.* Bloomington: Indiana University Press.

Okamura, Jonathan. 1998. *Imagining the Filipino American Diaspora: Transnational Relations, Identities, and Communities.* New York: Garland.

———. 2008. *Ethnicity and Inequality in Hawaii.* Philadelphia: Temple University Press.

Perlmann, Joel. 2005. *Italians Then, Mexicans, Now: Immigrant Origins and Second-Generation Progress, 1890 to 2000.* New York: Russell Sage Foundation.

Perlmann, Joel, and Roger Waldinger. 1997. Second Generation Decline? Children of Immigrants, Past and Present—A Reconsideration. *International Migration Review* 31 (4): 893–922.

Portes, Alejandro, Patricia Fernández-Kelly, and William Haller. 2005. Segmented Assimilation on the Ground: The New Second Generation in Early Adulthood. *Ethnic and Racial Studies* 28 (6): 1000–1040.

Portes, Alejandro, and Rubén G. Rumbaut. 2001. *Legacies: The Story of the Immigrant Second Generation.* Berkeley: University of California Press and New York: Russell Sage Foundation.

Portes, Alejandro, and Min Zhou. 1993. The New Second Generation: Segmented Assimilation and Its Variants among Post-1965 Immigrant Youth. *Annals of the American Academy of Political and Social Sciences* 530 (1): 74–98.

Potter, Robert. 2005. "Young, Gifted and Back": Second-Generation Transnational Return Migrants to the Caribbean. *Progress in Development Studies* 5 (3): 213–23.

Robbins, Joel. 2004. *Becoming Sinners: Christianity and Moral Torment in a Papua New Guinea Society.* Berkeley: University of California Press.

Rumbaut, Rubén G. 2002. Severed or Sustained Attachments? Language, Identity, and Imagined Communities in the Post-immigrant Generation. In *The Changing Face of Home: The Transnational Lives of the Second Generation*, Peggy Levitt and Mary C. Waters, eds., pp. 43–95. New York: Russell Sage Foundation.

———. 2005. Turning Points in the Transition to Adulthood: Determinants of Educational Attainment, Incarceration, and Early Childbearing among Children of Immigrants. *Ethnic and Racial Studies* 28 (6): 1041–86.

Rumbaut, Rubén G. and Alejandro Portes (eds.). 2001. *Ethnicities: Children of Immigrants in America.* Berkeley: University of California Press.

Smith, Robert Courtney. 2006. *Mexican New York: Transnational Lives of New Immigrants.* Berkeley: University of California Press.

Spickard, Paul. 1996. *Japanese Americans: The Formation and Transformations of an Ethnic Group.* London: Prentice Hall International.

Suárez-Orozco, Carola, Marcelo Suárez-Orozco, and Irina Todorova. 2008. *Learning in a New Land: Immigrant Students in American Society*. Cambridge, MA: Belknap Press of Harvard University Press.

Takahashi, Jere. 1997. *Nisei/Sansei: Shifting Japanese American Identities and Politics*. Philadelphia: Temple University Press.

Takamori, Ayako. 2010. Rethinking Japanese American "Heritage" in the Homeland. *Critical Asian Studies* 42 (2): 217–38.

Tsuda, Takeyuki. 2001. When Identities Become Modern: Japanese Immigrants in Brazil and the Global Contextualization of Identity. *Ethnic and Racial Studies* 24 (3): 412–32.

———. 2003. *Strangers in the Ethnic Homeland: Japanese Brazilian Return Migration in Transnational Perspective*. New York: Columbia University Press.

———. 2009a. *Diasporic Homecomings: Ethnic Return Migration in Comparative Perspective*. Stanford, CA: Stanford University Press.

———. 2009b. Global Inequities and Diasporic Return: Japanese American and Brazilian Encounters with the Ethnic Homeland. In *Diasporic Homecomings: Ethnic Return Migration in Comparative Perspective*, Takeyuki Tsuda, ed., pp. 227–59. Stanford, CA: Stanford University Press.

———. 2012. Whatever Happened to Simultaneity? Transnational Migration Theory and Dual Engagement in Sending and Receiving Countries. *Journal of Ethnic and Migration Studies* 38 (4): 631–49.

Ueda, Reed. 2002. An Early Transnationalism? The Japanese American Second Generation of Hawaii in the Interwar Years. In *The Changing Face of Home: The Transnational Lives of the Second Generation*, Peggy Levitt and Mary C. Waters, eds., pp. 33–42. New York: Russell Sage Foundation.

van Niekerk, Mies. 2007. Second-Generation Caribbeans in the Netherlands: Different Migration Histories, Diverging Trajectories. *Journal of Ethnic and Migration Studies* 33 (7): 1063–81.

2 CONFRONTING IDENTITIES AND EDUCATING FOR LEADERSHIP AMONG ASIAN YOUTH

Caroline B. Brettell

Some of the most important questions in recent research on the immigrant second generation explore the conflicts between parents and children that erupt when two sets of values confront one another; the implications of the varying legal statuses of parents and their offspring within the immigrant family; and the role of schools, labor markets, citizenship regimes, and racial and class hierarchies in shaping the opportunities for the second generation (Zhou 1997, 1999, 2009; Kasinitz, Mollenkopf, and Waters 2004; Kasinitz, Mollenkopf, Waters, and Holdaway 2008; Qin 2006; Foner 2009; Alba and Waters 2011; Foner and Dreby 2011; Yoshikawa 2011).[1]

With regard to the political incorporation of immigrants in the United States in particular, previous scholarship has suggested that it is not fully realized until the children of immigrants come of age. Thus, researchers have increasingly been exploring how the children of immigrants confront issues of racism, address identity politics, acquire knowledge about the political sphere, and become civically and politically engaged (Geron et al. 2001; Min 2002; Marwell 2004; Junn and Masuoka 2008; Lopez and Marcelo 2008; Stepick, Stepick, and Labissiere 2008; Wray-Lake et al. 2008; Maira 2009; DeJaeghere and McCleary 2010). Using the term "immigrant youth," Stepick and Stepick (2002: 248) have observed that the children of immigrants are characterized by an "alienation from an unhyphenated 'American' identity" that emerges in response to their confrontation with discrimination and prejudice. They cite the Elian Gonzalez incident in Miami and the Proposition 1987 debate in California as two examples of heightened ethnic and political consciousness among immigrant youth in the United States. To this, we could add the anti-immigrant debates of the spring of 2006 that resulted in the participation of many young people in solidarity marches in cities across the United States. Similarly and more recently, the fight to pass the DREAM Act has galvanized some immigrant youth, several of them at great personal legal risk, to become visible in order to tell their stories and argue the case for passage of this act.[2] These forms of mobilization are not new. Ueda (1999: 663) has described how the civic inequality confronted by first-generation Japanese immigrants mobilized their children toward "full participation in American public life and to represent their community in the public realm, in short to achieve civically and politically what had been denied to their parents."

Some scholars have pointed to the significance of educational institutions and organizations in mobilizing immigrant youth and the children of immigrants to political and civic action, and perhaps even to identity politics. They argue that schools foster civic engagement among these young people, not only through formal learning, but also through community service requirements and other forms of civic activism (Stepick and Stepick 2002). They also observe gender differences in the civic engagement of immigrant youth, acknowledging however that research on this topic is limited (Albuquerque 2000; Bedolla 2000). Although Kasinitz, Mollenkopf, Waters, and Holdaway (2008: 286) found "a pervasive cynicism about politics" among immigrant youth in New York City, they also found that more than half of the respondents in their study across several different national origin populations belonged to some ethnic or youth organization. Marwell (2004) shows how second-generation Dominicans "learn politics." She argues that neighborhood political contexts act as strong mediating influences and focuses her attention on a Young Dominicans organization in one neighborhood that encourages community involvement. In another study of the new "contestatory politics" among Dominican youth in New York City, Aparicio (2007) explores the social and racial justice projects in that city that have involved Dominican youth and describes the process by which they construct a new political identity through their activities.

For the children of immigrants of Asian background whose parents were born in China, Korea, or various countries of Southeast Asia or South Asia, there is a growing literature not only with regard to their political participation (Kiang 2001), but also on issues of identity (Kibria 2002; Maira 2002, 2004; Min 2002; Lee 2004; Lee and Zhou 2004), modes of incorporation (Rumbaut and Portes 2001), and education (Zhou and Bankston 1998; Louie 2004b; Súarez-Orozco, Súarez-Orozco, and Todorova 2008). One gap in the literature, however, is a thorough discussion of leadership training for this population. Concerns about the need to provide leadership training and mentoring support for Asian youth are often voiced within Asian immigrant communities, by Asian political activists, and even by corporate managers. There are many venues for such training, and they often involve bringing speakers who have been active leaders in public and community service, in professional careers such as medicine, and in small business and corporations to share their perspectives with a younger generation. One aim of such events is to help the children of Asian immigrants to develop the leadership skills necessary for making a difference through political and public service. Another is to recognize that young people need to become comfortable with who they are, including their ethnic background, and to develop the necessary skills to deal with discrimination as well as with the challenges of operating in a bicultural world where they may have to negotiate conflicting sets of values and behaviors, or, as Tuan (2002: 210) has phrased it, a social terrain "where others define them as neither real Americans nor real Asians."

This chapter offers a description and analysis of one venue in which Asian youth—defined here as the children of Asian-origin immigrants who were born either abroad or in the United States—in the Dallas–Fort Worth metropolitan area (DFW) learn to confront issues of identity and develop their leadership skills. The research involved participant observation at the 2006 annual meeting of the Asian American Leadership and Education Conference (AALEC), which took place on a local university campus.[3] Indeed, it is in the university environment in particular that the children of immigrants can begin to learn leadership skills within organizations that they create rather than in organizations created by their parents or toward which their parents direct their children's time. I begin with a brief discussion of how primarily South Asian students become involved in campus organizations in general and what such activities mean to them. This is followed by the case study of the AALEC meeting and how it can be read both as a space of identity and as a community of practice for leadership training.[4]

CAMPUS ORGANIZATIONS, IDENTITY AND LEADERSHIP

Scholars who focus on ethnic student organizations within universities have emphasized their role as "sources of cultural familiarity, vehicles for cultural expression and advocacy, and venues for cultural validation" (Museus 2008: 576). They are the spaces that "second-generation college students most often use symbolically to affirm and perform identity" (Maira 2002: 126). The degree of involvement in such organizations can range from active leadership roles to almost complete disengagement (Maira 2002: 126). While the research described here did not explore students who were not involved in campus organizations, we did survey those who were active in ethnic organizations on campus, specifically the Indian Student Association.

Among the thirty-one respondents to this survey, 52 percent were female and 45 percent were male (one student did not provide his/her sex), and the median age was twenty years old with a mean age of 21.5 years. Fifty-five percent of these students were born in the United States. The remaining participants were born in India (23 percent), Pakistan (10 percent), Bangladesh (3 percent), the United Kingdom (3 percent), Kuwait (3 percent), and Denmark (3 percent) and are hence members of the 1.5 generation. Among those not born in the United States the median age of arrival was five years old, and the mean age was 6.31 years old. Eighty-one percent of the respondents were US citizens. Fifty-two percent of the survey participants said they were Hindu, and 42 percent said they were Muslim. All these students had command of the language of their parents' place of origin whether Hindi, Urdu, Punjabi, Malayalam, or any other number of South Asian languages. The majority of these students were majoring in business and engineering, but some were pursuing majors in the sciences, political science, international relations, and journalism.

About half the students in this survey indicated that they belonged to other organizations in addition to the Indian Student Association—for example, the Muslim Student Organization, AALEC, Relay for Life, the Asian Council, the Hindu Student Organization, Alpha Epsilon Delta pre-med honor society, or Islamic Relief. Similarly about 75 percent of the students indicated that they had participated in clubs in high school—the most reported being a sports club, the student council, the National Honor Society, and Rotary/Interact.

When asked about the reasons why they were involved in the Indian Students Association, 92 percent said that making friends was either very important (65 percent) or somewhat important. Sixty-five percent said that the volunteer opportunities were somewhat important (12 percent indicated this was very important). Forty-six percent indicated that having their participation on a resume was somewhat important, while 23 percent said it was very important, and 27 percent said it was not important. Similarly 46 percent indicated that learning about their heritage was somewhat important to their participation while 27 percent indicated it was very important. Students commented further on this issue of heritage, providing responses such as "it is very important to know your roots," "it is very important to interact with others in my same ethnic heritage," and "it is very important to keep in touch with our culture." They recognized the chance that this organization gave them to share common values, interests, and characteristics. Indeed the major event staged by the Indian Students Association on this particular campus is a Diwali festival, clearly a venue where these shared characteristics can be expressed (Brettell and Nibbs 2009). Most of these respondents were involved with the Diwali program in some capacity with the officers of the organization taking the leading role. When asked about their ethnic identity, 65 percent ranked a single ethnicity (Indian, Pakistani, Bangladeshi, etc.) first as the way they mostly think of themselves, while 16 percent ranked Asian American first, and only 6 percent ranked American first. But 26 percent ranked American second, while 23 percent ranked Asian second, and 16 percent ranked Asian American second.

It was the students who participated in the focus groups, all of whom were involved in one organization or another, who had the opportunity to speak in more detail about some of the dimensions of their leadership experiences. These students view their organizational activities within "role model" and or "civic activism" frameworks. One, for example, made the following observation with reference to participation in a program called "Connect":

It's a mentorship thing. It focuses on minorities who connect with high school seniors who plan on entering college. I think that's important because some people who come to college come for the wrong reasons. Upperclassmen can tell them about mistakes they made so you won't make the same mistakes. I discovered this club in college. I was attracted to it because I wanted to be a role model. I've been connecting to high school Indians. I've had three mentees, and they have all been Indian. I think of it as giving back to the community, and . . . I definitely think of what I am doing as being a good citizen.

Another student had assumed a leadership role as student body officer at the law school where she is enrolled.

I did it because it is my last year at school and I really wanted to give back to the school. I wanted to work as a liaison between faculty and students. . . . I really enjoyed it, but I did it to give back to the school, to help organize all the events.

A third described the decision-making process in which she engaged to find an associational space that suited her.

The biggest thing I'm involved in here is the marathon that raises money for pediatric AIDS. I got involved because I just wanted to help out and give back to the children. When I came to college I had trouble deciding what association to be in. I didn't want to do something cultural [Indian]; I tried it for a day, and it didn't work out. I wanted to be an active participant, and this organization allows me to make a direct impact. I sadly learned about America that there is a lot of apathy against disease and the minorities here. My role has been in education and outreach.

While leadership responsibilities and civic activism constituted one thread of discussion regarding involvement in student organizations, the other thread had to do with spaces of identity, and here ethnic organizations were very much at the center of discussions. Thus, one student said that she joined the Indian Student Association

mainly because all the other brown people joined. I was a part of all the activities. I went to a private Episcopal school. There were only ninety-four people in my graduating class, only three other Indians, not enough to form a club. We had a diversity club, and I was involved in its leadership. The campus organization also allows me an organized outlet for my culture. It's almost like family.

Another talked about his role in the Asian Council:

I am the new treasure of the Asian Council. That club integrates all the other associations and cultural communities together. Our aim is to bring them all together and make them aware of all the diversity issues and provide a ground to understand those issues. It's been such an interesting year. We aim at freshman because they leave the university because they don't feel comfortable here. It's been interesting to make a difference in their lives. I've learned more about what's going on against our society, because I've learned about a lot of hate crimes that goes on here on campus, or on other campuses. It helps us dialogue about these issues.

Other students talked about these pan-Asian organizations as a vehicle for learning what they have in common with other "Asian" students—the fact that they are not Caucasian and that many of the family values cross over. One female student linked her involvement to broader issues of racism, again illustrating a growing awareness about societal complexity during the transition from high school to college:

In high school I was involved in a lot of organizations like Student Congress, and Habitat for Humanity. I like leadership. When I came to college, I was exposed to more racism, not on this campus but in the news, etc. I am very aware of racism; I have had terrible experiences. . . . I think what a lot of minority students face when they come to a campus like this is they see a lot of sororities, and the majority is Caucasian. The point is that when I came to college one of the things that drew me to the ISA was that I felt like I could belong to something as a group. There was a place for everyone. Even though you don't see a lot of Indian people in the sororities, there is a place for you to belong if you want to. Certain groups, but not all groups.

Another chimed in that there are new challenges at college that "make us more aware of our foreignness." Others agreed by observing that one might join an ethnic organization because it helps to maintain culture but that when issues of race or discrimination arise they are grateful to have a group to lobby. One student went on to observe in this regard that when the student senate on campus launched an initiative to get rid of the four "minority seats," claiming it was racist to have them, the ethnic organizations moved into action, arguing that without these seats they would have no chance of becoming involved or being represented. Putting this in to the framework of a lesson learned, one male student observed, "We learn America is a salad bowl, but you have to stand up to maintain your identity. There is a sense of right and wrong." In this particular focus group these latter comments led to the issue of sororities and fraternities as organizations from which they were for the most part excluded. Commented one young woman, "Even if I did want to join a sorority, I wouldn't fit their profile. So, I don't want to subject myself to the rejection."

Clearly, being involved in campus organizations offers college-age students a space where they can work out who they are apart from their parents, broaden their knowledge of the challenges they will face in the broader US society, and develop leadership and organizational skills. All these dimensions are equally manifest in the AALEC meeting, a convention run by these college students for a broad range of high school students of various Asian backgrounds.

THE ASIAN AMERICAN LEADERSHIP AND EDUCATION CONFERENCE

AALEC was established in 1997 by a group of students and educators on the campus where this research was conducted. Its mission was to "provide leadership and educational training to encourage young minds to explore, grow and lead the way to success." Although it began as a program for college students, AALEC has become (as of 2001) a program for Asian high school students sponsored by the Asian Council, another student organization on this particular university campus. Students serve on the executive board, but they recruit group leaders from other campuses in the area. The aim of the annual AALEC meeting as represented on one of its affiliated websites is to "educate and reach out to the tremendously growing population of Asian American Students" as well as to "bridge the communication gap and the cultural gap which continuously challenge the Asian-American community"). A search on the Internet reveals that AALEC is one of any number of such conferences or events (with different names and acronyms) that take place on university campuses around the country and that often reach out to area high school students of Asian background. Further, these conferences should be viewed in relation to the programs of broader national organizations such as LEAP (Leadership Education for Asian Pacifics, Inc.). LEAP was founded in 1982 with the mission to "grow leaders" within the Asian and Pacific Islander community and has sponsored innumerable workshops and programs in corporate and university settings to foster leadership skills.[5] LEAP's basic approach, one that is reflected in AALEC, is that "Asian and Pacific Islanders can retain their unique cultures, identities and values while developing new and vital skills that will make them effective leaders within their own organizations, their communities and the broader society" (*www.leap.org*).

Each year, AALEC formulates a theme for the meeting. The theme of the eighth annual AALEC meeting in 2006 (when participant observation was carried out) was "True Identity—A Journey Inward."[6] That year, JR, an Indian American student (he was born in the United States, but his parents are Christians from Kerala), a sophomore, was serving as the chair of the event. He had attended an AALEC program when he was in high school and enjoyed it, saying that it was "eye-opening" for exposing him to stereotypes that are pervasive in the broader culture.

In his freshman year he was asked to be the recruitment director for the program—his job was to visit area high schools to "drum up" attendees. Although he did not apply to be chair the next year, no one else wanted to do it so he stepped up to the plate. JR described himself as very active in high school and said that he has continued this high level of activity in college "so as not to be bored." But clearly, by his own involvement in organizational decision-making, JR was also developing his own leadership and civic skills and his own ability to foster positive change. Thus as an organizer and leader, rather than a participant—where he started out—he has moved to the center of this community of practice but continues to learn new skills that will serve him well in his own process of broader civic and political engagement in the wider public sphere of the United States. Certainly it served him well on the university campus. The year following his leadership of AALEC, JR served as a student assistant in the Office of the President of the university—clearly locating himself at the power center of the university.

The purpose of the AALEC annual meeting is to expose Asian youth to different opportunities and career paths—that there are "more than two set-tracks to success," the university's director of Asian programs commented in an interview. A second purpose is to teach young people about how to build on who they are as Asians as they move outside their comfort zones and into positions of leadership. JR emphasized that Asian parents do not push their children toward leadership roles, but they do emphasize excelling academically. He suggested that often Asian youth internalize false stereotypes and act like the stereotype rather than like themselves. He brought up the example of sports. Since there are so few Asians in sports, Asian youth think they are not good athletes. AALEC, he suggested, teaches them that they can do different things and that this is just one of many false stereotypes. AALEC also tries to help young Asian youth to overcome their problems with public speaking by teaching them that if they are invited to speak it is because someone recognizes that they have something to say and that this should give them confidence. AALEC has identified some of the recurring problems shared by Asian immigrant youth and attempts to address them in the context of the annual meeting.

LEARNING AND PRACTICE IN MEETING ACTIVITIES

Each annual meeting lasts for two days and involves a number of interactive group activities, breakout sessions led by student leaders, speakers, collective meals, and some recreational activities like Casino Night and DJ and an early-morning scavenger hunt. At the 2006 AALEC meeting, one of the more interesting group activities was a session labeled the "Wall of Prejudice" moderated by the university's Women's Center Director, a white woman, who between 2000 and 2006 served as the coordinator for Asian American Student Services within the Office of Student

Activities and Multicultural Student Affairs (henceforth referred to as the moderator).[7] The Wall of Prejudice exercise focuses on cultural values and stereotypes. The session began with a general conversation about what it means to be Asian American, what values are important to Asian Americans, and why one should care. One student replied it was important so you know your history; another said that if you are close to your culture it makes you close to who you are. When talking about values one person said that his father was "mean" (the moderator translated that as "a disciplinarian"). Then they talked about "mother," and one student said mother "was everything"; another said "the cook"; a third said his mother still had a big role in his life. Students then tossed out other values—one said self-respect and suggested you have to respect yourself before others respect you. Another talked about appreciating what you have got; and another suggested that you don't know what you have until it's gone. One of the group leaders (a Muslim Indian) said she thought people were happiest if they make the best of what comes their way. They also talked about honoring their parents as an important value of Asian culture (filial piety), as well as the importance of maintaining ties with the homeland. And one student mentioned food—"you are what you eat."

The moderator then distributed a blue sheet to each student with a word on it and involved them in a form of pile-sorting. On the board at the front of the room she had posted the word *Asian* on one end, *American* on the other end, and *Asian-American* in the middle. The students were asked to come forward with their blue sheet, pick up a piece of tape, and post their word up, all in thirty seconds. In the categories at the end of the short flurry of activity were the following:

Asian: humble, studious, patient, powerful, quiet, overachievers, hides emotions, loyal, conformity, independence, works best alone, strong, discipline

American: proud, flexible, deliberate, dreamer, impatient, spontaneous, outspoken, question authority, individual, casualness, thinks on feet, reluctant, risk-taking, destiny

Asian-American: harmony, respect, reliable, works well in a group, looking to be #1, listens well, clumsy, trustworthy, pig-headed, collective decision-making, friendly, tolerant, ambitious, inner strength, perseverance, shows emotions

The moderator then asked the students, who were now sitting in their seats again, if they wanted to move any of the words. One wanted to move powerful to the Asian American category. One wanted to move independent from Asian to American but the group decided not to. Proud was moved to the middle. Respect was moved to the Asian category from the Asian American category. The phrase "shows emotions" was moved to the American category from the Asian American category. What was most intriguing about this exercise and the discussion that followed was that these young people appear to accept the positive stereotypes of Asians and Asian Americans, but to be less comfortable with what they perceive as the negative ones. The moderator talked with them about the middle category and the question of reconciling extremes. How do you have an Asian American identity, she asked; how do you balance contrasting values? One student suggested that there would always be a bit of imbalance. "Everyone has a strong and a weak side," offered another student. A third said, "there is a time and a place for everything," which the moderator translated as "having flexibility" and then suggested that this can be a benefit. This was followed by a discussion of what to do when confronted with stereotypes as well as of what labels are out there. One student mentioned the term "FOBS" (fresh off the boat) as the way to label people who showed some Asian characteristics. "Traditional" and "introverted" were also offered as other words used to describe those leaning to the Asian side. Those leaning to the American side they said were confronted with such labels as "whitewashed," "easy going," "crazy," "arrogant," "Abercrombie and Fitch." The students were then asked how they find the middle ground. One student suggested they should speak up; others said you should tell the person to stop; a third suggested that you should work to show both sides. In a later conversation, the moderator explained that the Wall of Prejudice exercise "allows us to own the stereotypes and prejudices that we see and hear (and may feel), but then to talk about ways that those hurt us, and then allow participants to tear it all down."

This practice activity teaches Asian youth to confront stereotypes and labels as well as to forge their own understanding of who they are as individuals. While it is set up as a multicultural exercise with preestablished categories, there is room in the exercise for students to think about and challenge the meanings that have been assigned to these categories and to realize which ones they have perhaps internalized.

The next activity involved exposing these young people to positive role models—particularly individuals who have assumed leadership roles in different social contexts. In the field research that Deborah Reed-Danahay and I have conducted focused on the civic engagements of Vietnamese and Indian first-generation immigrants (Brettell and Reed-Danahay 2012), we have taken note of the importance of banquets and other community events as places where community leaders and politically active individuals address their coethnics, narrating their own personal stories of climbing the ladder to leadership and greater civic participation. At the AALEC meeting, a similar mechanism is used. At the 2006 conference, during the luncheon on the first day, a Korean-origin manager from Frito Lay (whose corporate headquarters are in Dallas) addressed the students. He offered the model of a path to success within the business world, suggesting that anyone in the room could rise to the managerial level if they had the ambition and determination to do so. This speaker started by relating his own experience to that of his audience. "I am an Asian, and I am supposed to be good at math," he joked. He talked about his parents, small business owners, who worked hard so that he could be a success in school—again a story with which some of the young people in the audience would be familiar. He then turned to another stereotype and turned it on its head. Several of you, he observed, probably play in your school orchestra. This involves a team environment, he emphasized, "something applicable to the real world." The more general message to these young people was that they should "pursue their own interests, based on their own strengths and talents and in the long run these will pay off." He invoked the overall theme of the 2006 conference by encouraging his audience to "know who you are and what you want to do; and be strategic because leadership involves strategic thinking and access." However, he also shared some of the other dimensions of leadership, from his point of view: honesty, candidness, being a good listener, working with others, and celebrating the success of others.

The second speaker was Joe Chow, the Chinese-born mayor of Addison, an inner-ring suburb of Dallas. Chow, who often appears at Asian events in the DFW area, described his own background—arriving in the United States in 1979 to pursue a degree at a university in Oklahoma, taking a job as a waiter and then various other positions in the restaurant industry until he opened his own restaurant in the DFW area in 1986. He then branched out into the real estate and insurance businesses and in 2002 ran for and was elected to the Addison city council. Chow said that many people told him he could not win—that he had no base and that he had never engaged in a leadership program or served on a voluntary board. But he persisted. "I knocked on every door of Addison two or three times," he said, and once elected, he claimed that he worked harder than others. Chow became mayor pro-tem in 2004 and then, having built up his own confidence, he ran for and was elected mayor in 2005.[8] He described some of the business boards on which he has served, including the Greater Asian American Chamber of Commerce, and stressed the importance of "giving back to one's community." He acknowledged that few Asian parents encourage their children to "go help someone." "They want you to be physicians, attorneys, and engineers." But his message was different—"Get into service." He concluded by telling the assembled youth that because they were members of the second generation they had the language skills and American civic knowledge that many of their parents did not and that this would serve them well.

The first day of this meeting ended with a "privilege walk" exercise. This exercise is a standard component of diversity training that is meant to reveal the economic and social inequalities that are behind the privileges extended to some in our society by comparison with others. It offers a visible representation of different life experiences. But perhaps most important, it had the result of highlighting differences in experience within the "Asian" category. At the beginning of the exercise at the 2006 AALEC meeting, all the students were asked to stand in an even line and hold hands. Then a series of questions were read out by a facilitator, one by one, and the students were told to take X many steps forward depending on how they responded to the question as applicable to themselves. The line begins to break apart. One question, for example, was "Are you a white male?" and the instruction was to take five steps forward if the answer in your case was "yes." Another was "Did either of your parents or another family member ever spend time in a refugee camp?" and the instruction was to take three steps backward; others had to do with the level of education of parents, if they had traveled, if there were books in their house, if their family expected them to go to college, and if they had ever been asked to speak for all the people of their ethnic group. This exercise went on for several minutes, and then the students were asked to stop and look around. The lone white male in the group was the furthest ahead. On his tail were several Indian girls, something that indicates the class selectivity of Indians in this country. Several of the Vietnamese students were at the back because they had parents with little education or parents or a family member who had been in refugee camps. The students were asked to talk about how they felt being at the front, the back, the middle. The group was not that talkative so some of the facilitators (the college students who were serving as role models to their younger peers) jumped in, a response that perhaps reflects the very issue that this conference was meant to remedy or may simply have been a function of this being at the end of a long and intense day. But the message of the day was clear—that Asian American youth should "find" themselves in a blend of both cultures, that they should confront discrimination and prejudice, and that they should be aware of the diversity of life experiences that they and their families represent within the "Asian" category.

CONCLUSION

Alex Stepick and Carol Stepick (2002: 254) have suggested that while we may not know much yet about immigrant youth attitudes toward civic engagement, "we do know that responses to discrimination will play a critical role and that immigrant youth's complex identities will probably promote multiple forms of engagement." Campus student organizations in general, and events such as the Asian American Leadership Education Conference in particular, are communities of practice where Asian American youth can work out some of these issues. They are also made aware of what they have in common as well as of how they are different. Lisa Lowe (1991: 28) has stressed the heterogeneity of Asian Americans (by class, gender, and national difference) "as part of a strategy to destabilize the dominant discursive construction and determination of Asian Americans as a homogenous group." This dominant construction, she suggests, often resulted in exclusion. AALEC tries to provide members of the second generation with the self-awareness and leadership skills that will help them to challenge this exclusion.

A good deal of scholarly attention has been paid to the apparent "political docility" of Asian immigrants in the United States (see, for example, Lien 2001). In an early article, Moon (1984: 584) pointed out that "Asian Americans have remained unassertive, indifferent, and even fatalistic in political matters. Their lack of participation in civil movements on their own behalf and in support of other minority groups has been conspicuous." He challenged the prevailing views that this is due to cultural values among Asians and argued instead that it is better explained as a reaction to discrimination and connected to the scientific and technological career paths taken by many Asian immigrants. The activities and speakers at the AALEC meetings are instructive not only in offering strategies for dealing with discrimination, including establishing a sense of who they are as Asians, Asian Americans, and Americans, but also in opening the arena of possibilities with regard to career paths and in encouraging engagement in the civic sphere.

Clearly an important implication of this research, and a next step for future inquiry, would be to explore how leadership training such as that discussed in this chapter might influence how Asian youth become involved not only in corporate leadership, but also in national issues and electoral politics as they grow to maturity. What issues will galvanize their attention in ways that are parallel to the mobilization of Latino youth around the DREAM Act? Will the issues vary depending on national origins, reflecting the diversity within this population that emerged from the "privilege walk" exercise? Or will pan-ethnic concerns shared across Asian groups in America be drivers for civic and political action? Further, to what extent will the involvement of Asian youth in the civic and political spheres of the United States be guided by homeland issues, something that clearly influences the political activities of many first-generation Asian immigrant groups—for example, Hindu nationalism among Indian immigrants or anticommunism among Vietnamese immigrants? The children of Asian immigrants are beginning to stake their claims and make their place in local, state, and national politics—in some cases moving to national prominence—as the examples of the governors of Louisiana (Bobby Jindal) and South Carolina (Nikki Haley), both the children of immigrants from India, indicate. And nationwide, as is evidenced by the number of articles on the voting patterns of Asian Americans in the 2010 election, the media is beginning to draw attention to the role of this population in American political life.[9]

Finally, this consideration of AALEC raises some interesting issues in relation to diversity training and multiculturalism more broadly and as matters of policy. In the European context, policies of multiculturalism are currently hotly debated and controversial (Wikan 2002; Grillo 2010). While the debate is less heated in the

United States, there certainly are subtexts regarding cultural difference—especially in relation to language—present in public discourse. The communities of practice that I have described in this chapter provide a context in which Asian youth can both be themselves and acquire the skills that will allow them to succeed within and potentially lead within the broader multicultural public sphere.

NOTES

1. The terms "second generation," "immigrant youth," or "children of immigrants" are often loosely and imprecisely applied, not only to quite distinct populations from a variety of national origin backgrounds but also to young people who may or may not have been born in the host-society. Some young people are immigrants; others are not.

2. See "Undocumented Immigrant Youth Support DREAM Act by Coming Out of the Shadows," *Latin America News Dispatch*, May 5, 2011. (*www.latindispatch.com/2011/ 05/05/undocumented-immigrant-youth-support-dream-act-by-coming-out-of-the-shadows/*). Accessed September 5, 2011.

3. This research for this paper was part of a project supported by the Russell Sage Foundation. Deborah Reed-Danahay was the co–principal investigator on this project. Any ideas developed in this chapter are those of the author alone and do not reflect the opinions of the co-PI or the Russell Sage Foundation. Although the project primarily focused on first-generation immigrants (Brettell and Reed-Danahay 2012), we did gather data on the children of immigrants (1.5 and second generation) on two college campuses by means of a short survey focused on high school and campus organizational activities, several focus groups, and participant observation at several student organization meetings.

4. For further discussion of the concept of "community of practice," see Lave and Wenger 1991; Wenger 1998, 2006.

5. Information on LEAP can be found at *www.leap.org*.

6. Each year there is a different theme. The theme for the 2008–2009 year was: "Creative Minds: Imagine, Innovate, Influence."

7. This woman's education and professional experience had primarily been with Asian and Asian American cultures. She also helped to found the Diversity Education program (DEP) at her university and taught the training classes from 2000 to 2006 and was succeeded by the coordinator for African American Student Services in 2006. As of the fall of 2007 there is a new director of all the Asian organizations who is of Asian background. The Asian organizations on this campus include the Asian Council, the East Asian Students Association, the Hindu Students Association, the Indian Students Association, the Persian Students Association, and the Vietnamese Students Association. It was often impossible to tell the national origins of the students participating although there were more East and Southeast Asians than Indian students.

8. Chow has been reelected two more times as mayor of Addison, the maximum number of terms he can serve.

9. For an excellent overview of Asian immigrants in the United States, see the recent report from the Pew Center (2012).

REFERENCES

Alba, Richard, and Mary C. Waters (eds.). 2011. *The Next Generation: Immigrant Youth in Comparative Perspective*. New York: New York University Press.

Albuquerque, Rosana. 2000. Political Participation of Luso-African Youth in Portugal: Some Hypotheses for the Study of Gender. *Papers*. Universidade Aberta, Centro de Estudos das Migrações e das Relações Interculturais, pp. 167–82. Lisbon.

Aparicio, Ana. 2007. Contesting Race and Power: Second-Generation Dominican Youth in the New Gotham. *City and Society* 19 (2): 179–201.

Bedolla, L.G. 2000. They and We: Identity, Gender and Poitics among Latin Youth in Los Angeles." *Social Science Quarterly* 81: 106–66.

Brettell, Caroline B., and Faith G. Nibbs. 2009. Lived Hybridity: Second-Generation Identity Construction through College Festival. *Identities: Global Studies in Culture and Power* 16 (6): 678–99.

Brettell, Caroline B., and Deborah Reed-Danahay. 2008. "Communities of Practice" for Civic and Political Engagement: Asian Indian and Vietnamese Immigrant Organizations in a Southwest Metropolis." In *Civic Hopes and Political Realities: Immigrants, Community Organizations, and Political Engagement*, S. Karthick Ramakrishnan and Irene Bloemraad, eds., pp. 195–21. New York: Russell Sage Foundation.

———. 2012. *Civic Engagements: The Citizenship Practices of Indian and Vietnamese Immigrants*. Stanford, CA: Stanford University Press.

DeJaeghere, Joan G., and Kate S. McCleary. 2010. The Making of Mexican Migrant Youth Civic Identities: Transnational Spaces and Imaginaries. *Anthropology and Education Quarterly* 41 (3): 228–44.

Espiritu, Yen Le. 1994. The Intersection of Race, Ethnicity, and Class: The Multiple Identities of Second Generation Filipinos." *Identities* 1 (2–3): 249–73.

Foner, Nancy (ed.). 2009. *Across Generations: Immigrant Families in America*. New York: New York University Press.

Foner, Nancy, and Joanna Dreby. 2011. Relations between the Generations in Immigrant Families. *Annual Review of Sociology* 37: 545–64.

Geron, Kim, Enrique de la Cruz, Leland T. Saito, and Jaideep Singh. 2001. Asian Pacific Americans' Social Movements and Interest Groups. *PS: Political Science and Politics* 34 (3): 618–24.

Grillo, Ralph. 2010. An Excess of Alterity? Debating Difference in a Multicultural Society. In *Anthropology of Migration and Multiculturalism: New Directions*, Steven Vertovec, ed., pp. 19–38. New York: Routledge.

Hall, Kathleen D. 2002. *Lives in Transition: Sikh Youths as British Citizens*. Philadelphia: University of Pennsylvania Press.

Junn, Jane, and Natalie Masuoka. 2008. Identities in Context: Politicized Racial Group Consciousness among Asian American and Latino Youth. *Applied Developmental Science* 12 (2): 93–101.

Kasinitz, Philip, John H. Mollenkopf, and Mary C. Waters (eds.). 2004. *Becoming New Yorkers: Ethnographies of the New Second Generation*. New York: Russell Sage Foundation.

Kasinitz, Philip, John H. Mollenkopf, Mary C. Waters, and Jennifer Holdaway. 2008. *Inheriting the City: The Children of Immigrants Come of Age*. New York: Russell Sage Foundation.

Kiang, Peter Nien-chu. 2001. Asian Pacifc American Youth: Pathways for Political Participation. In *Asian Americans and Politics*, Gordon Chang, ed., pp. 230–57. Stanford: Stanford University Press.

Kibria, Nazli. 2002. *Becoming Asian American: Second-Generation Chinese and Korean American American Identities*. Baltimore: Johns Hopkins University Press.

Lave, Jean, and Etienne Wenger. 1991. *Situated Learning: Legitimate Peripheral Participation*. Cambridge: Cambridge University Press.

Lee, Jennifer, and Min Zhou. 2004. *Asian American Youth*. New York: Routledge.

Lee, Sara S. 2004. Class Matters: Racial and Ethnic Identities of Working- and Middle-Class Second Generation Korean Americans in New York City. In *Becoming New Yorkers: Ethnographies of the New Second Generation*, Philip Kasinitz, John H. Mollenkopf, and Mary C. Waters, eds., pp. 313–38. New York: Russell Sage Foundation.

Lien, Pei-te. 2001. *The Making of Asian America through Political Participation*. Philadelphia: Temple University Press.

Lopez, Mark Hugo, and Karlo Barrios Marcelo. 2008. The Civic Engagement of Immigrant Youth: New Evidence from the 2006 Civic and Political Health of the Nation Survey. *Applied Developmental Science* 12 (2): 66–73.

Louie, Vivian. 2004a. Becoming and Being Chinese American in College: A Look at Ethnicity, Social Class, and Neighborhood Identity Development. In *Immigrant Life in the US: Multi-disciplinary Perspectives*, Donna Gabaccia and Colin Leach, eds., pp. 113–29. New York: Routledge.

———. 2004b. *Compelled to Excel: Immigration, Education, and Opportunity among Chinese Americans*. Stanford, CA: Stanford University Press.

Lowe, Lisa. 1991. Heterogeneity, Hybridity, Multiplicity: Making Asian American Difference. *Diaspora* 1 (1): 24–44.

Maira, Sunaina. 2002. *Desis in the House: Indian American Youth Culture in New York City*. Philadelphia: Temple University Press.

———. 2004. Youth Culture, Citizenship and Globalization: South Asian Muslim Youth in the United States after September 11th. *Comparative Studies of South Asian, Africa and the Middle East* (24) 1: 18–30.

———. 2009. *Missing: Youth, Citizenship, and Empire after 9/11*. Durham, NC: Duke University Press.

Marwell, Nicole. 2004. Ethnic and Postethnic Politics in New York City: The Dominican Second Generation." In *Becoming New Yorkers: Ethnographies of the New Second Generation*, Philip Kasinitz, John H. Mollenkopf and Mary C. Waters, eds., pp. 227–56. New York: Russell Sage Foundation, 2004.

Min, Pyong Gap (ed.). 2002. *Second Generation: Ethnic Identity among Asian Americans*. New York: AltaMira.

Moon, H. Jo. 1984. The Putative Political Compacency of Asian Americans. *Political Psychology* 5 (4): 583–605.

Moon, Seungsook. 2003. Immigration and Mothering: Case Studies from Two Generations of Korean Immigrant Women. *Gender and Society* 17 (6): 840–60.

Museus, Samuel D. 2008. The Role of Ethnic Student Organizations in Fostering African American and Asian American Students' Cultural Adjustment and Membership in Predominantly White Institutions. *Journal of College Student Development* 49 (6): 568–86.

Pew Research Center. 2012. *The Rise of Asian Americans*. Social and Demographic Trends. Washington, DC: Pew Research Center.

Qin, Desiree Baolian. 2006. "Our Child Doesn't Talk to Us Anymore": Alienation in Immigrant Chinese Families." *Anthropology and Education Quarterly* 37 (2): 162–79.

Rumbaut, Rubén G., and Alejandro Portes (eds.). 2001. *Ethnicities: Children of Immigrants in America*. New York: Russell Sage Foundation.

Shankar, Shalini. 2008. *Desi Land: Teen Culture, Class and Success in Silicon Valley*. Durham, NC: Duke University Press.

Suárez Orozco, Carola, Marcelo M. Suárez Orozco, and Irina Todorova. 2008. *Learning in a New Land: Immigrant Students in American Society*. Cambridge, MA: Belknap Press of Harvard University Press.

Stepick, Alex, and Carol Dutton Stepick. 2002. Becoming American, Constructing Ethnicity: Immigrant Youth and Civic Engagement. *Applied Developmental Science* 6 (4): 247–57.

Stepick, Alex, Carol Dutton Stepick, and Yves Labissiere. 2008. South Florida's Immigrant Youth and Civic Engagement: Major Engagement: Minor Differences. *Applied Developmental Science* 12 (2): 57–65.

Tuan, Mia. 2002. Second-Generation Asian American Identity: Clues from the Asian Ethnic Experience. In *Second Generation: Ethnic Identity among Asian Americans*, Pyong Gap Min, ed., pp. 209–37. Walnut Creek, CA: AltaMira.

Ueda, Reed. 1999. Second-Generation Civic America: Education, Citizenship, and the Children of Immigrants. *Journal of Interdisciplinary History* 29 (4): 661–81.

Wenger, Etienne. 1998. *Communities of Practice: Learning, Meaning, and Identity*. Cambridge: Cambridge University Press.

———. 2006. Communities of Practice: A Brief Introduction. *www.ewenger.com/theory/*. Accessed July 26, 2011.

Wikan, Unni. 2002. *Generous Betrayal: Politics of Culture in the New Europe*. Chicago: University of Chicago Press.

Wray-Lake, Laura, Amy K. Syvertsen, and Constance A. Flanagan. 2008. Contested Citizenship and Social Exclusion: Adolescent Arab-American Immigrants' Views of the Social Contract. *Applied Developmental Science* 12 (2): 84–92.

Yoshikawa, Hirokazu. 2011. *Immigrants Raising Citizens: Undocumented Parents and Their Young Children.* New York: Russell Sage Foundation.

Zhou, Min. 1997. Growing Up American: The Challenge Confronting Immigrant Children and Children of Immigrants. *Annual Review of Sociology* 23: 63–95.

———. 1999. Segmented Assimilation: Issues, Controversies, and Recent Research on the New Second Generation. In *The Handbook of International Migration: The American Experience,* Philip Kasinitz, Jose DeWind, and Charles Hirschman, eds., pp. 196–212. New York: Russell Sage Foundation.

———. 2009. Conflict, Coping, and Reconciliation: Intergeneraitonal Relations in Chinese Immigrant Families. In *Across Generations: Immigrant Families in America,* Nancy Foner, ed., pp. 21–46. New York: New York University Press.

Zhou, Min, and Carl L. Bankston III. 1998. *Growing Up American: How Vietnamese Children Adapt to Life in the United States.* New York: Russell Sage Foundation.

3 "MY FRIENDS MAKE ME WHO I AM"

The Social Spaces of Friendship among Second-Generation Youth

Lisa Haayen

While there is a significant and growing amount of literature about the second generation, little if any attention is paid to the role of friendship in these youths' lives. In this chapter, I delve into this understudied social relationship, exploring the ways that second-generation youth draw on their friendship networks to produce and perform aspects of their personal identities.

British sociologist Graham Allan argues that friendship is not independent of other aspects of life, but rather that patterns of friendship reflect and are built around social locations and identities. Patterns of friendship vary by gender, class, ethnicity, age, and social location and are therefore broadly revealing in terms of illuminating the way friendships shape and are shaped by the broader contexts of social organization. Recent work, albeit conducted primarily among adults, shows that friendships play an important role in molding, reinforcing, and challenging individual identities (Allan1996). Despite the fact that friendship has not been a commonly used concept for analysis, Hruschka (2010) argues that there are descriptions of friendship "hidden away" in the ethnographic record. A survey of ethnographic literature about Mexico-US migrants reveals that social scientists are already capturing instances of the way friendship shapes concepts of personal identity (see O'Connor 1990; R. Adler 2004; Smith 2006; Gomberg-Munoz 2011). While ethnographers studying second-generation youth sometimes superficially observe the roles friends play in helping youth reach educational or economic goals, these relationships are rarely taken as a concept for analysis, and scholars have seldom if ever considered a link between friendship and identity. My analysis in this chapter brings the study of friendship "into" the study of second-generation youth and hence provides a new analytical lens that can be used to examine and theorize dimensions of the second-generation experience, in particular that of their identities.

SECOND GENERATION IDENTITY CONSTRUCTION

A body of literature about the children of post-1965 migrants explores the ways these youth actively construct "identities" that are rooted neither exclusively in the United States, nor in their parents' countries of birth, but based on their location between the two. In anthropology, the concept of identity is largely explored in terms of "ethnicity," meaning "how individuals associate themselves or are associated by others with a particular category or group of people based on ethnic or cultural markers" (Brettell and Sargent 2006). This holds true when it comes to the second generation, and social scientists exploring "identity" have largely examined where and how youth delineate the boundaries of their ethnic identities (Waters 1999; Kibria 2002; Maira 2002; Dhingra 2003; Warikoo 2004). Scholars generally agree that this process of ethnic identification is dialogic (Tseng 2002), in that it is constantly created, maintained, and re-created by agentive individuals (Brettell and Sargent 2006).

Those who study second-generation youth in the United States argue that rather than assimilating into a mainstream notion of what it means to be "American," youth are developing a more hybrid, polyglot, cosmopolitan or ethnic conception of the word (Jones-Correa 2002; Warikoo 2004, 2011). Brettell and Nibbs (2009) use the term "lived hybridity" to describe ways that second-generation youth create a hybrid culture that defines who they are and how they fit into the contested racial and ethnic hierarchies of U.S society. This term, which emphasizes the agency of youth, captures the ways that second-generation identities are now theorized to be fluid, multiple, and contextual—and is also framed primarily in terms of ethnicity (Banks 1996; Jenkens 1997; Hall 2002; Brettell and Sargent 2006).

THE RESEARCH CONTEXT: SECOND-GENERATION YOUTH IN PLEASANT PARK

This research is situated in Pleasant Park,[1] a small neighborhood in the heart of Dallas, Texas. Dallas is among the ten largest cities in the United States, and it has been labeled an "emerging gateway city" of immigration as it has experienced a fast and sustained rate of immigration over the past twenty-five years (Hardwick 2008). Dallas was among the top ten US cities showing the greatest population gains between 1990 and 1999, and these gains were achieved entirely from international migration (Frey 2000). Residents of Hispanic or Latino descent account for well over 50 percent of the Pleasant Park neighborhood population, and Mexican immigrants with varying legal statuses make up the vast majority of this group.

The Pleasant Park neighborhood is one of the most densely populated and ethnically diverse neighborhoods in the United States. It comprises almost one hundred apartment complexes; about one hundred small businesses, many family run; and only a handful of single-family homes. Pleasant Park is adjacent to one of

Dallas's most affluent neighborhoods, Green City.[2] Pleasant Park's many apartments were built in the 1960s and 1970s to attract Dallas's young, single, affluent professionals. The neighborhood boomed through the early 1980s and became known to local Dallas residents as a "yuppie" haven (Minora 2012).

However, the population of Pleasant Park started to shift dramatically in the 1980s. The singles the neighborhood originally attracted married and followed a pattern of "neighborhood succession" typical to Dallas (Kemper 2005), leaving the area to seek more spacious single-family homes in the northern suburbs. The year 1988 was a critical one in Pleasant Park, and macroeconomic forces impacted the neighborhood in two ways. First, the housing market suffered a downturn, which depressed rents and property values in what had become an overbuilt market. This left property owners with a glut of empty apartments and no pipeline of young singles to fill them. Second, the federal Fair Housing Act, which barred apartment complexes from discriminating against families, was amended to increase enforcement, and this made Pleasant Park unable to maintain its niche as an exclusive playground for affluent singles. In the early 1990s, many lower-income families began moving into Pleasant Park to take advantage of a large inventory of very affordable apartment housing. Through the 1990s, problems began to plague the neighborhood, and Pleasant Park became an increasingly unsafe and chaotic place to live. There were rising rates of violent and aggravated crime, a preponderance of drugs, an influx of liquor stores coupled with little attempt to limit the sale to those over age twenty-one, and the emergence of neighborhood gangs and prostitution businesses. Property owners put minimal money into maintenance, and many buildings fell into extreme disrepair. Ultimately, Pleasant Park developed a reputation among many Dallasites as a neighborhood to be avoided. Beginning in 2000, the city of Dallas became safer overall, and the Pleasant Park neighborhood followed suit. However, the neighborhood remains a challenging place to live, and residents frequently describe it to me as a place "you want to leave as soon as you can."

Mexican immigrants made up a significant portion of the Pleasant Park population. Dallas has a lengthy history as a receiving context for Mexican immigration. New arrivals first came at the beginning of the twentieth century during the railroad boom, and Dallas saw a new surge of arrivals both during and before the Mexican Revolution. By the 1920s, a significant Mexican "community" had developed (Corchado and Trejo 1996; R. Adler 2005). In 1986, the Immigration Reform and Control Act (IRCA) included an amnesty provision that granted amnesty to more than 3.1 million immigrants, most of whom were of Mexican origin, and one result of this legislation was to increase further the Mexican migrant presence in Dallas, as in many other parts of the country (Adler 2005).

Immigrants from Mexico were attracted to Dallas during the 1990s because of a booming economy and steady work, and they were drawn to the affordable housing that became available in Pleasant Park. The principle of "chain migration" (Massey et al. 1987) is evident in the neighborhood, where many apartment complexes are populated almost entirely with residents from a particular town or village. Many parts of Mexico are represented, including both urban and rural regions. Frequently, my young respondents note that their fathers were the first members of the family to migrate to Dallas. Some also report coming alone with their mothers, or joining their mothers or parents in Dallas after a time, all of which are patterns that have been well established in the migration literature (Hondagneu-Sotelo 1992, 1994, 2001; Hondagneu-Sotelo and Avila 1997; Pessar 1998). The geography of Pleasant Park has developed a distinctly "Mexican" character. Neighborhood shopping centers are lined with Mexican grocery stores, taquerias, pastelerias, and heladerias. It is possible to spend an entire day in Pleasant Park and never encounter the need to speak English, or even to use US dollars. Few residents are able to travel back to Mexico because of increasingly tight enforcement at the border, but friends and family from Mexico frequently visit, and goods, food, and news circulate freely.

In the past five years, the character of Pleasant Park has changed once again, owing to the fact that the International Rescue Committee began resettling significant numbers of refugee families in the neighborhood. The neighborhood has received an influx of new residents from many countries in Africa, the Middle East, and Southeast Asia. Currently, the residents of Pleasant Park represent forty countries from around the world, and local school administrators count at least twenty-seven languages spoken within the small, 3.5-mile area. The arrival of residents from all over the world has made the neighborhood a "superdiverse" context.[3] Some Mexican immigrants, including some of the youth who participated in my research, feel resentment about the changing dynamics of their community. Many have shared with me that they feel the refugee residents are "handed" everything by the government and neighborhood service providers. They contrast this with their parents, who they have seen work hard and struggle over many years to achieve a certain level of stability. As one respondent described to me, "our parents [his and those of other children of Mexican immigrants] came here and worked really hard for every single thing they have, and we have helped them. Now, we have all these new people coming, and they get a laptop, and a phone, and checks coming from the government. And it doesn't seem right. It just doesn't seem fair."

Approximately one-third of Pleasant Park residents are youth under the age of eighteen, and a large subset of this group naturally comprises the second-generation children of the Mexican immigrant community. These youth attend one of four Independent School District (DISD) elementary and middle schools in the neighborhood, all of which feed into Bradford High School.[4] Bradford is among the poorest-performing schools in the city, a fact not lost on many parents who say they migrated to seek better educational opportunities for their children. Second-generation youth of Mexican descent experience their neighborhood's superdiversity as they navigate school, work, and family life, making it a unique site for a study of youth friendships.

THE RESEARCH SAMPLE AND THE PROBLEMATIC LABEL "SECOND GENERATION"

Within Pleasant Park, I conducted ethnographic fieldwork with a group of high school aged second-generation youth. The youth in the sample, who ranged in age from fourteen to nineteen, were all the children of immigrant parents from Mexico. Most of their parents immigrated directly to Pleasant Park, meaning that almost all the youth have lived in their neighborhood for as long as they can remember. Most in fact have spent their entire lives living in the same apartment complex, or perhaps moving between two complexes in close proximity.

The label "second generation" is used to identify children of immigrant parents who were born and raised primarily in the United States or other immigrant-receiving countries (Getrich 2008; Alba and Waters 2011). The label "1.5 generation" is used to describe youth who were born abroad but educated primarily in their receiving country (Smith 2006). Some scholars use the age of twelve as the point of delineation for membership in this group (Kasinitz et al. 2008). The youth in my sample fall into both of these categories. Many were born in the United States to parents who emigrated from Mexico to Dallas in the 1990s. At least one-third were born in Mexico and traveled to Dallas with their parents when they were younger than five years old. Most of these youth lack visas that allow them to be in the country.

An important body of literature documents the many ways that the everyday experiences of the 1.5 generation differ from the US born, or those with a visa (Coutin 2000; Gonzales 2008a, 2008b, 2011; Gonzales and Chavez 2012). Once 1.5-generation youth who lack legal status leave the safe haven of public school, they face a world where their options for further education, employment, and economic stability are severely limited. Some research has found that they live in constant fear of detection by the authorities and deportation. However, the issue of legal status did not weigh heavily on the minds of most youth in my sample. This is perhaps due to the context of their neighborhood, which is home to a large population of migrants of varying legal status from all over the world. Undocumented youth in my sample feel surrounded by others whom they perceive to share their situation. Many are able to secure "informal" employment working for family members who are entrepreneurs and so are unconcerned about being able to find work. They view police raids to be possible but relatively infrequent. Most have heard that they will be able to apply for state-funded college assistance in Texas. And many also feel that their legal status will not hinder them from settling in Pleasant Park and marrying, or starting a family if that is what they choose to do. Gonzales and Chavez (2012) found that young people "awake to the nightmare" of their illegal status as they move from adolescence to adulthood, meaning they gradually become aware of the way it restricts their options. While the youth in my sample, the oldest of whom were just beginning their senior year of high school when this research was completed, may be on the cusp of this awareness, few if any had yet realized it as a serious concern.

My research also revealed that the concept of "generation" does not resonate with the youth themselves. My informants do not characterize or organize their network of friends in terms of country of birth or legal status, and they do not self-identify or draw any type of social boundaries on this basis. As one informant explained to me, "If you become good enough friends with someone, you kind of get a sense of whether they have papers or not, but it really does not matter." Another quickly noted, "It's not something you ever talk about openly. That would be awkward and even a little rude."

Therefore, in this chapter, as is common in much of the literature,[5] I use the label "second generation" to describe all the youth in my sample, including those born in the United States and those who arrived as young children. The chapter will not tease out differences between "second-generation" youth and the theoretical "1.5 generation," a topic that is less germane to my inquiry about how the identities of youth born to immigrant parents are emically constructed.

DATA COLLECTION METHODS

The data for this study was gathered during fieldwork conducted between 2010 and 2013, using methods including individual structured interviews, individual unstructured interviews, group discussions, projective drawing and speaking exercises about friends, and extensive participant observation with youth, their friends, and their families. These data were collected by identifying various types of sites where it was possible to observe over time the way friendship relationships are developed and maintained. These included spending extended amounts of time at a college readiness program attended during three summers; neighborhood churches; swimming pools and apartment complexes around the neighborhood; sports and school clubs, such as soccer and tennis teams and the Student Council; neighborhood fairs and festivals; and social gatherings at the homes of my respondents.

This research proceeded from an emic definition of friendship; during interviews, conversations, and participant observation, I asked youth to identify, engage with, and talk about their relationships with their "friends" and "close friends," and the work proceeded along the (admittedly sometimes fuzzy) boundaries that they themselves identified. By engaging second-generation youth in Pleasant Park in the process of visually representing their networks (Galaskiewicz and Wasserman 1993) of friends, I was able to gain an understanding of the complex set of friendship relationships that each maintains. Youth's friends are often compartmentalized into different groups, based on contexts of interaction, including "school" friends, "sports or club" friends, "work" friends, and "cousins," just to name a few. Youth use technology, including Facebook and group text messaging, to maintain a large group of people who in some way or another fit into their notion of what a "friend" is.

However, most youth also have a smaller group of five to seven "close friends," and within this circle, a handful of one to three individuals with whom they have frequent and sustained contact outside of school.

The following sections explore my findings, including a discussion of (1) who second-generation youth befriend and (2) the way friendship serves as a space for the construction and performance of personal identity.

WHO DO SECOND-GENERATION YOUTH BEFRIEND?

Conversations about "close friends" revealed that there is a high degree of homogeneity in youths' friendship networks. The majority reported that most of their friends are close to their same age and live within their same neighborhood. Frequently, youth described a process whereby they meet and become close to a next-door neighbor or friend who lives within their same apartment complex and then begin to spend time with them at school and other places. Since most of the youth do not have vehicles or driver's licenses and since safety concerns keep most (especially girls) close to home, geographic proximity makes it easy to spend time with someone, and youth note that it often facilitates the development of a close friendship relationship. As one respondent explained, "Pablo moved in next door, and we have spent most of our time together ever since. It's easy, because I can just knock on his door when I want to hang out or talk, and my mom doesn't worry about where I am."

Because families within Pleasant Park tend to occupy a similar socioeconomic "class" location, forging friendships primarily with same-age friends who live in the neighborhood means that second-generation youth count among their close friends other high school aged youth who are also members of "working poor" families. This fact is not lost on many youth, who sense that they and their friends are different from other "Americans." As one youth put it, "I dated a white girl from Preston [an affluent suburb] once, and it was just different. She had really different customs—her whole family did. Their house was huge, and they all sat around watching TV together in the evenings. I don't know, I just never felt really comfortable there." Another echoed this sentiment adding that "[white] Americans are just different. They live in big houses with lots of space. Their neighborhoods are more controlled. They can go to sleep earlier than we can and not worry about what is happening outside in the street. The city protects them more than us. There are big differences in the way we all live. I went in the house of a white coworker once, and I was kind of just amazed."

In addition to sharing their age, neighborhood location, and social "class," youth in my sample reported that almost all their close friends shared their "Mexican" ethnicity. Most estimated that 90 percent to 100 percent of their friends are "Mexican like me." One youth noted, "Yeah, my friends are pretty much all Mexican like me. When I was younger, like in elementary school, I had a couple of African American friends, but some moved away, and I kind of drifted apart from the others as I got older." And, another added that coworker "100 percent of my friends are Mexican like me. We just have the same point of view about most things. They have the same traditions, they are Catholic, they dress the same way and eat the same foods as me. We just fit together better."

I asked youth to consider why this is the case, and their responses were enlightening. Some, who have absorbed the broader discourses about multiculturalism (Kymlicka 2001), were reticent to address this subject, lest they appear racist. A few maintained that there is no particular reason for the lack of diversity, and that it is just "happenstance." However, when probed to truly reflect, youth described a myriad of reasons that it is better to be friends with someone who is "Mexican too." The most commonly cited reasons included the fact that this kind of friend "speaks your language," "faces the same experiences," "feels more at ease around your family, and "just understands your culture better." Many youth expressed the feeling that it is just more "comfortable" to be friends with people who are also "Mexican." A few comments from the youth themselves further explicate their feelings on this issue: "It's easier to be friends with people who talk the same language. You can tell jokes and stories in Spanish and not have to remember to speak only English or worry that they won't understand." "At school, I see Mexicans hanging out with Mexicans, black kids hanging out with blacks, and foreign kids hanging out with kids from their same country. I think it's just because they have more in common and feel more comfortable around each other." "I think I am friends with mostly other Mexicans because we all face common experiences. You know, on the first day of school, I will tend to go toward someone who looks something like me, and we will almost immediately have some things to talk about." "Someone Hispanic is just more likely to be like you are or to face something you are also facing. This is especially true for girls—Hispanic girlfriends are much more likely to get along with your parents and family than other kinds of friends."

Overall, it can be said that the friendship networks of second-generation Mexican youth in Pleasant Park are almost universally marked by the traits of age, geographical, social class, and ethnic "homophily" (McPherson et al. 2001). Homophily refers to the idea that contact between similar people occurs at a higher rate than contact among dissimilar people, and it has been attached to the common adage "birds of a feather flock together." Because most second-generation youth in Pleasant Park spend the majority of their time at home or at school, it is perhaps not surprising that the majority of their friends tend to be other high school–age youth who attend their high school and live nearby. The literature supports the fact that the structure of urban living means that youth are most likely to befriend those with whom they have regular contact (Moore 1990: 729). However, the almost universal trend toward ethnic homophily is perhaps more surprising and striking because it does not necessarily square with the superdiverse quality of the neighborhood; while Mexican American second-generation youth could choose to befriend youth from many different ethnic backgrounds, most form their close friendships with others whom they perceive to share their Mexican ethnicity.

This finding about ethnic homophily provides an ethnographic point of view that challenges frequently repeated conventional assumptions about the lives of the second generation—that they are growing up in increasingly diverse schools, neighborhoods, and worksites and rapidly acquiring multicultural points of view (Kasinitz et al. 2008; Warikoo 2011). For example, Helena Wulff observes that a mixed ethnic group of young teenage girls in South London has grown up "acquiring the habit of multiracial friendship, which is bound to have an increasing political impact in the long run" (1995). By contrast, my findings suggest that while youth in the ethnographic context of one extremely heterogeneous American neighborhood do live, work, and attend school among an increasingly diverse group of peers, it is in some ways more accurate to say that they live "alongside" but not "with" their ethnically diverse neighbors.

When capturing this tendency toward ethnic homophily, it is critical to avoid essentializing a level of ethnic "sameness" that does not actually exist within the "Mexican" community in Pleasant Park. Stuart Hall (1996: 4) noted that "identification" is "constructed on the back of a recognition of some common origin or shared characteristics with another person or group . . . and with the natural closure of solidarity and allegiance established on this foundation." In this way, many of my youth respondents self-identify with friends they perceive to be "Mexican like me" based on the imagining a shared point of origin in Mexico. However, Hall cautioned against the "naturalism" of identity, arguing that identities are "never unified and, in late modern times, increasingly fragmented and fractured; never singular but multiply constructed across different, often intersecting and antagonistic discourses, practices, and positions." Further, they are "constantly in the process of change and transformation" (4). This is undoubtedly the case in Pleasant Park. There is not one fixed concept of "Mexicanness," but rather this is a concept that is constantly in flux and that of course varies within and between individuals and families based on different points of reference, a dynamic that has been well established in the literature of Mexican migration (Cintron 1997; Trueba 1999; Hirsch 1999; Smith 2006). However, for the purposes of this research, the important finding is that at a certain "scale," my youth respondents draw a boundary based on their "Mexicanness." While important in their own eyes, it is undoubtedly a "constructed form of closure" (S. Hall 1996: 4)—one that should never cloud or mask the multiple and constantly shifting points of identification that exist among individuals of Mexican descent living in Pleasant Park.

Although I approached this study intending not to focus on ethnic boundaries, I soon found that ethnic homophily is an important part of social life for my respondents. To understand the ways that these youths' identities are shaped by friends, it is extremely important to first understand that their friendship relationships are social fields within which personal identity is being received, shaped, and sanctioned by close friends whom they perceive themselves to share a similar ethnic point of view.

WHAT DO FRIENDS DO: CLOSE FRIENDSHIP AS SPACE FOR PERSONAL IDENTITY PRODUCTION AND PERFORMANCE

My youth respondents of both genders generally talked about their relationships with their close friends in positive terms. This contrasts with a body of literature that highlights less positive aspects of friendships (Vigil 1988, 2002; Cepeda 2003; Barash 2007; Mendoza-Denton 2008). My respondents maintained that a high degree of loyalty and trust is exactly what makes a friendship "close." A youth's "close friends" are distinct from other members of their broader friendship group precisely because they do not have to worry that they will stab them in the back, tell their secrets, "narc" on them, let them down, or steal their boyfriend or girlfriend. Of course, close friends do betray, and when this happens they are quickly removed from a youth's inner circle. Close friendships are extremely rare. Not every youth in my study professed to have close friends, and many had only one. They are often described through a metaphor of family ("like a sister/brother to me") or in terms of a matrimony (my "wifey"). This makes close friendship a unique social space that affords the performance and production of identity, and the findings below focus on the positive aspects of this type of relationship, while not ignoring the conflict and tension that can take place within such spaces.

Second-generation youth in Pleasant Park commonly expressed the sentiment that "my friends make me who I am." This powerful declaration illustrates the fact that friendship relationships do indeed serve as social spaces within which youth can work out their unique and shifting understandings of their personal identities. Specifically, friends help second-generation youth produce them both by validating their unique understandings of their "self" and also by helping to develop or evolve these self-understandings over time, and in response to shifting situational contexts.

When youth reflect on the role friendships play in their lives, the phrase "the real me" frequently surfaces. Second-generation youth in my study believe that a friend, by definition, is someone who "knows the real me" and who "understands me like no one else." These declarations highlight the fact that transparency is an important aspect of a friendship. For second-generation youth in Pleasant Park, a friend is someone from whom "I don't have to hide anything." Close friends are those you trust enough to engage in unfiltered conversations, and they provide social spaces where it is safe to let your guard down. Your friends, youth in this study assert, don't judge, and therefore, you can tell them anything. They know everything you have done, but yet they still see you for the "real" you. This aspect of friendship goes to the heart of the way friends help produce an individual youth's unique understandings of their true "self." In some ways, second-generation youth believe that they exist as people, because their friends know that they do. As one youth described it, "When you are with friends, it is the one place you can be your-self. You don't have to fake it, or live up to their expectations, or act a certain way because it is expected. You are free to just be yourself."

Sociologist Dorothy Jerrome (1992) makes a similar observation in a study of the ways that the activities associated with friendship shape the lives of a group of elderly women in a retirement community in Sussex, England. Friendships "locate" individual women within a framework of shared values and attitudes, and in this way confirm "who" each woman believes she is and who she can credibly "claim to be." In a similar fashion, friendship relationships in Pleasant Park are spaces within which second-generation youth develop their own, egocentric ideas about their unique personal identities. Their overlapping and constantly evolving beliefs, desires, attitudes, and ideas—about their guiding principles and values, their orien-tation toward school, their aspirations for the future, their role as "Americans," their gendered roles as men or women, and their roles within their families and their ethnic communities—all can be expressed to friends in raw and unfiltered ways. In response, youth can rely on their friends to validate these understandings about personal identity, by locating them, receiving them, believing them, and responding to them. In a Hegelian sense, youth believe they "are," because their friends know them as unique people. Second-generation youth assert that: "My family members don't even know me as well as my close friends do. Friends know the good, the bad, and even the very worst side of me. My family, especially my parents may know what is best for me, but my friends take the time to try to see who I really am, what I really think and want." "You always need to have close friends, because they will be on your side. They will know you and support you in everything you try to do. In this neighborhood, you can't go it alone." "My friends know me, and they don't judge me. They are just there for me to let me be the person I want to be and help along the way as much as they can."

This use of spaces of friendship for the confirmation and validation of iden-tity calls to mind Goffman's ideas about social drama (1990 [1959]), which pro-vided a foundation for the field of social-interaction theory. Youth's observations about friendship and interactions with their friends suggest that close friendships are "backstage" spaces, where youth can comfortably and confidently "work out," the identities that they will perform for the other audiences they encounter. The trusting bond that is established with close friends means youth feel less pressure to perform in the ways that other audiences (peers, teachers, parents, or community members) expect, and instead feel free to define and express themselves on their own terms. This points to a powerful role for friendships in the lives of second-generation youth.

Not only do friendships help youth produce their personal identities by vali-dating their conceptualizations of themselves; they also function as social spaces where identities can be developed. Youth rely on close friends to serve the important role of working through issues and "talking things out." For example, when they face a crossroads or need to make a decision, it is important to them to be able to confer with friends, compare viewpoints, and reach their own opinion. Youth recount this type of advice sharing and interaction about a range of issues, including things like how to resolve problems with romantic relationships, how to handle disputes or differences of opinion with parents, and how important it is to stay in school. For example, several young girls described to me a process of hashing out their views about pregnancy and motherhood with friends, to reach their own opinions on the issue. One respondent, Sara, recounted that this was a regular topic of conversation with a close friend who had very different views than she did. Both girls had mothers who felt that pregnancy at a young age was an expected part of life and something to be celebrated. Although Sara was committed to graduating high school and attending college before considering motherhood, and thought it might feel "shameful" to become pregnant before doing so, she was frequently faced with a need to confront the beliefs of other women in her family and uncertain of her own stance on this important issue concerning her future. Conversely, her best friend thought that handling pregnancy and high school with parental support was manageable and "not that big of a deal."

Through frequent conversation, the girls agreed to disagree. However, their conversation and interaction left Sara feeling clear on her own beliefs; after working through the issue with her friend, she was more committed than ever to putting off motherhood until at least after high school. Importantly, it was the social space of her friendship relationship with her best friend that allowed her to work out her own personal beliefs and gain clarity on this issue.

Many of the young males I have come to know describe using their friendships as a means to work out decisions about their future aspirations. In Pleasant Park, as mentioned above, alcohol and drugs are ubiquitous. Young males in particular feel almost daily pressure to engage in the use of these substances, which often is bound up in gang activity. Male second-generation youth are forced almost daily to choose between a path that includes drinking, drugs, and violence or one that includes staying in school, participating in extracurricular activities, and steering clear of the authorities. Young boys recount that interaction with friends tangibly shapes the way they view these choices and the decisions they make.

One respondent, Jose, recounts that he is a member of a small group of friends, who are soccer buddies who have a pact to "make it." The boys regularly get together to discuss the pressures they face and to remind each other to stay "on the right track." By doing so, they provide not just positive peer pressure, but social validation that one can choose to steer clear of the allure of partying, drug use, and gangbanging but still find a credible social role within the neighborhood.

Anthropologist Marianne Gullestad (1984) highlights a similar dynamic among a group of young, married women raising children in a middle-class neighborhood in Norway. In observing the way these women provide sociability and support to each other through what she dubs their "kitchen table society," she observes that, through friendships, women develop a common understanding of how to handle their roles as young wives and mothers. Not only do they provide support, they use gossip and other measures to apply warnings and sanctions to friends who step beyond the boundaries of what is acceptable (for example, unacceptable flirting with another woman's husband in public). Ultimately, Gullestad (1984: 256) argues that women's friends "can be seen as mediating between family and marriage and the outside world. . . . Women give each other permissions, support, sanctions, warnings and interpretations" while navigating through their everyday lives. In the same way, second-generation youth rely on their friends to help them mediate their somewhat liminal roles as the children of Mexican immigrants living within an ethnically diverse neighborhood. Together, in collaboration and sometimes conflict, friends help individual youth develop and shape their understandings of who they are, apart from their friends, family, or ethnic community. Further, friendship relationships serve as spaces where these identities can be maintained, even in the face of pressure to shift them in response to outside dynamics.

Second-generation youth also count on their friends to help them perform their unique self-identities for others around them. Because, as Kathleen Hall (2002) points out, youth face the need to interact with so many "others" who seek to define and project identities on them, friendship relationships take on a new importance as a powerful social space with a unique and important role. Second-generation youth in Pleasant Park do indeed encounter the kinds of identities from "without" that Hall identifies. As noted above many youth proudly self-identify as "Mexican," and this produces an identity that they feel carries specific expectations about how they will spend their time, how they will perform in school, when and how they will begin earning a living to help support the family, when and how they will enter into parenthood, and how they will perform their roles as gendered members of their families and extended families. It is important to note again that there are likely countless ways that a "Mexican" identity can be produced within the neighborhood, and that these constantly shift and take form in response to changing contexts, as all identities do. However, it is equally important to consider that second-generation youth themselves use what they perceive as their "Mexicanness" as one point of reference, which they juxtapose against their larger, ethnically homogenous neighborhood, and which helps them to make sense of how they should and want to engage with the social worlds of family, school, work, and community. The expectations that they believe accompany being a "Mexican" in Pleasant Park can often conflict with or challenge youths' understandings of their unique "personal selves," which are shaped through experiences and messages received at school, at work, in the neighborhood, or in the country at-large. In some ways this is captured by the trope of being "caught between two worlds," which is common in the literature of migration (Kibria 2002). Conversely, in relation to "others" in their diverse school or neighborhood, second-generation youth are acutely aware of those who seek to cast them as "just Mexicans," who should occupy a particular role. For many, this means encountering teachers and administrators who they believe do not fully expect them to succeed, or bosses who they feel will always think of them as "just" a busboy or dishwasher. Further, in relation to discourses within the larger nation, the youth believe they encounter many who seek to cast them—along with their families—as people who are undeservingly in the United States regardless of their legal status, a discourse Leo Chavez (2008) has described as the narrative of the "Latino threat." For example, one observes, "So many white people think all Mexicans are just in this country illegally. I feel like they meet me and expect me to be all drunk and disorderly and unruly. I feel like I already have something to prove to them before they even really get to know me." And, another explains, "My coworkers are mostly white, and they go to fancy schools and are headed to college. They all act like we are friends, but deep down I know they all think I will always be the busboy."

Each of these identities is fluid, reflexive, and situational and has its own dynamics. Yet they are also similar to one another in that they are imposed on second-generation youth from the outside. In the face of each, friendships empower and provide agency to youth, by providing safe spaces within which they can answer the question of "who they are" on their own terms. In doing so, youth are free to build on, transform, or depart from the identities they form in relation to the expectations of parents and family members, in relation to the reference point of their Mexican community, and from the ways they are defined by the racial and social discourses circulating in their schools, workplaces, and neighborhood. Further, they can use the social spaces of their friendship relationships to perform their unique personal identities, which are then validated and sanctioned by their friends.

The interactions within a small group of friends who are part of a college readiness program called the "Eagle Scholars" aptly illustrate this point. The youth have come together to support and sanction the goal of "making it." For these youth, "making it" refers to the shared aspiration to complete high school and college, find a job "I like," and create a life "better than my parents have." The friends believe an ultimate articulation of this dream will be to one day have people look up to them, the way they look up to a small handful of adult mentors and role models in their own lives. The youth, many of whom hope to be the first members of their family to graduate high school, face very real obstacles to achieving these goals. For one, many find that other friends or family members, including older siblings or cousins living in the neighborhood, constantly discourage them from pursuing this path. In doing so, individuals often seek to use gendered ideas about what is appropriate for a "Mexican" girl or boy to do or become. Others may find that their desires for further education and white-collar employment bump up against ideas that their parents or adult family members have about the path they should pursue. For example, one respondent recounted: "My dad's side of the family is always telling me that

I am being silly. That I just need to get married and get pregnant like Mexican girls are supposed to do." However, another quickly added: "My cousins and other friends are always telling me I am not going to make it. But I don't even listen to them. I have my Eagles friends, and we know that someday we will have the last laugh." In clinging to their goal, they often use the shared site of their friendship to resist others—other youth, family members, or parents—who assert that they cannot or should not achieve these goals.

The young girls within the circle employ the space of their friendship in a uniquely gendered way. I discovered this one day when I overheard them talking about their relationships with their mothers, many of whom emphasize the importance of learning to run a household, including learning what the girls view as "traditional" skills like planning and cooking meals, cleaning, taking care of laundry, and facilitating family social gatherings. Several of the mothers tell their daughters they want them to have the option to get married and start a family young, should they be unable to achieve their desire to go to college, or change their minds after meeting the right boy. While the girls resent what they view as the implication that they are going to fail and need to "fall back" on the skills they would need to be a young mother and housewife, they agreed among each other that it was important to learn to take care of a household, because it would allow them to be "independent," and not need to "count on anybody else for anything." In so doing, they used the social space of their friendship to transform their mothers' insistence that they learn "traditional skills" into social agreement that it was important to learn skills that would help them become "an independent American women." The space of their friendship, in the form of a conversation and the resulting conclusion, became a way to help the girls perform their shared self-identities as hardworking American students, while also deal with and mediate family expectations, in this case the expectations of their mothers.

In other instances, youth describe friends acting as "mediators" when their personal identities clash with what is expected by parents or family members. One youth, Jesse, described the ways that she teamed up with her best friend, Lupe, to help convince her mother to let her join the high school basketball team. Neither girl felt that she could stick it out on the largely African American team without the support of a good friend. However, Jesse's mother was afraid that frequent practices and late games would be too much of a time commitment and take her daughter away from her responsibilities at home, which included cooking, housework, and caring for her younger siblings. Ultimately, the girls successfully convinced this mother that participating on the team was important for Jesse. They made the case that it was more than acceptable for girls to play sports at their school, that this activity would help Jesse stay involved in and stick with school, and that it would serve the important role of providing an extracurricular activity for her to list on her college applications. Together, the friends successfully meld the mother's expectation of what was appropriate for her teenage daughter with their own understandings of how a young, "Mexican" girl in Pleasant Park should spend her free time. In the process, the social space of their friendship became a venue for the performance—and protection—of a unique personal identity. In a similar fashion, this research reveals the ways that second-generation youth use the spaces of friendship to perform their unique, personal identities, in part by resisting or transforming discourses from "without" that seek to shape their understandings of who they are, whether these come from family members, teachers, peers, neighbors, or discourse within the nation at-large.

CONCLUSION

This study provides several important insights about the social relationships of friendship among second-generation youth. First, it reveals that youths' friendships are not just sites of superfluous social interaction. Rather, they are dynamic social spaces where personal identity can be produced, developed, and performed. Friends validate individual youth's notions of who they "are" as unique individuals. They provide forums where aspects of personal identity can be collaboratively worked out or developed. And, friendships serve as social fields where personal identity can be performed, or expressed to the outside world, in part in response to identities that "others"—including family members, teachers, peers, community members, and fellow citizens—seek to impose on second-generation youth from the outside. In this way, friendships serve as sites of agency for youth, who are able to use them to resist, transform, or critique outside notions of the people they "are" and the people they would like to "become."

As a growing sociological literature considers the ways youth move through school systems, gain jobs, and achieve upward mobility, anthropologists have an opportunity to draw from ethnographic methods and anthropological theory to consider the lives and growth of second-generation youth on a more intimate and personal level. Further research should continue to examine personal identity construction, by broadening the range of contexts and groups of youth studied while continuing to consider the ways that friendships serve as spaces for the development of youth's unique understandings of their personal selves. For example, do friendship relationships in other superdiverse neighborhoods tend to have the same homophilic qualities? Among other groups of friends, both within the same ethnic group and without, do the same dynamics of personal identity development surface? How can this understanding be brought into the now-prevalent study of second-generation outcomes, to provide a fresh lens for thinking about the trajectories of second-generation youth through high school and into adulthood?

In policy terms, this research is timely in light of debates taking place about the futures of second-generation youth, both in the United States (Schumacher-Matos 2010) and other countries of immigration (Wikan 2002). The United States received large numbers of migrants in the 1990s and 2000s, and policy experts argue that this means the country must now shift from an immigration policy with an emphasis on keeping newcomers out, to one with an emphasis on encouraging those who are already settled there to "integrate into the social fabric" (Myers 2012). This research offers an understanding about ways that second-generation youth form identifications against the context of the broader society, thereby providing a perspective that could help policy makers and citizens at-large to answer the call to facilitate their integration. In particular, the findings call attention to the power of friendships to shape youth's trajectories. Friends validate youth's concepts of "self" and in the process play a role in shaping their future goals and aspirations, their senses of right and wrong, and their ideas about how to participate as citizens of their schools, neighborhoods, and country. While not focused on academic outcomes explicitly, the research could be particularly helpful for those wishing to help youth improve their school performance. It sheds light on the ways that networks of friends can either help or hinder educational progress, and this understanding could inspire the development of new programs or the refinement of existing programs that seek to create an environment for positive support among friends.

By engaging with youth who live in a superdiverse neighborhood, this research also highlights the need for policy makers to pay more attention to this type of context, which is an increasingly common one for youth around the country and the world. Researchers within many disciplines tend to be focused on the ties and practices within particular migrant ethnic groups, or on differences among different ethnic groups. Meanwhile, the diverse settings where educational orientation is negotiated through everyday interactions between a number of different ethnic groups remain seriously understudied. This research has begun to illuminate the discourses of race, gender, and class that second-generation students (and their families) navigate as they approach the path to adulthood, and it also indicates that there is much more work to be done.

NOTES

1. The pseudonym "Pleasant Park" has been used to protect the identities of informants and the community.
2. The pseudonym "Green City" has been used to protect the identities of informants and the community.
3. The concept of superdiversity refers to the fact that migrants around the world, including in Pleasant Park, increasingly settle and interact not in ethnic enclaves (Zhou 1992; Stepick et al. 2003), but in areas characterized by extreme diversity of country of origin, ethnic identification, immigration status and corresponding rights, labor market experiences, gender and age profiles, and reception by service providers and residents (Vertovec 2010).

4. The pseudonym "Bradford High School" has been used to protect the identities of informants and the community.

5. For example, see Suarez-Orozco and Suárez-Orozco 2001; Smith 2006; Getrich 2008; Alba and Waters 2011.

REFERENCES

Achor, Shirley. 1978. *Mexican Americans in a Dallas Barrio.* Tucson: University of Arizona Press.

Adler, Patricia A., and Peter Adler. 1998. *Peer Power: Preadolescent Culture and Identity.* New Brunswick, NJ: Rutgers University Press.

Adler, Rachel H. 2004. *Yucatecans in Dallas: Breaching the Border, Bridging the Distance.* Boston: Pearson/Allyn and Bacon.

———. 2005. ¡Oye Compadre! The Chef Needs a Dishwasher: Yucatecan Men in the Dallas Restaurant Economy. *Urban Anthropology and Studies of Cultural Systems and World Economic Development* 34 (2/3): 217–46.

Alba, Richard, and Victor Nee. 2003. *Remaking the American Mainstream: Assimilation and Contemporary Immigration.* Cambridge, MA: Harvard University Press.

Alba, Richard, and Mary C. Waters. 2011. *The Next Generation: Immigrant Youth in a Comparative Perspective.* New York: New York University Press.

Allan, Graham. 1996. *Kinship and Friendship in Modern Britain.* Oxford: Oxford University Press.

Amit-Talai, Vered. 1995. The Waltz of Sociability: Intimacy, Dislocation and Friendship in a Quebec High School. In *Youth Cultures: A Cross-Cultural Perspective*, Vered Amit-Talai and Helena Wulff, eds., pp. 145–63. London: Routledge.

Banks, Marcus. 1996. *Ethnicity: Anthropological Constructions.* London: Routledge.

Barash, Susan Shapiro. 2007. *Tripping the Prom Queen: The Truth about Women and Rivalry.* New York: Griffin.

Barth, Frederik. 1969. *Ethnic Groups and Boundaries: The Social Organization of Cultural Difference.* London: Allen and Unwin.

Basch, Linda G., Nina Glick Schiller, and Cristina Szanton-Blanc. 1994. *Nations Unbound: Transnational Projects, Postcolonial Predicaments, and Deterritorialized Nation-States.* Lanhorne, PA: Gordon and Breach.

Bell, Sandra, and Simon Coleman (eds.). 1999. *The Anthropology of Friendship.* Oxford: Berg.

Brettell, Caroline B., and Faith G. Nibbs. 2009. Lived Hybridity: Second-Generation Identity Construction through College Festival. *Identities* 16 (6): 678–99.

Brettell, Caroline B., and Carolyn Sargent. 2006. Introduction, Migration, Identity, and Citizenship: Anthropological Perspectives. *American Behavioral Scientist* 50 (1): 3–8.

Carsten, Janet. 2000. *Cultures of Relatedness: New Approaches to the Study of Kinship.* Cambridge: Cambridge University Press.

Chavez, Leo R. 2008. *The Latino Threat: Constructing Immigrants, Citizens, and the Nation.* Stanford, CA: Stanford University Press.

Cintron, Ralph. 1997. *Angels' Town: Chero Ways, Gang Life, and Rhetorics of the Everyday.* Boston: Beacon.

Corchado, Alfredo, and Frank Trejo. 1999. Urban Renewal: Dallas' Mexican Population Brings Boom Times to Once-Dying Areas, Creates Challenges. *Dallas Morning News,* September 20, p. 1A, 6A–7A.

Coutin, Susan Bibler. 2000. *Legalizing Moves: Salvadoran Immigrants' Struggle for US Residency.* Ann Arbor: University of Michigan Press.

Davidson, Elsa. 2011. *The Burdens of Aspiration: Schools, Youth, and Success in the Divided Social Worlds of Silicon Valley.* New York: New York University Press.

Desai, Amit, and Evan Killick (eds.). 2010. *The Ways of Friendship: Anthropological Perspectives.* New York: Berghahn.

Dhingra, Pawan. 2003. Being American between Black and White: Second Generation Asian American Professionals' Racial Identities. *Journal of Asian American Studies* 6 (2): 117–47.

Frey, William H. 2000. The New Urban Demographics: Race Space and Boomer Aging. *Brookings Review* 18 (3): 20–23.

Galaskiewicz, Joseph, and Stanley Wasserman. 1993. Social Network Analysis: Concepts, Methodology, and Directions for the 1990s. *Sociological Methods and Research* 22 (1): 3–22.

Getrich, Christina. 2008. *American by Birth, Mexican by Blood: Cultural Citizenship and Identity among Second-Generation Mexican Youth.* PhD diss., University of New Mexico.

Glick Schiller, Nina, and Georges Fouron. 2001. *Georges Woke Up Laughing: Long-Distance Nationalism and the Search for Home.* Durham, NC: Duke University Press.

Goffman, Erving. 1990 [1959]. *The Presentation of Self in Everyday Life.* New York: Doubleday.

Gomberg-Muñoz, Ruth. 2011. *Labor and Legality: An Ethnography of a Mexican Immigrant Network.* New York: Oxford University Press.

Gonzales, Roberto G. 2008a. *Born in the Shadows: The Uncertain Futures of the Children of Unauthorized Mexican Migrants.* PhD diss., University of California, Irvine.

———. 2008b. Left Out but Not Shut Down: Political Activism and the Undocumented Student Movement. *Northwestern Journal of Law and Social Policy* 3 (2): 219–39.

———. 2011. Learning to Be Illegal: Undocumented Youth and Shifting Legal Contexts in the Transition to Adulthood. *American Sociological Review* 74 (4): 602–19.

Gonzales Roberto G., and Leo R. Chavez. 2012. "Awakening to a Nightmare": Abjectivity and Illegality in the Lives of Undocumented 1.5-Generation Latino Immigrants in the United States. *Current Anthropology* 53 (3): 255–81.

Gullestad, Marianne. 1984. *Kitchen-Table Society: A Case Study of the Family Life and Friendships of Young Working-Class Mothers in Urban Norway.* Oslo: Universitetsforlaget.

Hall, Kathleen D. 2002. *Lives in Translation: Sikh Youth as British Citizens*. Philadelphia: University of Pennsylvania Press.

Hall, Stuart. 1996. Introduction: Who Needs Identity? In *Questions of Cultural Identity*. P. Du Gay and Stuart Hall, eds., pp. 1–17. Thousand Oaks, CA: Sage.

Hardwick, Susan W. 2008. Place, Space, and Pattern: Geographical Theories in Institutional Migration. In *Migration Theory: Talking across Disciplines*. 2nd ed. Caroline Brettell and James Hollifield, eds., pp. 161–82. New York: Routledge Taylor and Francis.

Hess, B. 1972. Friendship. In *Aging and Society*. Vol. 3, *A Sociology of Age Stratification*, M.W. Riley, ed., pp. 357–96. New York: Russell Sage Foundation.

Hirsch, J.S. 1999. En el Norte la Mujer Manda: Gender, Generation, and Geography in a Mexican Transnational Community. *American Behavioral Scientist* 42 (9): 1332–49.

Holy, Ladislav. 1996. *Anthropological Perspectives on Kinship*. London: Pluto.

Hondagneu-Sotelo, Pierrette. 1992. Overcoming Patriarchal Constraints: The Reconstruction of Gender Relations among Mexican Immigrant Women and Men. *Gender and Society* 6 (3): 393–415.

———. 1994. *Gendered Transitions: Mexican Experiences of Immigration*. Berkeley: University of California Press.

———. 2001. *Doméstica: Immigrant Workers Cleaning and Caring in the Shadows of Affluence*. Berkeley: University of California Press.

Hondagneu-Sotelo, Pierrette, and Ernestine Avila. 1997. "I'm Here but I'm There": The Meanings of Latina Transnational Motherhood. *Gender and Society* 11 (5): 548–71.

Hruschka, Daniel J. 2010. *Friendship: Development, Ecology, and Evolution of a Relationship*. Berkeley: University of California Press.

Jerrome, Dorothy. 1984. Good Company: The Sociological Implications of Friendship. *Sociological Review* 32 (4): 696–718.

———1992. *Good Company: An Anthropological Study of Old People in Groups*. Edinburgh: University Press Edinburgh.

Jones-Correa, Michael. 2002. The Study of Transnationalism among the Children of Immigrants: Where We Are and Where We Should Be Headed. In *The Changing Face of Home: The Transnational Lives of the Second Generation*, Peggy Levitt and Mary C. Waters, eds., pp. 221–52. New York: Russell Sage Foundation.

Kasinitz, Philip, John H. Mollenkopf, Mary C. Waters, and Jennifer Holdaway. 2008. *Inheriting the City: The Children of Immigrants Come of Age*. New York: Russell Sage Foundation.

Kemper, Robert V. 2005. Dallas-Fort Worth: Toward New Models of Urbanization, Community Transformation, and Immigration. *Urban Anthropology and Studies of Cultural Systems and World Economic Development* 34 (2/3): 125–49.

Kibria, Nazli. 2002. *Becoming Asian American: Second-Generation Chinese and Korean American Identities*. Baltimore: Johns Hopkins University Press.

Kymlicka, Will. 2001. *Politics in the Vernacular: Nationalism, Multiculturalism, and Citizenship*. Oxford: Oxford University Press.

Lamphere, Louise. 2007. Migration, Assimilation and the Construction of Identity: Navajo Perspectives. *Ethnic and Racial Studies*: 30 (6): 1132–51.

Levitt, Peggy, and Mary C. Waters (eds.). 2002. *The Changing Face of Home: The Transnational Lives of the Second Generation*. New York: Russell Sage Foundation.

Maira, Sunaina. 2002. *Desis in the House: Indian American Youth Culture in New York City*. Philadelphia: Temple University Press.

———. 2009. *Missing: Youth, Citizenship, and Empire after 9/11*. Durham, NC: Duke University Press.

Massey, Douglas S., Rafael Alarcón, Jorge Durand, and Humberto González. 1987. *Return to Aztlan: The Social Process of International Migration from Western Mexico*. Berkeley: University of California Press.

McPherson, Miller, Lynn Smith-Loing, and James M. Cook. 2001. Birds of a Feather: Homophily in Social Networks. *Annual Review of Sociology* 27: 415–44.

Minora, Leslie. 2012. The Remaking of Vickery Meadow. *Dallas Observer*, February 9.

Moore, Gwen. 1990. Structural Determinants of Men's and Women's Personal Networks. *American Sociological Review* 55 (5): 726–35.

Myers, Dowell. 2012. The Next Immigration Challenge. *New York Times*, January 12, A27.

O'Connor, Mary I. 1990. Women's Networks and the Social Needs of Mexican Immigrants. *Urban Anthropology* 19 (1): 81–98.

Ortner, Sherry B. 2003. *New Jersey Dreaming: Capital, Culture, and the Class of '58*. Durham, NC: Duke University Press.

Pessar, Patricia R. 1998. The Role of Gender, Households and Social Networks in the Migration Process: A Review and Appraisal. In *Becoming American/America Becoming*, Josh DeWind, Charles Hirschman, and Philip Kasinitz, eds., pp. 35–52. New York: Russell Sage Foundation.

Portes, Alejandro, Patricia Fernández-Kelly, and William Haller. 2009. The Adaptation of the Immigrant Second Generation in America: A Theoretical Overview and Recent Evidence. *Journal of Ethnic and Migration Studies* 37 (7): 1077–104.

Reed-Danahay, Deborah. 1999. Friendship, Kinship and the Life Course in Rural Auvergne. In *The Anthropology of Friendship*, Sandra Bell and Simon Coleman, eds., pp. 137–54. Oxford: Berg.

Schneider, David. 1984. *A Critique of the Study of Kinship*. Ann Arbor: University of Michigan Press.

Schumacher-Matos, Edward. 2010. Denying Citizenship for Illegal Immigrants' Children Is a Bad Idea. *Washington Post*, June 27.

Shankar, Shalini. 2008. *Desi Land: Teen Culture, Class, and Success in Silicon Valley*. Durham, NC: Duke University Press.

Smith, Robert C. 2008. Horatio Alger Lives in Brooklyn: Extrafamily Support, Intrafamily Dynamics, and Socially Neutral Operating Identities in Exceptional Mobility among Children of Mexican Immigrants. *Annals of the American Academy of Political and Social Science* 620 (November): 270–90.

Smith, Robert Courtney. 2006. *Mexican New York: Transnational Lives of New Immigrants.* Berkeley: University of California Press.

Stanton-Salazar, R., and S. Spina. 2003. Informal Mentors and Role Models in the Lives of Urban Mexican-Origin Adolescents. *Anthropology and Education Quarterly* 34 (3): 231–54.

Stepick, Alex, Guillermo Grenier, Max Castro, and Marvin Dunn (eds.). 2003. *This Land Is Our Land: Immigrants and Power in Miami.* Berkeley: University of California Press.

Suárez-Orozco, Carola, and Avary Carhill. 2008. Afterword: New Directions in Research with Immigrant Families and Their Children. *New Directions for Child and Adolescent Development* 121: 87–104.

Suárez-Orozco, Carola, and Marcelo M. Suárez-Orozco. 2001. *Children of Immigration.* Cambridge, MA: Harvard University Press.

Suárez-Orozco, Carola, Marcelo M. Suárez-Orozco, and Irina Todorova. 2010. *Learning a New Land: Immigrant Students in American Society.* Cambridge, MA: Belknap Press of Harvard University Press.

Trueba, E.T. 1999. *Latinos Unidos: From Cultural Diversity to the Politics of Solidarity.* Lanham, MD: Health.

Tseng, Yen-Fen 2002. From "Us" to "Them": Diasporic Linkages and Identity Politics. *Identities: Global Studies in Culture and Power* 9 (3): 383–404.

Vertovec, Steven. 2010. Super-diversity and Its Implications. In *Anthropology of Migration and Multiculturalism: New Directions*, Steven Vertovec, ed. Oxford: Routledge.

Vigil, James Diego. 1988. *Barrio Gangs: Street Life and Identity in Southern California.* Austin: University of Texas Press.

———. 2002. *A Rainbow of Gangs: Street Cultures in the Mega-city.* Austin: University of Texas Press.

Warikoo, Natasha. 2004. Cosmopolitan Ethnicity: Second Generation Indo-Caribbean Identities. In *Becoming New Yorkers: Ethnographies of the New Second Generation*, Philip Kasinitz, John H. Mollenkopf, and Mary C. Waters, eds., pp. 361–92. New York: Russell Sage Foundation.

———. 2011. *Balancing Acts: Youth Culture in the Global City.* Berkeley: University of California Press.

Waters, Mary C. 1999. *Black Identities: West Indian Immigrant Dreams and American Realities.* New York: Russell Sage Foundation.

Wikan, Unni. 2002. *Generous Betrayal: Politics of Culture in the New Europe.* Chicago: University of Chicago Press.

Wulff, Helena. 1995. Inter-racial Friendship: Consuming Youth Styles, Ethnicity and Teenage Femininity in South London. In *Youth Cultures: A Cross-Cultural Perspective*, Vered Amit-Talai and Helena Wulff, eds., pp. 65–77. London: Routledge.

Zhou, Min. 1992. *Chinatown: The Socioeconomic Potential of an Urban Enclave.* Philadelphia: Temple University Press.

———. 1997. Growing Up American: The Challenge Confronting Immigrant Children and Children of Immigrants. *Annual Review of Sociology* 23: 63–95.

4 "TOO WHITE AND DIDN'T BELONG"

The Intra-ethnic Consequences of Second-Generation Digital Diasporas

Faith G. Nibbs

How second-generation children of immigrants develop a sense of themselves as part of an ethnic group is a question that has been explored for over half a century in the United States (Zhou 1997; Portes and Rumbaut 2001; Rumbaut and Portes 2001; Alba and Waters 2011), and more recently in Germany (Kecskes 2000; Heckmann, Lederer, and Worbs 2001; Haug 2002; Worbs 2003; Riphahn 2003; Kristen, Cornelia, and Granato 2007).

Kenneth Karst (1986) has described two distinct paths that foreigners, and by extension, their children, follow to satisfy their need to belong: turning inward to group solidarity, or outward toward the mainstream community. Most recently, attention has turned to what Block and Buckingham (2007) regard as the third significant socializing influence in the life of second-generation youth life: the media. Existing research on negotiating group solidarity and group identities through media in migrant communities has mainly focused on its usefulness as a starting point for collective resistance to outside assimilating forces or injustices (Miller and Slater 2000; Kasinitz et al. 2002; Block and Buckingham 2007; Plaza 2010). But I have argued elsewhere (Nibbs 2014) that constructs of belonging using media technology are not just negotiated in relation to the society to which one migrates, but also within one's own culture group. As young people are likely to be the most prolific users of this technology, it may be useful to think of their need to belong through these constructs not just in terms of insider/outsider–either/or, but as a demonstration of a combination of both.

The social processes by which intragenerational gaps or peer acculturation gaps in the second generation are created, and the internal boundaries they reflect, have been studied to a lesser extent and generally appear in two bodies of literature. One set can be found in the literature on intragenerational gaps in immigrant youth and is rooted in oppositional theory (Ogbu 1990). This literature (see Waters 1994;

Zhou 1997) suggests that oppressed minorites form identities that are bound in opposition to the successful mainstream. The second body of literature also emphasizes ideas of opposition but more directly in relation to the idea of "acting white." Originally formulated in reference to African Americans, this framework, derived from Fordham and Ogbu (1986) suggests that for African American youth, being accused of acting white is tantamount to being told one does not belong in the black race (Neal-Barnett 2001), and thus, is one of the most negative charges that can be hurled against a youth by his or her peers. The social consequences for acting white can be so debilitiating to youth identity that it has resulted in young people hiding their intelligence, withdrawing from white friends, or from black youth society (Fordham and Ogbu 1986; Graham 1995; Kunjufu 1988). More recently, acting-white theorizations have been extended to discussions of Asian Americans. Pyke and Dang (2003), for example, in their work with Korean and Vietnamese children of immigrants, suggest that these youth use terms like *FOB* (fresh off the boat) and *whitewashed* as classificatory shemes by which coethnic peers identify each other as similar or different. They note how such categories "mark not only symbolic boundaries but also interactional boundaries that are internally maintained" (p. 162). As Internet technology is relatively new, we do not as yet understand how these boundaries are maintained or negotiated in the new kinds of social spaces created in cyberspace. I have found that both oppositional and dissonance theories can be useful in understanding how the second-generation children of Hmong immigrants are defining their identity and creating its boundaries on the Internet.

This comparative study is based on an ethnographic investigation into second-generation Hmong engagement with online social networking in the United States and Germany within the discourse of "acting white" on YouTube, Hmong-specific blogs, Facebook web postings, the text created within each site, sound files, and any visual images found. I am defining the second generation to mean children who were born in the United States or Germany to at least one parent who was born in another country. In this specific case study, it happened that all the second-generation participants had two foreign-born parents, making this particular group distinct in that it can particularize the participants experience from those with only one foreign-born parent. To properly contextualize and compare the various social interactions that became part of these online identities, I simultaneously engaged in conventional face-to-face ethnographic fieldwork in the United States and Germany. My approach aligns with S. Wilson and Peterson (2002: 457), who suggest the virtual is merely a "continuum of communities, identities, and networks that exist" in the real, and that "the integration of ethnographic methods, both conventional and virtual, can be helpful in developing rich comprehensive understandings of relationships between online and off-line cultural life" (B. Wilson 2006: 309).

An emerging mode of social control or boundary maintenance that is especially prevalent in second-generation youth is social networking on the Internet. Digital storyteller Brenda Laurel (1990: 93) referred to earlier forms of these social networks as "vibrant new villages of activity within the larger cultures of computing." Today, estimates suggest that 97 percent of all two-way telecommunication in the world is coming through the Internet and active Facebook users engaged in social networking villages are upward of eight hundred million people (Ferguson 2011). Arturo Escobar (1994: 217) was among the first anthropologists to raise questions about how people were being socialized by their experiences in these new technological spaces. In migration research we have come to understand how web spaces facilitate diasporic bonds (Karim 1998; Wong 2003; Hiller and Franz 2004; Ignacio 2004; Leepreecha 2008; McCaskill 2008; Nibbs 2014), and how those constructed by the more tech-savvy children of immigrants are helping their generation maintain a transnational identity (Plaza 2010). These studies have raised the importance of looking anthropologically at the Internet's potential not only as a tool that links people together, but as a new public sphere.

The second-generation Hmong who have resettled in the West have heavily engaged in Internet use. This chapter will draw from the racial identity literature to examine how second-generation Hmong have adaptively responded to racial categories by reproducing the derogatory stereotype of being "whitewashed" among coethnic peers in online spaces. Using the Internet as my principal site of investigation, I will explain how web-based social networking is being used to perpetuate this intra-ethnic othering, and thereby as a form of social control and as a leveling pressure to define Hmongness within the Hmong community.

The data used in this analysis include observations conducted online over the course of three years of fieldwork in Hmong communities in the United States and Germany that included semistructured interviews and participant observation. The sample Internet posts investigated were constructed and maintained by second-generation Hmong youth in both countries. A Google search for "Hmong" and "Whitewashed" yielded over two hundred hits. The websites analyzed as part of this study had to be active within the previous twelve months of this study. As a result of this sampling criterion, one hundred posts were selected: eighty-five originating in the United States, and twenty originating from Germany. In addition to examining websites, I conducted interviews with thirty second-generation youth from the United States and Germany who self-identify as Internet users ranging in age from sixteen to twenty-six years old. Interviews were conducted online, over the phone, and face-to-face. Participants were recruited by sending e-mail requests on the basis of the web content, and by asking members of my personal research network within the second-generation Hmong demographic in both countries about their experiences within the discourse of acting white on the Internet.

ACTING WHITE OR BEING HMONG

While the exact origins of the Hmong are unknown, China is the first place where they appear in historical records, with many migrating from China to Southeast

Asia during the nineteenth century. During the Vietnam War era, many Laotian Hmong participated in covert US military operations and in the resistance against encroaching communist forces in Laos. When US forces withdrew from the region, Hmong people faced reprisals from the emerging communist regime known as the Pathet Lao. Thousands of Hmong refugees began fleeing Southeast Asia in 1975, immigrating to North America and other parts of the world.

After arriving in the West, Hmong collective identity, in part, was shaped by the various intersecting forms of subordination they experienced. In America that meant not only in opposition to the social identity of their white-dominant hosts, but also in opposition to their more successful East Asian "model minority" counterparts. Aihwa Ong (1999) argues that this resulted in an "ideological whitening" of middle-class East Asians and an "ideological blackening" of the poorer Southeast Asian refugees. Pyke and Dang (2003: 150) have more recently argued that neither category makes them "honorary whites" nor frees them from racial oppression," but alternatively puts them in a "stratified space between black and whites," wherein they construct "sub-ethnic identities." One distinction between Asian Americans and African Americans, from where the acting white literature first derived, is that Asians Americans are perpetually seen as "ethnic" as opposed to "American," thus confounding race and ethnicity in a more complex way (150). This can be seen in the kinds of press that followed the Hmong's arrival in the West. Not being white was telegraphed in terms of cultural elements, as they were described as "rural, preliterate, patriarchal, clannish, and traditional" (Lee 2005: 3). Thus, being cultural Hmong was seen by their Western hosts, among other things, as not being white.

Nagel (1994: 154–55) suggests that immigrant populations enlist or impose different identities depending on their symbolic appropriateness and strategic utility. The second-generation Hmong are an appropriate group to evaluate in order to understand how these racialized identities are internalized and used strategically. As with all immigrant groups before them, Hmong youth had to assess which of their parent's cultural practices they had to give up or hide in order to merge into society. Of the cultural characteristics they decided to keep as a part of their identity, some emerged with a hyperimportance and became performative standards for Hmong authenticity. They took the form of an invisible line drawn in the sand that, if crossed, transports the offender from authentically ethnic to American, from embracing one's heritage to "selling out," from Hmong to whitewashed. The resulting distrust and isolation toward those who cross this line is a practice Pyke and Dang (2003) refer to as "intraethnic othering."

In contrast, the second-generation Hmong whose parents were resettled in Germany were bought up in what is considered a "post-racial" society, where racial hierarchies have not been an organizing principle of social order for over sixty years (Fehrenbach 2008). In Germany, postwar distinctions of social inclusion and exclusion have come to be understood more in terms of "religion and culture rather than biology and phenotype" (Fehrenbach 2008: 934). This does not mean that expressions of racism are not manifest in that society, but rather that "whiteness" is not a part of the discourse in the same way that it is in the United States. Being Hmong in Germany, or Asian, is an ethnic categorization—not racial. Those who cross the lines in the sand drawn around second-generation Hmongness in that country cross from authentically ethnic to German, but not from Hmong to white. At least that is the way it has been for the past twenty-five years. Today, with the proliferation of Internet exchanges between US and German Hmong, there is evidence that American Hmong discourses about being whitewashed have had an effect on the identities of their German coethnics and how they see themselves vis-à-vis their hosts and each other. In the sections that follow, I describe some of the meanings attached to Hmongness and whiteness, how Internet use is reproducing these forms of racialization in other Hmong communities, and with what consequences.

ON BEING HMONG

The Hmong are first and foremost a clan people whose kinship network has served as a social safety net and their primary means of cultural integration for centuries. Even prior to their arrival in the West, kinship gave the Hmong their sense of being connected to one another. In light of Hmong history and their way of life, which has scattered them over southern China, northern Vietnam, Laos, Thailand, and nine countries of refugee resettlement, it is surprising that a collective identity distinct from non-Hmong has remained as strong as it has. Their strong identity has been attributed to their tradition of marrying within Hmong society (Millett 2002: 49). As a result of their emphasis on marrying within the group, they have become more or less genetically "closed." Pierre Van den Berghe (1987: 24) argues that this perception of ethnicity is at its core "made up of people who know themselves to be related to each other by a double network of ties of descent and marriage." And because Hmong cosmology continues these relationships in the afterlife, it is this web of ties that helps set them apart in their minds from other groups. As such, marrying outside the group is often seen as a deliberate act of disruption and hence an attack on Hmongness.

The Hmong second generation, while identifying with other Westerners in many ways, has largely chosen to maintain a preference toward marriage with other Hmong. Pressures to behave within these boundaries are put on youth by casting those who violate these norms as outsiders. One Hmong second-generation woman whose parents were resettled in Germany experienced it this way: "When I told my family I was marrying a German, my father told me that it would be the end. I knew what he meant. I would be out—out of the family, out of their spiritual protection, out of everything. After the wedding we barely saw each other or talked. The Hmong say that by marrying a German I chose to abandon our people, that I am no longer Hmong." A second-generation Hmong woman whose parents were resettled in America shared her frustration of how this act has also caused others in her peer group to question her Hmongness:

> I have been labeled too white, and told that I didn't belong. I've been criticized of not being Hmong enough. Why? My husband is not Hmong. . . . I am more Hmong than some Hmong people who claim to have "Hmong pride." Just because my husband isn't Hmong doesn't make me less Hmong. Doing so doesn't mean you're more Hmong. I educate myself in the Hmong culture and teach others about it. I am Hmong!

In the American example, marrying outside the ethnic group was framed as "acting white"; thus, young women who act white are displaying a premonitory sign that they will look outside their ethnic group for a spouse. Marrying outside the group is seen as a moral failing that brings shame to a family, and hence a young person's action in this direction is subject to critique by the community.

Another symbolic qualifier of Hmongness in opposition to whiteness that has developed is being able to speak the Hmong language. To protect the uniqueness of their ethnic identity and maintain cultural boundaries, it is not surprising that maintaining knowledge and use of the Hmong language has become "insider" behavior, and therefore appropriate. The loss of language falls outside of this cultural framework. I find it particularly interesting that this emphasis on language remains important in the second generation, particularly because other research among other immigrant populations has found that even among young people who strongly identify with their ethnic group nevertheless prefer to speak English rather than their parent's native languages (Portes and Rumbaut 2001). For the second-generation Hmong, however, it is not a preference to speak their language that seems to make one an insider, but rather maintaining the ability to do so.

One consequence of this boundary marker is a marginalization of women. In my own online sample, I found five times as many young men accused young women of this disintegration of Hmongness than the reverse. One female youth shared her experience with this gender differential:

> I have seen people, mostly girls, try to express their concern about how some people are trying to exclude them from being Hmong based on things like speaking English instead of Hmong around Hmong people. . . . I've seen guys attack girls who say they are too conceited or proud to keep their own heritage, or they think they are too good to be Hmong. I witnessed a guy at a Hmong New Year fest who overheard a girl say she was proud to be Hmong, go up and force her to try to speak Hmong. And when he exposed that she could not do it fluently, he laughed and made a big public deal saying she really had no Hmong pride.

This gendered language ideology is not unique to the Hmong. Similar gendered language differentials have been found among other immigrant groups effecting processes of changes in or resisting changing from indigenous languages to languages of wider communication. In this case, the application of being whitewashed could be attributed to the high value placed on Hmong-to-Hmong marriage. A male who speaks better Hmong can accuse a female of being whitewashed, and her assimilative behavior is seen as a threat to marry outside the ethnic group. Thus, the loss of face asserts a form of social pressure on the female youth to behave within certain peer-imposed boundaries if they wish to remain eligible to marry Hmong. This follows Weber's (1946: 405) assertion that status, or quality of social honor, directly influences social class, and that maintaining social honor within a group may require the maintenance of a specific style of life and the rejection of others. These core values regarding what it means to be Hmong are monitored by means of the Internet, which has become a vital means of communication. But maintaining those boundaries in the age of Internet technology is messy.

INTERNET BROWBEATING

High connectivity of immigrant youth over the Internet has provided a new space for social interaction and for monitoring dimensions of identity and the maintenance of core values among the second generation. Prior to the ubiquitous use of Internet, studies have suggested that second generation children of immigrants act "American" or by extension, "German" or "pan-ethnic" in the mainstream, public spheres and "ethnic" or "racial" in marginal, private ones. For Internet users, the private sphere gets muddled with the public as home videos, photos, or behaviors displayed on social networking sites are put out in virtual space for all to see. Multiple studies have been conducted on how this technology binds diasporic people together and creates emotional bonds (see Bernal 2005; Brinkerhoff 2009; Alonso and Oiarzabal 2010), while less attention has been given to how much agency individuals have to switch between identities in this context. Moreover, little is known about how the muddling of public and private identity spheres impacts ethnic consciousness in a way that members experience disapproval, or even ostracism from coethnics.

Social networking through Hmong-specific blogs, Facebook, or even forums such as YouTube has created new spaces to reinforce peer definitions of whiteness and provide another public platform to uphold the boundaries of group authenticity. Even though users can use pseudonyms to try to mask specific identities, or communicate in the private sphere through invited networks of friends, users have had little trouble unmasking one another and exposing exactly who is doing the blogging. Moreover, in cases where friends "friend" other friends, intimately shared information can quickly disseminate to unintended peripheral networks numbering in the thousands, all reading in on a once private conversation. In a small ethnic community such as the Hmong, where a high premium is placed on reputation or face maintenance, the Internet can become a new medium through which one can quickly lose face.

One set of online conversations among second-generation Hmong that particularly attracted my attention were those regarding whiteness in relation to how much Hmong an individual spoke. Take, for example, this entry from a participant's Facebook page: "One thing I must say is that it is quite shameful to see Hmong people who are unable to speak Hmong. To me, it seems as though they look down on their culture, throwing it out the window. There are acceptations [*sic*] like those who are adopted, maybe, but I believe those who have parents who are Hmong should able to speak Hmong or understand it." Another Facebook entry situated the Hmongness of peers squarely within use of Hmong language: "I have witnessed too many small Hmong children who are ignorant about their culture. Too many Hmong children don't speak their native tongue and don't even recognize the Hmong language when they hear it. Too many Hmong children don't know what the essence of being 'Hmong' is about nor do they have pride that they are Hmong." In this particular entry, referring to Hmong women competing in Miss Hmong pageants, where girls are judged on their ability to emulate "traditional" cultural values, not being able to communicate in their parent's native language is a source of public shame: "The ones who can't speak properly just sound funny . . . but the ones that can are actually really good. . . . Take [Miss Hmong] pageants for an example. . . . You can totally tell who's good and who's not. The ones, who aren't good, are made fun of, and the ones that are good, are being complimented." Finally, in this Facebook entry, a youth's ability to speak Hmong is related to class: "I'm a Hmong American and I hate the fact that Hmong oldies keep on asking me why I speak Hmong so clearly? Now I know, it is 'cause Hmong teen[s] these days can't even speak Hmong fluently or not even at all. Hmong teens these days have to realize that we are Hmong and we don't have a country. If we want to improve, we should fight for a country and show that we are not low classes like other countries think we are."

Besides Facebook, there are a several other popular websites that have adopted social network features. One such site is YouTube. YouTube began as a video-sharing platform but has expanded to offer spaces to comment on the posted video and the ability to broaden viewer access to videos through "friending"—or sharing the video with other networks of people. Patricia Lange (2008) has noted how young people are using these channels to project identities that affiliate with particular social groups. However, these public/private comment forums also offer a unique opportunity for peer critique. Again, using Hmong-language proficiency as an example, in one particular YouTube post, there are some Hmong girls horsing around, as youth do, in their own backyard, or what would otherwise be a safe space in the domestic sphere. They are talking to each other in Hmong. Someone, other than the girls playing shot the video and posted it on the web. As Hmong young people began to view it, the thread of comments under the video turned to how well the girls spoke Hmong. "Come one Girls (*sic*)," one post reads, then the text switches to all capital letters connoting a shout, "DON'T EVEN TRY TO SPEAK HMONG!" This was followed by other youth commenting on their Hmongness based on their language proficiency: "What is that? Chinese?"

Another YouTube video that was posted showed some Hmong youth helping their peers with the language. The comment posted by the person who uploaded the video read: "Attempting to teach Hmong to white-washed kids." Comments posted by viewers ranged from noting the entertainment value of Hmong who can't speak their own language "LMAO" [laughing my ass off], to disgust and sorrow over the state of the one trying to regain some language fluency: "So sad, So white . . . we really do all need to learn the language." One youth in an interview said that she is very cautious not to post videos where she is speaking Hmong because she knows that despite its content, it will ultimately be judged on how white or Hmong she is. For the same reason, others spoke of fearing their friends will post video taken unsuspectedly from their phones that depicts them "acting white."

Similar discussions associating whiteness with language are being debated on Hmong blog sites. One website that pitches itself as "your virtual Hmong community" has a thread going called "Hmong who can't speak Hmong." Whiteness and outsidership are specifically ascribed to those in the second generation who cannot speak the language. Take, for instance, a blogger who wrote: "I know a few Hmong who can't speak their own language . . . so sorry for them. However, it is their fault, 'cause they *choose* not to speak it. . . . Anyway, me and some friend[s] of mine always tease and make fun of them. . . . They are all white washed."

Another subscriber directly equates Hmong pride with use of the Hmong language: "hell yeah!! hmong pride or u die!! show no fear, and show no mercy to those who look down on us hmong. (but wats up wid those white wash hmong foke who band hmong pride and never teaches there kids any hmong! there freakn killing us hmong peeps!!)" In this post, a male youth explicitly states that self-ascription to Hmongness is not enough—they must speak the language: "If someone is of Hmong descent but can't speak Hmong, i do not consider them Hmong. . . . To me, they're Hmong In Name Only (HINO's) because they're of Hmong descent, but they're no longer part of the culture and people of Hmong. They are White!" One young lady, who was brought up in a small town with parents who spoke only English, tried to explain in a blog that her commitment to multiple identities did not cross racial lines, explaining that while she may be "English-washed," she was not white. This was countered by another respondent who wrote:

> To actually try and compare your white washed wannabe-Hmong lifestyle to English-washed is completely absurd! So you hang with Hmong people? Okay, congrats on having Hmong friends. You're still white washed. The only person

who believes in a category of English-washed is you. If it makes you feel like the Hmong you desperately want to be, so be it. Just remember, you can call an orange and apple, but it's still an orange. But guess what: You are white washed! Accept it.

Turning now to Germany, although the Hmong population is quite small (approximately 150 people), its second generation is very actively engaged with the Internet, and social networking has played a significant role as a symbolic bridge in connecting this small group to other Hmong in the diaspora. As Internet use is international, Levitt and Jaworsky (2007: 34) found that country-specific identifications of racial identities can affect "migrant trajectories." By extension, US-based discussions of whiteness have the potential to influence Hmong in other countries of the diaspora, such as in Gammertingen, Germany, where those identifications may have a weaker or altogether different meaning. Messages being sent and received over the Internet need to be contextualized in the diverse experiences of the second generation from the various localities where they have been resettled. Second-generation Hmong Germans for example, position themselves differently from Hmong Americans because they have been racialized in different ways. Those youth who were raised in America in areas where communities had been inundated with large numbers of Southeast Asians that came over with their parents experienced well-documented instances of racism, whereas the second-generation Hmong who had been brought up in southern Germany have been regarded as a model minority of sorts, assimilating to some ideal of the German middle-class mainstream in a way that has weakened their racial status. How do these ethnic differences impact diasporic discussions of whiteness over the Internet?

It has only been in the last two years that Facebook, blogging, and other forms of diasporic web-based communication have come into fashion in the German Hmong community, and they are now the spaces where the second generation do the majority of their social networking. For the young girls in particular, whose courtship traditions leave them waiting to be found by a Hmong man, they see these sites as an additional opportunity to showcase their Hmongness or marriageability to the rest of the diaspora. For the young men, it is an additional site to scout out a wife. The American Hmong have been engaging in these types of events longer, are more proficient at them, and thus have created most of the Hmong-related blogs that the Germans network in. However, new social networking sites like Facebook, YouTube, and self-made web pages create new spaces where the German Hmong can control and disseminate information about their situated Hmongness to coethnics outside their small community.

One example of this comes from the website of a young female German Hmong. It opens within the rules of Hmong communication with the woman clearly communicating her clan affiliation. This is to avoid violating the incest taboo, that is, inadvertently attracting a Hmong man from the same clan. The communication is followed by general musing about what Hmong life in Germany is like, a list of likes and dislikes, and links to her photo gallery filled with uploaded pictures showcasing her in business, casual, and traditional attire. Besides e-mail contact information, she has a place for visitors to blog or chat with her. One Hmong, who describes himself as a Hmong American "teen," wrote on her wall "Dang that's amusing, I never knew there were Hmong in Germany. I will call you guys Nazis for fun."

It is comments like this that pressure the German second generation to prove their Hmongness to the diaspora. One way the Internet has improved their position in this regard is through an American Hmong–created Facebook application called "How Hmong Are You?" On this link, respondents are asked to rate a set of questions, similar to a Likert scale, on how well they identify with certain statements like: "You speak the Hmong language"; "You like having lots of people around"; "Your family is huge"; "You know some things about the history of your people [but] you never really cared too much to study it"; and, "Hmong videos are hilarious, especially the really bad special effects." Even though this Facebook application was originally constructed as a joke, or a parody of the parental generation, the German Hmong that I follow on Facebook don't know this. This quiz, originally forwarded to one of them by a relative in Wisconsin, got passed around from youth to youth in Germany, who took this quiz with earnestness. One of the unique aspects of the German Hmong is how well the second generation speaks the Hmong language. Not surprisingly, their average scores were very high, most scoring "a full 90% Hmong"—which, according to this app, means they "enjoy the Hmong customs and abide to tradition. You speak the language frequently and can converse with the old folks without using English." They began posting these results with pride on their Facebook profiles for everyone in their American Hmong network to see. I was told by several German Hmong that it proves they weren't "white washed." Curious, I asked where they got that phrase from and, repeatedly, was told that they saw other American Hmong who could not speak Hmong being called this on the Internet. This showed not only that they engaged with other Hmong websites originating from America, but also that they used these websites as a form of empowerment to position themselves inside the diasporic parameters of Hmongness.

SUMMARY AND IMPLICATIONS

From the experiences of the Hmong second generation we can garner a better understanding of how the children of migrants deal with being ethnic, racial, and Western at the same time and how the Internet becomes a space for negotiating these various aspects of self. Participating in collective behaviors binds them together in an ethnic intimacy that perpetuates important cultural values. Certain factors, such as Hmong kinship and cosmology, form the oppositional cultural framework for a Hmong social identity that separates them from their hosts. Learning English or German to the exclusion of Hmong or marrying a non-Hmong are interpreted as efforts to transgress important cultural boundaries, and hence as deliberate acts of betrayal worthy of casting someone outside of the group. Given the influence of the parents' ethnic identity on their children, it follows that the second generation ratifies a comparable definition of Hmongness. In direct response to racial discrimination, the second generation also adopts a sense of Hmongness that is formed in opposition to whiteness. Thus, claiming Hmongness for these youth depends not only on their lineage, but also on their cultural image as not white. This poses a double dilemma for these youth who may simultaneously consider their ethnicity to be a stigma because of racism and cultural differences from whites while also experiencing a stigma from coethnic peers for being too white.

There are several implications of this analysis. The first is that prior to ubiquitous Internet use, these youth could segregate their identities in different spheres, the public and private. However, the Internet has brought the private into the public, melding these worlds in a way that is limiting users' agency to create group boundaries between insiders and outsiders as they choose. This is having a particular effect on women. Because of the dynamics of face in Hmong culture, there are social implications for marriage within these networks, particularly if a woman's identity is seen as drifting too far outside of one sanctioned by her peers. In this way, this technology is becoming a boundary-maintaining mechanism and a mechanism for social control, especially for the male youth who are using it to exert social pressure on those in their potential marriage pool. Since whiteness is being linked to, or impedes, a woman's marriageability, and is being associated disproportionally with women, I assert that a certain feminization of whiteness is being formed among these second-generation youth. This is a subject that needs more thorough examination than is possible in this chapter.

Second, cyberspace territories, like real territories, provide a site where the meaning of ethnic identity is shaped beyond the local territory or country where the messages originate. The German "How Hmong Are You" example demonstrates how one country may have power over creating a diasporic ideal identity, which has to be reconciled with other diasporic Hmong identities. Other researchers have argued that norms and values within an ethnic group are dependent on the extent to which individuals participate in the social relationships with those who also hold those norms and values (Zhou 1997: 997). From this we might understand that while computer-mediated communication can transcend the limitation of small and isolated diasporic communities to connect them to other coethnics, it is limited to those who possess the technology and to those who live in countries where Internet policies are not restricted by socialist governments. Therefore the more that second-generation Hmong participate in Internet-based social networking with members of their own group around the diaspora, the more I expect the normative conformity to these behavioral standards. This is something particularly to watch for as the Hmong youth in China gain freer access to mediums such as Facebook.

Min Zhou (1999) has stressed that the second generation, unlike their parents, evaluate themselves and construct identities in relation to the meanings and standards of their new society. Internet spaces have brought them in contact with broader diasporic societies who do not necessarily occupy "singular, uncomplicated spaces of identity, but speak from intersecting subject positions" (Block and Buckingham 2007: 75). The web-based "new villages of activity" that Laurel (1990: 93) once imagined have become an important social sphere where these different diasporic subjectivities can be communicated and contested. In this way, the experiences of the Hmong second generation in the United States and Germany add to our understanding of how the myriad social positions and cultural boundaries that exist across diasporas are shaped and reshaped through computer-mediated spaces, and their experiences highlight the importance of studying virtual spaces in relation to identity formations among the children of immigrants.

NOTES

1. See Kulick 1998; Echeverria 2003; Cavanaugh 2006.
2. The project "Diasporic Networks and Processes of Incorporation among the Hmong in the US and Germany" was supported by the Cultural Anthropology Program of the National Science Foundation (NSF/BCS 0849055). Any opinions, findings, conclusions, or recommendations expressed in this paper are those of the authors and do not necessarily reflect the views of the National Science Foundation.

REFERENCES

Alba, Richard. 2005. Bright vs. Blurred Boundaries: Second-Generation Assimilation and Exclusion in France, Germany, and the United States. *Ethnic and Racial Studies* 28 (1): 20–49.

Alba, Richard, and Mary C. Waters (eds.). 2001. *The Next Generation: Immigrant Youth in Comparative Perspective.* New York: New York University Press.

Alonso, Andoni, and Pedro Oiarzabal. 2010. *Diasporas in the New Media Age: Identity, Politics, and Community.* Reno: Nevada University Press.

Archdeacon, Thomas J. 1983. *Becoming American: An Ethnic History.* New York: Free Press.

Barker, C. 1999. Empowerment and Resistance: Collective Effervescence and Other Accounts. In *Transforming Politics: Power and Resistance*, P. Bagguley and J. Hearn, eds., pp. 11–31. London: Macmillan.

Becker, Howard. 1995. Visual Sociology, Documentary Photograph and Photojournalism: It's (Almost) All a Matter of Context. *Visual Sociology* 10 (1): 5–14.

Bennett, A. 2004. Virtual Subculture? Youth Identity and the Internet. In *After Subculture: Critical Studies in Contemporary Youth Culture*, A. Bennett and K. Khan-Harris, eds., pp. 162–72. New York: Palgrave.

Bernal, V. 2005. Eritrea On-Line: Diaspora, Cyberspace, and the Public Sphere. *American Ethnologist* 32 (4): 660–75.

Block, Liesbeth de, and David Buckingham. 2007. *Global Children, Global Media: Migration, Media and Childhood.* New York: Palgrave.

Brinkerhoff, Jennifer. 2009. *Digital Diasporas: Identity and Transnational Engagement.* New York: Cambridge University Press.

Canter, Rachelle J., and Suzanne S. Ageton. 1984. The Epidemiology of Adolescent Sex-Role Attitudes. *Sex Roles* 11 (7/8): 657–76.

Castles, M. 1997. *The Power of Identity.* Oxford: Blackwell.

Cavanaugh, Jillian. 2006. Little Women and Vital Champions: Gendered Language Shift in a Northern Italian Town. *Journal of Linguistic Anthropology* 16 (2): 194–210.

Chafetz, J.S. 1978. *Masculine/Feminine or Human?* 2nd ed. Itasca, IL: Peacock.

Clark, Kenneth B., and Mamie P. Clark. 1939. The Development of Consciousness of Self and the Emergence of Racial Identification in Negro Pre-school Children. *Journal of Social Psychology* 10 (4): 591–99.

———. 1947. Racial Identification and Preference in Negro Children. In *Readings in Social Psychology*, T.M. Newcomb and E.L. Hartley, eds., pp. 169–78. New York: Holt.

DeVos, George. 1975. Ethnic Pluralism: Conflict and Accommodation. In *Ethnic Identity: Cultural Continuities and Change*, George DeVos and Lola Romanucci-Ross, eds., pp. 5–41. Mountain View, CA: Mayfield.

Dhingra, Pawan. 2007. *Managing Multicultural Lives.* Stanford, CA: Stanford University Press.

Dublin, Thomas. 1996. *Becoming American, Becoming Ethnic: College Students Explore Their Roots.* Philadelphia: Temple University Press.

Echeverria, Begona. 2003. Language Ideologies in (En)Gendering the Basque Nation. *Language in Society* 32 (3): 383–404.

Escobar, Arturo. 1994. Welcome to Cyberia: Notes on the Anthropology of Cyberculture. *Current Anthropology* 35 (3): 211–23.

Fehrenbach, H. 2008. Review of Timothy L. Schroer, Recasting Race after World War II: Germans and African Americans in American-Occupied Germany (Boulder: University Press of Colorado, 2007). *American Historical Review* 113 (3): 934–35.

Ferguson, Niall. 2011. World on Wi-Fire. *Newsweek*, October 3.

Fordman, Signithia, and John Ogbu. 1986. Black Students' School Success: Coping with the "Burden of 'Acting' White." *Urban Review* 18 (3): 176–206.

forums.hmoob.com. Virtual Hmong Community. *www.forums.hmoob.com/showthread.php?s= d9c9a88eaecedfd2ff753ba537f6e4b0&t=8075&page=2.* Accessed October 10, 2011.

Gamson, W.A. 1992. *Taking Politics.* Cambridge: Cambridge University Press.

Goffman, Erving. 1955. On Facework. *Psychiatry* 18 (3): 213–31.

Graham, Sandra. 1995. Narrative versus Meta-analytic Reviews of Race Differences in Motivation: A Comment on Cooper and Door. *Review of Educational Research* 65 (4): 509–14.

Haug, S. 2002. Familienstand, Schulbildung und Erwerbstaetigkeit Junger Erwachsener: Eine Analyze der Ethnischen und Geschlechtsspezigischen Ungleichheiten—Erste Ergebnisse des Integrationssurveys des BiB. *Zeitschrift fuer Bevoelkerungswissenschaft* 27 (1): 115–44.

Heckman, F., H. Lederer, and S. Worbs (in cooperation with the EFFNATIS research team). 2001. "Effectiveness of National Integration Strategies towards Second-Generation Migrant Youth in a Comparative European Perspective." Final Report to the European Commission, Bamberg, Germany.

Hiller, H. H., and T.M. Franz. 2004. New Ties, Old Ties and Lost Ties: The Use of the Internet in Diaspora. *New Media and Society* 6 (6): 731–52.

Ho, David. 1976. On the Concept of Face. *American Journal of Sociology* 81 (4): 867–84.

Ignacio, Emily Noelle. 2005. *Building Diaspora: Filipino Cultural Community Formation on the Internet*. New Brunswick, NJ: Rutgers University Press.

Karim, Karim H. 1998. *From Ethnic Media to Global Media: Transnational Communication Networks among Diasporic Communities*. Oxford, England: Transnational Communities Programme, University of Oxford.

Karst, Kenneth. 1986. Paths to Belonging: The Constitution and Cultural Identity. *N.C.L. Review* 64: 303.

Kasinitz, Philip, Mary C. Waters, John H. Mollenkopf, and Merih Anil. 2002. Transnationalism and the Children of Immigrants in Contemporary New York. In *The Changing Face of Home: The Transnational Lives of the Second Generation*, Peggy Levitt and Mary C. Waters, eds., pp. 96–122. New York: Russell Sage Foundation.

Kecskes, R. 2000. Soziale und Identifikative Assimilation Tiirkischer Jugendlicher, Berliner. *Journal fiur Soziologie* 10 (1): 61–78.

Kristen, Cornelia, and Nadia Granato. 2007. The Educational Attainment of the Second Generation in Germany. *Ethnicities* 7 (4): 343–66.

Kulick, Don. 1998. Anger, Gender, Language Shift and the Politics of Revelation in a Papua New Guinean Village. In *Language Ideologies: Practice and Theory*, Bambi Schieffelin, Kathryn Woolard, Paul Kroskrity, eds., pp. 87–102. New York: Oxford University Press.

Kunjufu, J. 1988. *To Be Popular or Smart: The Black Peer Group*. Chicago: African American Images.

Lange, Patricia. 2008. Living in YouTubia: Bordering on Civility. In *Proceedings of the Southwestern Anthropological Association Conference* vol. 2, by Southwestern Anthropological Association, pp. 98–106. San Jose, CA: California State University for the Southwestern Anthropological Association.

Laungaramsri, Pinkaew. 2008. Epilogue. In *Living in a Globalized World*, D. Mccaskill, P. Leepreecha, and H. Shaoying, eds., pp. 319–27. Chaing Mai, Thailand: Mekong Press.

Laurel, Brenda. 1990. *The Art of Human-Computer Interface Design*. Reading, MA: Addison-Wesley.

Lee, Stacet. 2005. *Up against Whiteness: Race, School, and Immigrant Youth*. New York: Teachers College Press.

Leepreecha, Prasit. 2008. The Role of Media Technology in Reproducing Hmong Ethnic Identity. In *Living in a Globalized World*, D. McCaskill, P. Leepreecha, and H. Shaoying, eds., pp. 89–113. Chaing Mai, Thailand: Mekong Press.

Levitt, Peggy, and Nadya Jaworsky. 2007. Transnational Migration Studies: Past Developments and Future Trends. *Annual Review of Sociology* 33 (1): 129–56.

Matute-Bianchi, M.E. 1986. Ethnic Identities and Patterns of School Success and Failure among Mexican-Descent and Japanese-American Students in a California High School: An Ethnographic Analysis. *American Journal of Education* 95 (3): 233–55.

McCaskill, Don. 2008. "Fix" and "Flux": The Transformation of Hmong Culture and Identity. In *Living in a Globalized World*, D. McCaskill, P. Leepreecha, and H. Shaoying, eds., pp. 277–318. Chaing Mai, Thailand: Mekong Press.

Miller, Daniel, and Don Slater. 2000. The Internet and Relationships. In *Making Sense of Language: Readings in Culture and Communication*, Susan Blum, ed., pp. 409–23. New York: Oxford University Press.

Millett, Sandra. 2002. *The Hmong of Southeast Asia*. Minneapolis: Lerner.

Nagel Joane. 1994. Constructing Ethnicity: Creating and Recreating Ethnic Identity and Culture. *Social Problems* 41 (1): 152–76.

Neal-Barnett, Angela. 2001. Being Black: New Thoughts on the Old Phenomenon of Acting White. In *Forging Links: African American Children; Clinical Development Perspectives*, Angela Neal-Barnett and Josefina Contreras, eds., pp. 75–112. Westport, CT: Praeger.

Nibbs, Faith G. 2014. *Belonging: The Social Dynamics of Fitting In as Experienced by Hmong Refugees in Texas and Germany*. European Monograph Series. Durham, NC: Carolina Academics Press.

Ogbu, John. 1990. Minority Status and Literacy in Comparative Perspective. *Daedalus* 119 (2): 141–68.

Ong, Aihwa. 1999. Cultural Citizenship as Subject-Making: Immigrants Negotiate Racial and Cultural Boundaries in the United States. In *Race, Identity and Citizenship: A Reader*, E. Torres, L. Miron, and J. Inda, eds., pp. 262–93. Malden, MA: Blackwell.

Oregon Business Report. 2009. 45% Employers Use Facebook-Twitter to Screen Job Candidates, Career Builer survey finds. Electronic document, *www.oregonbusinessreport.com/2009/08/45-employers-use-facebook-twitter-to-screen-job-candidates/*. Accessed October 28, 2011.

Plaza, Dwaine. 2010. Maintaining Transnational Identity: A Content Analysis of Web Pages Constructed by Second-Generation Caribbeans. In *Diasporas in the New Media Age*, Andoni Alonso and Pedro Oiarzabal, eds., pp. 151–69. Reno: University of Nevada Press.

Portes, Alejandro, and Rubén G. Rumbaut. 2001. *Legacies: The Story of the Immigrant Second Generation*. Berkeley: University of California Press; New York: Russell Sage Foundation.

Pyke, Karen, and Tran Dang. 2003. "FOB" and "Whitewashed": Identity and Internalized Racism among Second Generation Asian Americans. *Qualitative Sociology* 26 (2): 147–72.

Riphahn, Regina. 2003. Cohort Effects in the Educational Attainment of Second Generation Immigrants in Germany: An Analysis of Census Data. *Journal of Population Economics* 16 (4): 711–37.

Rodriguez, Richard. 1982. *Hunger of Memory*. New York: Bantam Books.

Rumbaut, Rubén, and Alejandro Portes. 2001. *Ethnicities: Children of Immigrants in America*. Berkeley: University of California Press.

Sawyer, Lena. 2008. "Voices of Migrants: Solidarity and Resistance." In *Identity, Belonging and Migration*, Ruth Wodak and Paul Jones Gerard Delanty, eds., pp. 241–60. Liverpool: Liverpool University Press.

Thomson, Mark, and Maurice Crul. 2007. The Second Generation in Europe and the United States: How Is the Transatlantic Debate Relevant for Further Research on the European Second Generation? *Journal of Ethnic and Migration Studies* 23 (7): 1025–41.

Van den Berghe, Pierre. 1987. *The Ethnic Phenomenon*. New York: Praeger.

Waters, Mary C. 1994. Ethnic and Racial Identities of Second-Generation Black Immigrants in New York City. *International Migration Review* 28 (4): 795–820.

Weber, Max. 1946. *From Max Weber*. Translated by H.H. Garth and C. Wright Mills. New York: Oxford University Press.

Weitzman, S. 1977. *Sex Roles: Biological, Psychological, and Social Foundations*. New York: Oxford.

Wilson, Brian. 2006. Ethnography, the Internet, and Youth Culture: Strategies for Examining Social Resistance and "Online-Offline" Relationships. *Canadian Journal of Education* 29 (1): 307–28.

Wilson, Brian, and M. Atkinson. 2005. Rave and Straightedge, the Virtual and the Real: Exploring On-line and Off-line Experiences in Canadian Youth Subcultures. *Youth and Society* 36 (3): 276–311.

Wilson, Samuel, and Leighton Peterson. 2002. The Anthropology of Online Communities. *Annual Review of Anthropology* 31: 449–67.

Witte, James, and Susan Mannon. 2010. *The Internet and Social Inequalities*. New York: Routledge.

Wong, L. 2003. Belonging and Diaspora: The Chinese and the Internet. *First Monday* 8 (4): 16.

Worbs, Susan. 2003. The Second Generation in Germany: Between School and Labor Market. *International Migration Review* 37 (4): 1011–38.

Zhou, Min. 1997. Segmented Assimilation: Issues, Controversies, and Recent Research on the New Second Generation. *International Migration Review* 31 (4): 975–1008.

———. 1999. Coming of Age: The Current Situation of Asian-American Children. *Amerasia Journal* 25 (1): 1–29.

5 POLITICAL SPACES

The Ambivalent Experiences of Italian Second-Generation Associations

Bruno Riccio

If in the 1980s Italians began to realize that Italy was no longer a country of emigrants, but had become a place that itself attracted immigrants from other parts of the world (King and Andall 1999; Grillo and Pratt 2002; Colombo and Sciortino 2002), they now need to understand that it has become home to second-generation children of the first-wave migrants (Ambrosini 2005; Chiodi and Benadusi 2006; E. Colombo, Leoninini, and Rebughini 2009; Colombo and Rebughini 2012; Miranda 2012). These young people are beginning to organize in sociocultural, religious, and, more relevant here, political terms via associations. Indeed, these associations are very dynamic and carry important political weight. For this reason they provide us with a new and different case by comparison with the immigrant associations formed by their parents that animated migration politics until the 1990s and were organized mainly on the basis of national, ethnic, and cultural differences (Però 2002; Caponio 2005; Carchedi and Mottura 2010). While first-generation immigrants tended to struggle for recognition through engagement in social activities based on Italian associational facilities and by interplaying with the economic and institutional system within specific localities, members of the second generation tend to fully address the highly contested issue of citizenship and tend to cross local and sometimes national boundaries (Salih 2004). As we will see, this kind of strategy proves to be crucial for youth who were schooled and socialized in Italian society, but who encounter barriers to social mobility and full citizenship rights (Andall 2002; Colombo, Domaneshci, Marchetti 2011).[1]

For the purposes of this chapter I will consider "second generation" in a loose sense, as comprising children of immigrant background who grew up in Italy as well as those who were actually born in Italy (see Andall 2002). I include in that definition those who were born in Italy and those who came as minors (under the age of fifteen) because both, as members of associations and as victims of discrimination, participate in the process that will be analyzed in this chapter. These "new Italians," as they often define themselves, try to strengthen their social position.

In their struggle for recognition, they often focus on the double meaning of representation (symbolic as much as political; see Grillo 1985). In order to enhance their access to social resources, as well as to political representation and participation, they contest and critique the widespread Italian representation that categorizes them as forever migrants. Indeed, Italian youth of migrant origin have reached adulthood at a time when Italian society is characterized by a serious "multiculturalism backlash" (Vertovec and Wessendorf 2009). Members of the second generation are often being depicted as "different" by the majority society, a phenomenon that is typical of contemporary cultural racism, which draws absolute boundaries to legitimize the incommensurability of cultures and hence normalizes social exclusion and discrimination.

The main objective of second-generation associations is to fight against such discrimination and to facilitate equal opportunities of social mobility for the youth of immigrant background. With this purpose in mind they are also well networked through the Internet and tend to be very active in their use of the Internet and new digital media. As we will see, although these associations are characterized by familiarity with new media and transnational connections, many second-generation leaders and members also find it crucial to interact and improve communication with local Italian institutions. Yet to realize these purposes they have to confront problems, which are typical of other associational experiences—even those of first-generation migrants—such as fears of exploitation, the frustrations of not ensuring active participation, or increase in recruitment together with financial sustainability and consequent organizational autonomy.

In order to establish a context for my discussion of second-generation associations, I begin this chapter with a discussion of contemporary multidimensional racism in Italy and the delicate issue of citizenship. After a description of the field site, the first-generation associational experiences, and the methodology adopted in this specific study, I then turn to a delineation of the main characteristics, objectives, and strategies of second-generation associations in Italy and in Bologna in particular, drawing largely from the experiences and perspectives of members, leaders, and outsiders. I emphasize the main challenges they face by focusing on the ambivalent tension between processes of "deterritorialization" and "reterritorialization" (Appadurai 1996) and reflect on what the experiences of second-generation associations teaches us about everyday practices of citizenship.[2] More specifically, I argue that the deterritorializing effect of having found a public space in the World Wide Web contrasts and needs to come to terms with the reterritorializing wish to concretely enter the local public space to realize an "enacted citizenship."[3]

RACISM, CITIZENSHIP, AND THE POLITICS OF EXCLUSION

Throughout Europe there have been various attempts to deport or exclude migrants who are regarded as disposable workers, but seldom as citizens entitled to access social welfare. It is now considered "normal" to allow free movement among the wealthy countries, but it is deemed dangerous to facilitate migration from countries that combine poverty and, more so after 9/11, Islam. In Italy illegal migration has become a focus of aggressive campaigns from the political right. This has contributed to the politicization of migration issues, and helped to increase the pressure for migration control and the "representation of migrants as problems" (Grillo 1985: 10). Furthermore, and more relevant here, the situation of ethnic minorities of immigrant origin, some of whom may be citizens or members of the second generation, has been badly affected by these anxieties.

There is a dangerous dialectic between government policy and public opinion already hostile to immigration. The media increasingly present immigration as a threat, contributing to the "moral panic" that negatively affects public opinion. In everyday political rhetoric, culture and cultural difference are increasingly politicized, and the opposition to foreigners is cast in terms of commonsense themes such as law and order and the defense of—sometimes national, sometimes local—economic interests. In other words, one witnesses the increasing cultural racism dominating right-wing (and other) ideologies. This kind of discourse underlines diversity resulting from cultural differences and concludes that, because of these cultural differences, integration is impossible. In 2008, for instance, the new mayor of Rome, talking about the Roma minority in the capital, explained that some of them are good citizens, but others, "also because of their culture," tend to steal and misbehave.[4] Furthermore, as Cole (1997) suggested some years ago based on research in Sicily to explore the emergence of the "new racism in Europe," popular hostility toward migrants is legitimized by depicting it as the natural response of people protecting their territories. More recently, comparing contexts as far away as Cameroon and Flanders, Ceuppens and Geschiere (2005) have argued that these discourses of "autochthony" not only reveal the obsession with belonging and the exclusion of strangers from day-to-day politics worldwide, but also easily switch from one target to another in their political attacks. The Northern League trajectory provides a good example here,[5] having moved through the 1980s to the 1990s from the stigmatization of the southern Italian to the stigmatization of international migrants. What is missing in the public space is a debate about the legitimization of exclusionary practices in everyday life that this new racist discourse creates.

As Andall's (2002) work in Milan has shown, "the very notion of the possibility of being both black and Italian remains a marginal concept within the broader framework of the contemporary immigration debate in Italy." In other words, "being black and being Italian were perceived as mutually exclusive categories. This view was not only evident at the institutional level of the police, but also amongst employers and by the gate-keepers of Italy's physical borders" (Andall 2002: 400). Therefore anti-immigrant sentiments are a matter not only of cultural racism but also of phenotypic characteristics that have become more and more relevant in constructing the internal boundaries of "Italianness." In 2008, a worrying sequence of events occurred involving occasional harassment by the police, violent attacks by informal as well as very organized but illegal groups such as the *camorra*, and a more mundane everyday discrimination in the labor market.[6] These events show that, in addition to the cultural racism mentioned above, very real everyday racialization also exists as part of contemporary Italian politics of exclusion. As Didier Fassin (2000: 6) explains when talking about France:

> If racism was previously seen as the rejection of foreigners, the discovery of internal boundaries dividing a French community which finds it increasingly difficult to perceive itself as national contrasts with the official discourse prevailing until the 1990s. Nationality no longer suffices to define the basis for exclusion of the Other: the concrete criteria according to which a landlord refuses housing, an employer rejects a job application, a policeman decides to check for identity papers . . . must be considered. These are phenomenological criteria that tend primarily toward appearance, particularly skin colour, and mainly target people not identified as European.

Contemporary Italian racism rhetorically conflates different kinds of stigmatizations in legitimizing social exclusion: cultural and religious difference, soil as much as blood, without forgetting racial difference. Indirectly it creates a "background noise" (Grillo and Pratt 2002) to the widespread resistance in granting citizenship to migrants and their children.

As Thomson and Crul (2007: 1038–39) argue, citizenship is an important tool of inclusion, endowing migrants and their children with rights equal to their peers. Yet they go on to observe that, "where more restrictive laws on citizenship exist, however, a discourse of exclusion is facilitated." The Italian citizenship law of 1992 made it easier for descendants of Italian emigrants to regain citizenship but also much more difficult for immigrants to apply for naturalization. This law on citizenship was also more restrictive with regard to the second generation, establishing that children born of foreign parents in Italy assume their parents' nationality and they can request Italian citizenship when they are eighteen years old only if they remain continually resident in Italy. This means that the children of migrants born in Italy do not automatically get Italian citizenship but have to apply for it and go through a complicated bureaucratic process. However, the really precarious condition is that of young people who came to Italy when they were children or as young adolescents only to discover that they are "foreigners" when they reach adulthood.

The need to change such a state of affairs concerning citizenship entitlement has spurred the birth of many of the second-generation associations, which I discuss in this chapter. However, as we shall see, the experience of various members and leaders we encountered taught us (myself and research assistant Monica Russo) about the need to go beyond the formal dimension of citizenship and also consider the everyday practices of citizenship (Riccio and Russo 2011), which I will discuss in further detail below. Some of these research participants offer substantiation for the emergent tendency in anthropological literature to broaden analytically the conception of citizenship to include its participatory dimension, which also depends on social everyday inclusion (Holston and Appadurai 1999; Glick Schiller and Caglar 2008; Reed-Danahay and Brettell 2008; Brettell and Reed-Danahay 2012). As Bloemraad et al. (2008: 162) have argued, immigrants can "make citizenship-like claims on the state and others, even in the absence of legal citizenship status, and perhaps even in the absence of legal residence." However, we should not forget that legal residence and the permit to stay might affect migrants' social life more than it does the granting of citizenship. The complex interplay of these factors is also anchored in the specific history of associational life in the local migration context.

FIELD SITE AND METHODOLOGY

The field research for this study was conducted in the city of Bologna, Italy. In research on second-generation integration in Europe and the United States the local level displays a particularly interesting context in which to appreciate the interplay between structure, culture, and personal agency.

By focusing on specific local conditions, it is possible to address concerns that structure describes only the more general, macro-level processes at work, that culture is all too easily reified, and that individual agency often appears to be neglected (Thomson and Crul 2007: 1030).

However, many studies of migrant associations focus on receiving states, their policies, and the political opportunity structure, sometimes running the risk of neglecting agency and, in our case here, how youth of immigrant background respond to, adapt to, or critique integration policies, and how their organizations and participation affect the meanings and practices of citizenship. Indeed, unlike the first immigrant organizations of the 1990s, second-generation associations show a more ambivalent and sometimes skeptical stance toward the opportunity offered by institutional networks in Bologna (Caponio 2005).

Bologna's economy has been historically characterized by the success of highly specialized small and medium-sized enterprises. Global restructuring processes and a very severe demographic decline of the local population are important processes affecting the city as well as the broader Emilia Romagna region (Salih and Riccio 2011). Immigrants who have settled in Bologna are mainly employed in small manufacturing industries, in the production of handicrafts, and in the metallurgical and mechanical industries. Although the majority are unskilled laborers (mechanics and laborers in small and medium-size firms), there are also an increasing number of skilled migrants who work below their skill level.

The immigrant population in Bologna is diverse. In 2007, there were 5,047 Romanians; 4,068 Filipinos; 3,477 Bangladeshis; 3,014 Moroccans; 2,302 Albanians; 2,220 Moldavians; 2,198 Chinese; and 2,175 Ukrainians; followed by residents coming from Pakistan, Sri Lanka, Senegal, and Eritrea. Foreigners aged under twenty-four numbered around eleven thousand, and the minors born in Italy to a family of migrant origin numbered around five thousand. The most numerous minors were: Filipinos (694), Chinese (592), Moroccans (573), Bangladeshis (540), Serbs (330), Romanians (297), and Albanians (220) (Osservatorio demografico comune di Bologna 2008).[7] The percentage of children with non-Italian background in schools (around 16 percent) is among the highest in the country, highlighting a stable phenomenon, mainly composed of families who settle, although maintaining quite substantial transnational links with their countries of origin.

Most of the first immigrant associations in the city of Bologna were founded in the mid-1990s, when the left-wing local administration started to promote a "multicultural integration policy" (Caponio 2005). Moreover, from the migrants' point of view, a multiplicity of organizational actors started to play an important role in the interface with Italian institutions as well as being crucial in maintaining transnational connections with the homeland. An important function was performed by migrants' national associations (such as the Pakistani, Albanian, or Senegalese associations), which are often shaped by migrants who are the most knowledgeable about the institutions in the receiving society. These are often the better educated, the elite who represent the foreign community only to some degree. Other potential forms of organizations developed, such as cooperatives and more focused social associations like the hometown associations. These tend to develop in the provinces, with many migrants coming from a specific town, and to become involved in projects of various kinds such as construction of a well or collecting funds to build places of worship, schools, and health centers back home (Riccio 2011).

Finally, one should note individual initiatives based on Italian associational structures, which allow socially active migrants to become involved in cultural and economic activities, networking with the actors of the economic and institutional system within specific localities. Associations involved in intercultural events (music, performances, etc.), but also those concerned with entrepreneurial projects, represent good examples of such initiatives. Individuals who address the broader issue of rights for migrants within the local context represent another example. Here one may encounter persons who prefer to participate within the trade union or the provincial or communal consultative councils for foreigners to seek to empower and enhance access to rights of migrants in general and not just in national or ethnic terms. This is to say that the myriad ways in which migrants have been entering Italian public space tends to overcome national, ethnic, and religious divisions (Carchedi and Mottura 2010).

Yet in the 1990s many of these associations—national and "intercultural" ones especially—were perceived by various migrants as imposed by the local government rather than the outcome of spontaneous mobilization. Furthermore, the sociopolitical participation that should have been facilitated by the establishment of the

Metropolitan Forum of Immigrant Associations favored the increase of migrants' associations, but these often involved unrepresentative leaders (Però 2002). On the other hand, facilities were provided in order to support migrant associational activities. One of the main problems encountered by migrants' associations was the access to public contracts and funding. After a comprehensive comparative study of local policies and migrant associations, Tiziana Caponio concluded that "the inexperience and structural weakness of immigrants' associations explains the distrust of public institutions, and in turn this distrust has the effect of keeping immigrants' associations even more inexperienced and structurally weak. Breaking this vicious circle does not appear to be an easy task" (Caponio 2005: 948).

However, in the last decade there has been a tremendous diversification of immigrant associations in Bologna and within the Italian landscape in general, with hometown associations transforming into regional associations or federations to better meet the challenges of codevelopment (Riccio 2011) or, with regard to the interplay with the receiving context, the birth of foreign women associations, foreign families associations, and mixed associations together with what are normally called second-generation associations.

The data presented in this chapter derives from a study of second-generation associations in the city of Bologna undertaken together with a postdoctoral student of mine (Riccio and Russo 2011). The study contributed to a broader research project, Urban Contexts, Migration Processes and Young Migrants (PRIN project 2006–2008; see also Callari Galli and Scandurra 2009; Guerzoni and Riccio 2009; Pazzagli and Tarabusi 2009; Falteri and Giacalone 2011) that explored the sociocultural experiences of young people of immigrant background in two urban and multicultural settings: Bologna and Perugia (both capitals of the two Italian regions with the highest ratio of young people of foreign origin in schools and society). From a methodological point of view, in our specific study we wanted to avoid essentialism and therefore did not assume that the members and leaders of these associations constituted a representative sample of the immigrant second generation as a whole. Besides looking up and down (leaders as well as members), we wanted to explore the view "inside out" and "outside in" (Grillo 1985), and thus we also interviewed migrants with a long associational experience as well as Bologna's local government personnel to gather a perspective from outside the second-generation associations. Furthermore, we conducted participant observation at public events and studied their websites and the digital products (short videos, etc.) one can download from them. Finally, in addition to twenty interviews with members and leaders of the second-generation associations and participant observation at public events we added two follow-up group discussions with eight of the interviewees, in which we focused on the main points emerging from the ongoing research. These included the internal as much as the external challenges these associations were facing in their activities, together with the importance given by many of the interviewees to issues of representation and discrimination.

Associations revealed themselves to be a particularly interesting lens through which to explore various social processes. Such processes include virtual as well as territorial strategies adopted to gain recognition and access to public space, and to support the struggle to improve the concrete and actual experience of being a citizen in contemporary Italian society.

SECOND GENERATION ASSOCIATIONS: BETWEEN DETERRITORIALIZATION AND RETERRITORIALIZATION

In Bologna one finds second-generation associations, which were born at the local level, together with local branches of associations that were born at the national level. Among the latter, the first and oldest second-generation association in Italy is the Giovani Musulmani d'Italia (GMI) association founded in 2001. It now has hundreds of members and several local branches in different towns and villages in Italy. The main aim of the organization is to become a point of reference for young Muslims born or brought up in Italy who want to be protagonists of their lives and in the society in which they live (Frisina 2008). The association maintains good relationships with the media and uses its website for circulating information (*www. giovanimusulmani.it*). As with cases of the second generation elsewhere in the world (see Levitt and Waters 2002), this youth population has a transnational life. The organization itself operates simultaneously on local, national, and transnational levels. As we shall see, residing in a specific local context may assume particular importance, for it is the arena where people's voices and concerns could be heard and developed into new demands of participatory citizenship. However, along with the local context, second-generation Muslims often emphasize the importance of transnational public spheres as a major context in which to direct their efforts, emphasizing the abandonment of the national as the main or the only political and discursive arena in which identity politics should be played out (Salih 2004). Indeed, the nation-state is increasingly understood by second-generation Muslims in Bologna and in Italy as a whole as operating through an exclusionary process, which not only denies them access to citizenship but also fails to acknowledge their complex identities. On the one hand, the state persists in crystallizing Muslims as permanent and essential "others," and on the other it offers them assimilation to the national community through a logic that restricts Muslim politics and identities to the private sphere (Salih and Riccio 2011).

The most popular second-generation organization in Italy, which is particularly active from a cultural and political point of view, is the G2 Second Generations network born in 2005, a national network of young Italians of immigrant background. As a leader of the network explained, during a meeting held in Bologna in 2007:

> The network is concerned with the condition of the so-called second generations, especially their access to rights and citizenship, that is not automatic, as you

know, but it foresees various complicated requisites, whereas we think we deserve it to be equal with our Italian peers with whom we have studied, played, and shared dreams, at least until our adult age. . . . We are often asked about our "integration" into Italian society, but we do not have this problem, we do not need to "integrate," we fully belong to this society, [and] we just need to be considered its citizens.

In addition to this political purpose an additional object is outlined on the organizational website; namely that of the cultural transformation of Italian society toward a more conscious one, able to recognize itself into all its children independently from their origin or background.[8]

Thus, it becomes crucial to work with Italian institutions politically and with Italian society culturally, because to obtain legal recognition without social recognition would be but a partial victory. Thanks to its website (*www.secondegenerazioni.it*) this organizational network provides members with a space for discussion and confrontation, as well as access to videos that deal with issues of citizenship rights, identity construction, and everyday discrimination. The website is a means of communication and a space of representation at the same time; the blog allows participants to share the frustrations of being a "foreigner on paper in a place we consider our home," whereas the forum is a "virtual square where we meet and confront on trivial as well as more serious matters." Similar to the G2 national observatory, this local branch through its website also offers a space where members' experiences with a lack of documents or with work problems due to Italian citizenship law are collected and recorded. As Dorothy Zinn has recently noted:

> One finds Italian youth slang, text-message language, emoticons and local dialects exactly as one would find among autochthonous Italian youths; at the same time, there are avatars, user names, foreign-language greetings and citations and, occasionally, national flags that all hint at non-Italian elements. Finally, on the basis of how often participants post, the forum administrator labels them with wry tags that play on the gamut of second generation situations: for example, "integrated G2," "undocumented migrant," "stay permit for study"; "stay permit being renewed." In short, the verbal and visual language simultaneously highlights Italian belonging, foreign cultural affiliations and the particular status identity of second generations: the medium of the G2 blog is truly its message. (Zinn 2011)

An important achievement of the G2 network has been the recognition it has received from political institutions as interlocutor on proposed changes to the citizenship and immigration laws. Furthermore, G2 has become an institutional consultant for the Ministry of Social Solidarity and for the Ministry of Public Instruction's Observatory on the Integration of Foreign Students and Intercultural Education (Zinn 2011). The respect accorded to the G2 network by national institutions partially translates into a springboard for local participants who also have their voices heard at the national level. G2 forum resembles the Chinese websites in Britain studied by Parker and Song, which "constitute emerging public spheres of growing importance as arenas of dialogic self-definition and elaboration" (2006: 592).

In Italy the children of Chinese migrants created a well-networked national association in 2005, called AssoCina (*www.associna.com*). It started as a small online chat group and in three years became an association of fifteen hundred members. Its aim is to represent young Chinese Italians, provide a bridge between the parents and the Italian society, and contest the dominant stereotypical representation of the Chinese in Italy. As an AssoCina leader put it at a public event we attended in Bologna:

> We want to realize a counterinformation. This is why we have realized the website, not only to create a place to encounter each other. There is a section called "news" where members write their own articles with the aim to counterinform about all the stereotypical ideas about the Chinese, like that of the Chinese who cook dogs in their restaurants, or that of the Chinese who never die. We also have articles on citizenship or simpler stories but told without all the distortions of the news.

As another member of the association, who is an activist in the local branch in Bologna, further exemplifies in an interview: "We are editing a new video on the electoral participation of naturalized citizens. . . . It is an electorate that the media normally do not consider and that people ignore. . . . We offer the possibility to let ourselves be known to the Italian audience who is interested . . . to let our everyday life be known like in a simple act of active citizenship as the political elections."

To deconstruct and reconstruct the public image of the Chinese youth means to facilitate a process of "normalization" of the presence of the second generation in the public sphere, especially at the local level. Parker and Song (2006, 2007) found similar processes among British Chinese youth in relation to the use of websites:

> The general concerns of 16–30-year-olds about belonging and inclusion, education and social mobility, parenting and family-building are given a culturally specific inflection. The following themes recur: ethnic boundaries between Chinese and non-Chinese are regularly questioned and reasserted; changing Chinese identity in the West is both celebrated and problematised; potentially conflicting loyalties to Britain and China are expressed; experiences of racism are compared and empathised with. (Parker Song 2007: 1048–49)

Beside those important national associations, which gradually founded a local branch in Bologna, other more strictly local associations also exist. For instance, Arcimondo is a second-generation association established in 2007 with the help of Arci (an Italian cultural association of the left) in Bologna, with the objective of fighting discrimination. Next Generation is another association founded in 2007 in a town (Imola) within the province of Bologna. This organization brings together young members of different national origin including Italians. For some years it also played the role of local referent for the G2 network. However the most interesting for our discussion is Crossing, formerly a local ethnically mixed association that has become a nationwide web TV channel: Crossing TV (*www. crossingtv.it*). This is a cosmopolitan TV channel that is very concerned with the problem of representation, and which aims to fight the "ethnic labeling and stereotypical rhetoric of Italian media," according to a cofounder of CrossingTV. Their goal to create a counterhegemonic representation is clear. According to one member, "CrossingTV was born to answer to an important need. In the media delirium in which white, black and yellow youth are involved, often in an instrumental and exploitative way, it is important to create a space which is pure, not labeled, not labelable and, more relevant, not labeling." Another member stated, "I do not want that when you hear my foreign name you think about crime and decay, I do not want that when you hear that I am Albanian you think of me being on the boats in the middle of the sea."

Like G2, AssoCina and Crossing, other associations also try to combine the outward communication aiming to challenge common representations with more internal reflections on cultural essentialism and on the need to recognize more complex forms of identification that are able to mediate their family experiences with everyday life within Italian society. In this regard, GMI, the association of young Italian Muslims, constitutes a crucial example. One member stated, "We were born to say that you can be comfortably Italian and Muslim, it is not a problem, neither a contradiction, they are not contrasting identities." Although with a different language, similar reflections can be found among young Chinese Italians: "Before knowing AssoCina, I used to define myself as an Italian by acquisition, then I realized that the concept of "second generation" includes your Chinese origin. . . . It is a mix between cultures where no one dominates the other. . . . It is important to live with both backgrounds." All these associations construct and look for the recognition of youths' multiple and situational identities. They publicly and intimately question the widespread essentialist rhetoric, which entraps youth of immigrant background in straightforward categorizations. In other words, they wish to have the opportunity to shape their future in Italian society by claiming more equality of rights and recognition of their difference at the same time.

For this purpose the Internet provided these young people with the space to elaborate the understanding of their social experiences and the place for alternative and critical communication toward Italian society. They represent what Brettell (2008) has recently called "netizens" to evoke social actors who are able to empower their everyday struggle to realize citizenship by navigating cyberspace. She uses the term "netizens" to describe "a group of individuals who are using the Internet to create a civically engaged community of practice . . . online" (2008: 228). Looking at those associations presented above by comparison with the first migrants' associations, one cannot underestimate the role of the competent use of Internet technology to shape communities out of a more fragmented population (E. Colombo, Leoninini, Rebughini 2009; Zinn 2011; A. Colombo and Rebughini 2012). As Parker and Song's (2006) research in Britain indicates, new public spheres are being created through Internet use. These authors note that "the Internet affords the expression of often previously unarticulated minority perspectives" (2006: 192), and these sites "could become the distinctive social institutions of these emerging British born generations" (2006: 589). Similar processes can be recorded in Italy. In 2008, the AssoCina website counted around seven hundred visits per day. Its visibility and neutrality in terms of boundaries are aspects of the virtual space that seem appreciated by its members. According to one AssoCina leader, "The forum is a free medium, without barriers, where those who register are not subjects to the prejudices we are used into everyday life. We want to reduce distances with Italian society; we are more similar to our peers that what appears and is commonly thought." The association's website becomes also the means through which to realize some of its objectives. As noted above, AssoCina aims at producing counterinformation, and one finds in the website provocative and ironic articles that deconstruct stereotypical representations of the Chinese community in Italy. Furthermore, the Internet facilitates a wide participation and a careful selection of topics covered at the same time. For instance, an activist of G2 explains: "We are politically relevant, but we do not follow any Italian political party; we exploit the democratic shape of the forum that allows everyone to participate, but we avoid responding to any provocative question that would associate us with one party or another."

For all these reasons (visibility, neutrality, freedom, democracy, participation, and inclusivity and selectivity at the same time), virtual space seems to play a crucial role in the development of second-generation associational life. But these organizations cannot and do not exist just virtually. We also see a need of "reterritorialization" by developing local branches in different towns. What I am arguing here is that, despite the many potentials of the Internet that undoubtedly facilitated an entry into (virtual) public space, the connection with engagement at the local level seems important for the participants (leaders and members) to ensure effective mobilization. This becomes clearer if we focus on the shifting perceptions of citizenship and the problems of interplay with Italian institutions at the local level.

As anticipated above, members of local second-generation associations in Bologna are more interested in realizing a citizenship in everyday practice rather than just on paper. They think that discrimination and social marginalization are the crucial issues to confront. One member of Arcimondo stated: "Yes, I am a foreigner, this is a fact. If they give me citizenship, that's a bureaucratic thing. I am always a foreigner. If I walk in the street, I am always a Moroccan, [I'm] not kidding; even if you show the red passport of Italian citizens, you are always a Moroccan. For the Italian law you are a full citizen, but for the Italian people you remain a foreigner." A member of GMI stated, "Among us we talk more about the meaning of citizenship, not about the bureaucratic piece of paper. I know that's important too, but the priority remains your recognition." Although the question of citizenship played the role of a springboard for most of the national associations of the second generation in Italy, the local branches of the national associations and the associations born in one locality seem to favor a broader objective: A member of GMI stated, "The campaign for the change of citizenship law is important, do not get me wrong, but if and when this will be granted, what will you do? Do you stop working? Do you cease the associational life? I think the second generation should go beyond formal citizenship and work on the sense of belonging to a territory and on the meaning of participating in its life."

The change of Italian citizenship law constitutes one important "battle," but the "war" to be won is much longer and addresses the transformation of Italian public representation of the second generation and its translation into antidiscriminatory practices. Indeed, the main objectives of second-generation associations remain the struggle against discrimination and the enhancement of equal opportunities of social mobility for the youth of immigrant background. This awareness is important and instructive from a policy-oriented point of view. Beside the change in the citizenship law, it seems that Italian institutions should look at affirmative action policies or other solutions that enable youth to enter and participate in Italian public space. The importance of the participatory dimension of citizenship has been recorded by other studies of the Italian second generation. For example, Colombo, Domaneshci, Marchetti (2011: 341) argue:

> For the young people interviewed who were born in Italy in particular, citizenship is not only reduced to its formal and instrumental dimension, but constitutes a central element of full and effective participation in social life. . . . More than to admittance, belonging is equivalent to involvement: the sense of being a part of situations and contexts that may have important effects on full self-realization, that require the recognition of autonomy and the active capacity of agency.

An important challenge for these associations is to find effective ways to combine the potential of virtual space with the need to concretely enter local everyday space. This is the reason why more recently one sees attempts to combine the two. For instance, in 2009 with the help of the Emilia Romagna region the regional network Together was created. It connects different associational experiences of different cities of the region through its website (*www.retetogether.it*), but it also supports projects in different high schools of the region with the aim at enhancing knowledge about and discussion of the situation of youth with an immigrant background in classroom contexts. The exchange among peers about issues of everyday discrimination is very effective in raising the understanding of the problems encountered by the children of migrants. Effecting social changes on the ground by normalizing and spreading the idea of what is to be a black Italian or an Italian Muslim seem to need long-term investments in face-to-face relations. The most meaningful fruits of these discussions become digital products to be uploaded on the website and thereby been consulted by a greater number of people.

Furthermore, the sharing of different experiences over the Internet can strengthen second-generation organization and facilitate their dialogue with Italian socializing institutions, such as schools, local Intercultural centers, and so on. Before this experiment, which has been facilitated by the Emilia Romagna region, the problem of who dictates the agenda was still very much felt. Despite the existence of some public funds targeting the second generation in 2007, most of the different second-generation associations' members displayed a certain degree of ambivalence if not suspicion about this funding. On the internal side, the majority felt the need to shape a stronger organizational identity. A member of Arcimondo stated,

> Before diving in we need to better understand who we really are; we need to strengthen our structure and our credibility at the local level (member of GMI). We are not ready yet, we need a better organization with more members, we cannot only be a small group of people.

On the external side, many expressed the fear of being manipulated and exploited by Italian local politicians or even by institutional personnel. The following comments manifest these concerns: A leader of Arcimondo stated, "The issue about the second generation is becoming fashionable, and we do not want to be used." A member of GMI and Arcimondo commented, "I do not like it when the personnel of the commune has already organized everything and only then call us to participate, but if you have done everything what should you need me for? I say no, thank you! Either you call me at the beginning and you take me as a serious interlocutor, or you only want to use me to play big with your potential electorate." "We do not want them to do things 'in our name,' we are sick and tired of being beneficiaries of local policies, [and] we want to be partners," stated a member of Next Generation.

The experience of these young people is different from that of their parents, who are often accused by their children of being unable to understand the main characteristics of Italian society on the one hand, and, on the other, to be begging for space and recognition. By contrast, the youth pretend to be interlocutors from the beginning and want to avoid being manipulated for political reasons. The project Together mentioned above offers an important counterexample of such manipulation. The funds of the Emilia Romagna region have been concretely used to strengthen the second-generation organization and to facilitate the concrete implementation of projects within a strategic space such as the schools.

Finally, another problem that constitutes an element of continuity in time with former migrant organizations (Però 2002; Caponio 2005), and in space with other second-generation political engagement such as that of the Secondo Movement in Switzerland (Wessendorf 2008), is that of representativeness, namely, the extent to which the leaders of the association are accorded a voice to represent the group, the rank and file, not to speak of the second generation as a whole. The leadership generally consists of politically aware, well-educated youth of immigrant background, mainly students, who engage in local cultural and social politics. As with many other organizations, this feature translates into problems of trust and recruitment. According to some activists, the worst problem is time. Most of the young workers of immigrant background do not find time to participate in associational activities. Furthermore, the difficulties of everyday life (permit to stay, work relations, salaries, rent) make the issues debated within the associations a bit remote for many members. On the other hand, at high school or university one develops different expectations of social mobility and contests diffuse discrimination. In other words, the subjects of this study are not representative of a general category of immigrant children; rather, they may constitute a political "vanguard" able to create a strategic place within Italian public space, which can reveal itself to be crucial for youth of immigrant background more generally (E. Colombo 2007).

The political organization of the children of immigrants is still a recent phenomenon, and most of the young people we have interviewed have shown themselves to be aware of the challenges discussed in this chapter. Clearly, we have seen that one of the main challenges is the strategic relevance of combining the potential of the Internet in conflating various and fragmented voices into a collective identity with concrete, on-the-ground mobilization that has as its purpose to create a citizenship practiced in the everyday life of local communities. Migrants' children, and those engaging in associations especially, share with their native peers the experience of navigating through virtual space. However, they are also a political minority that wants to change and affect Italian society, specifically to make it more accepting of their presence and right to belong. The familiarity with new technologies has allowed them to create new political spaces facilitating the emergence of a common political goal. The more recent strengthening of organizations has facilitated the implementation of more concrete and focused projects within educational and socializing institutions. Furthermore, from a policy-oriented perspective and from the viewpoint of Italian institutions, the experiences of these second-generation associations teach us that a new citizenship law needs to be accompanied by systematic antidiscrimination or even affirmative action policies within different everyday domains of Italian society. Creating a social environment where it is possible to be equal and different at the same time in Italian society is a slow and challenging process as well as one where activity in both real and virtual political spaces seem more and more necessary.

NOTES

1. A similar version of this chapter by Bruno Riccio and Monica Russo, "Everyday Practised Citizenship and the Challenges of Representation: Second-Generation Associations in Bologna," was printed with permission by Taylor and Francis Ltd., *www.tandfonline.com*, in *Journal of Modern Italian Studies* 16 (3): 360–72.

2. Appadurai (1996) and many other scholars (see also Papastergiadis 2000) use the term "deterritorialization" to evoke the transformation produced by migrant mobility together with the advances of the media and global communications technologies. Both processes are thought to be disrupting the linkage between culture and territory. For this reason, Appadurai suggests that we need to move away from earlier definition of culture, which stressed highly localized and holistic units. On the other hand, places remain important for people who dialectically engage in never ending processes of "reterritorialization" like the reproduction of home in a foreign environment (Little Italy, Chinatown, etc.).

3. Indeed this chapter draws on a paper delivered at the American Anthropological Association conference 2011 in Montreal and called "Reterritorializing 'Netizenship': The Ambivalent Experiences of Second Generation Associations in the City of Bologna (Italy)"; preliminary findings have been discussed at the Université Libre de Bruxelles ULB during the international workshop "The Others in Europe" in March 2009, and later at the Max Planck Institute for the Study of Religious and Ethnic Diversity (MMG) in Göttingen, where I gave older and different versions of the paper. I thank all the participants at the three events for their feedback and especially Saskia Bonjour, Ralph Grillo, and Susanne Wessendorf, who provided comments on the earlier version of the paper. For this chapter, as volume editors, Caroline Brettell and Faith Nibbs provided me with further comments and suggestions that were very valuable to strengthen the discussion, and I wish to thank them very much for their help. Finally I wish to thank my research assistant Monica Russo for allowing me to author this chapter, which is based on material we have gathered together.

4. *www.repubblica.it/2008/05/sezioni/cronaca/sicurezza-politica-3/alemanno-rom/alemanno-rom.html*

5. The Northern League is a populist party pretending to represent the local interests of the more economically productive regions of the North. It has been the champion of anti-immigration campaign, with its consensus growing throughout the 1990s, and it has participated as allies in Berlusconi's governments (1994, 2001, 2008). See Stacul 2006.

6. See *www.ricerca.repubblica.it/repubblica/archivio/repubblica/2008/09/17/abdoul-ucciso-dal-razzismo-milano-cattiva.html*; *www.repubblica.it/2008/11/sezioni/cronaca/caso-emmanuel-parma/caso-emmanuel-parma/caso-emmanuel-parma.html?ref=search*; *www.archiviostorico.corriere.it/2008/ottobre/05/Allarme_razzismo_immigrati_piazza_co_9_081005088.shtml*

7. Osservatorio demografico comune di Bologna (The Demographic Observatory of the Local Government) 2008. *www.comune.bologna.it/iperbole/piancont/index.html.*
8. *www.secondegenerazioni.it/about*

REFERENCES

Ambrosini, A. 2005. *Sociologia delle migrazioni*. Bologna: Il Mulino.

Andall, Jacqueline. 2002. Second Generation Attitude? African-Italians in Milan." *Journal of Ethnic and Migration Studies* 28 (3): 389–407.

Appadurai, Arjun. 1996. *Modernity at Large: Cultural Dimensions of Globalization.* Minneapolis: University of Minnesota Press.

Bloemraad, Irene, Anna Korteweg, and Gökçe Yurdakul. 2008. Citizenship and Immigration: Multiculturalism, Assimilation, and Challenge to the Nation-State. *Annual Review of Sociology* 34: 153–79.

Brettell, Caroline B. 2008. Immigrants as Netizens: Political Mobilization in the Cyberspace. In *Citizenship, Political Engagement, and Belonging: Immigrants in Europe and the United States*, Deborah Reed-Danahay and Caroline B. Brettell, eds., pp. 226–43. New Brunswick, NJ: Rutgers University Press.

Brettell, Caroline B., and Deborah Reed-Danahay. 2012. *Civic Engagements: The Citizenship Practices of Indian and Vietnamese Immigrants*. Stanford, CA: Stanford University Press.

Callari Galli, M., and G. Scandurra. 2009. *Stranieri a casa: Contesti urbani, processi migratori e giovani migranti*. Rimini: Guaraldi.

Caponio, Tiziana. 2005. Policy Networks and Immigrants' Associations in Italy: The Cases of Milan, Bologna and Naples. *Journal of Ethnic and Migration Studies* 31 (5): 931–50.

Carchedi, F., and G. Mottura (eds.). 2010. *Produrre cittadinanza: Ragioni, traiettorie e differenze nell'associazionismo dei migranti*. Milano: Franco Angeli.

Ceuppens, Bambi, and Peter Geschiere. 2005. Autochthony: Local or Global? New Modes in the Struggle over Citizenship. *Annual Review of Anthropology* 34: 363–84.

Chiodi, F., and M. Benadusi. 2006. *Seconde generazioni e località: Giovani volti delle migrazioni cinese, marocchina e romena in Italia*. Roma: Labos.

Cole, Jeffrey. 1997. *The New Racism in Europe: A Sicilian Ethnography*. Cambridge: Cambridge University Press.

Colombo, A., and G. Sciortino (eds.). 2002. *Stranieri in Italia: Assimilati ed esclusi*. Bologna: Il Mulino.

Colombo, Enzo. 2007. Molto più che stranieri, molto più che italiani: Modi diversi di guardare ai destini dei figli di immigrati in un contesto di crescente globalizzazione. *Mondi Migranti* 1: 63–85.

Colombo, Enzo, Lorenzo Domaneschi, and Chiara Marchetti. 2011. Citizenship and Multiple Belonging: Representations of Inclusion, Identification and Participation among Children of Immigrants in Italy. *Journal of Modern Italian Studies* 16 (3): 334–47.

Colombo, Enzo, Luisa Leonini, and Paola Rebughini. 2009. Different but Not Stranger: Everyday Collective Identifications among Adolescent Children of Immigrants in Italy. *Journal of Ethnic and Migration Studies* 35 (1): 37–59.

Colombo, Enzo, and Paola Rebughini. 2012. *Children of Immigrants in a Globalized World: A Generational Experience.* Basingstoke: Palgrave Macmillan.

Falteri, P., and F. Giacalone, F. (eds.). 2001. *Migranti involontari: Giovani 'stranieri' tra percorsi urbani e aule scolastiche.* Perugia: Morlacchi Editore.

Fassin, Didier. 2000. The Biopolitics of Otherness: Undocumented Foreigners and Racial Discrimination in French Public Debate. *Anthropology Today* 17 (1): 3–7.

Frisina, A. 2008. *Giovani Musulmani d'Italia.* Roma: Carocci.

Glick Schiller, Nina, and Ayse Caglar. 2008 "And Ye Shall Process It, and Dwell Therein": Social Citizenship, Global Christianity, and Non-ethnic Immigrant Incorporation. In *Citizenship, Political Engagement, and Belonging: Immigrants in Europe and the United States*, Deborah Reed-Danahay and Caroline Brettell, eds., pp. 201–25. New Brunswick, NJ: Rutgers University Press.

Grillo, Ralph D. 1985. *Ideologies and Institutions in Urban France.* Cambridge: Cambridge University Press.

Grillo, Ralph D., and Jeff C. Pratt. (eds.). 2002. *The Politics of Recognising Difference: Multiculturalism Italian-Style.* Aldershot: Ashgate.

Guerzoni, G., and B. Riccio, (eds.). 2009. *Giovani in cerca di cittadinanza: I figli dell'immigrazione tra scuola e associazionismo; Sguardi antropologici.* Guaraldi: Rimini

Holston, James, and Arjun Appadurai. 1999. Introduction: Cities and Citizenship. In *Cities and Citizenship*, James Holston, ed., pp. 1–18. Durham, NC: Duke University Press.

King, Rodney, and Jacqueline Andall (eds.). 1999. The Geography and Economic Sociology of Recent Immigration to Italy. *Modern Italy* 4 (2): 135–58.

Levitt, Peggy, and Mary C. Waters (eds.). 2002. *The Changing Face of Home: The Transnational Lives of the Second Generation.* New York: Russell Sage Foundation.

Miranda, A. (ed.). 2012 Etre étranger chez soi: Les jeunes d'origine immigrée en Italie. *Migrations Société* 24: 141–42.

Papastergiadis, Nikos. 2000. *The Turbulence of Migration.* Cambridge, UK: Polity Press.

Parker, David, and Miri Song. 2006. Ethnicity, Social Capital, and the Internet: British Chinese Websites. *Ethnicities* 6 (2): 178–202.

———. 2007. "Inclusion, Participation and the Emergence of British Chinese Websites. *Journal of Ethnic and Migration Studies* 33 (7): 1043–61.

Pazzagli, I., and F. Tarabusi. 2009. *Un certo sguardo: Etnografia delle interazioni tra servizi e adolescenti di origine straniera.* Rimini: Guaraldi.

Però, Davide. 2002. The Left and the Political Participation of Immigrants in Italy: The Case of the *Forum* of Bologna. In *The Politics of Recognising Difference: Multiculturalism Italian-Style*, Ralph D. Grillo and Jeff C. Pratt, eds., pp. 95–114. Aldershot: Ashgate.

Reed-Danahay, Deborah, and Caroline Brettell (eds.). 2008. *Citizenship, Political Engagement, and Belonging: Immigrants in Europe and the United States.* New Brunswick, NJ: Rutgers University Press.

Riccio, Bruno. 2011. Rehearsing Transnational Citizenship: Senegalese Associations, Co-development and Simultaneous Inclusion. *African Diaspora* 4: 97–113.

Riccio, Bruno, and Monica Russo. 2011. Everyday Practised Citizenship and the Challenges of Representation: Second-Generation Associations in Bologna. *Journal of Modern Italian Studies* 16 (3): 360–72.

Salih, Ruba. 2004. The Backward and the New: National, Transnational and Post-national Islam in Europe. *Journal of Ethnic and Migration Studies* 30 (5): 995–1014.

Salih, Ruba, and Bruno Riccio. 2011. Transnational Migration and Rescaling Processes: The Incorporation of Migrant Labor. In *Locating Migration: Rescaling Cities and Migrants*, Nina Glick Schiller and Ayse Caglar, eds., pp. 123–42. Ithaca, NY: Cornell University Press.

Stacul, Jaro. 2006. Neo-nationalism or Neo-localism? Integralist Political Engagements in Italy at the Turn of the Millenium. In *Neo-nationalisms in Europe and Beyond: Perspectives from Social Anthropology*. Andre Gingrich and Marcus Banks, eds., pp. 162–76. London: Berghahn.

Thomson, Mark, and Maurice Crul. 2007. The Second Generation in Europe and the United States: How the Transatlantic Debate Is Relevant for Further Research on the European Second Generation. *Journal of Ethnic and Migration Studies* 37 (3): 1025–41.

Vertovec, Steven, and Susanne Wessendorf. 2009. *Assessing the Backlash against Multiculturalism in Europe*. MMG [Max Planck Institute for the Study of Religious and Ethnic Diversity] Working Paper 09-04. Göttingen.

Wessendorf, Susanne. 2008. Culturalist Discourses on Inclusion and Exclusion: The Swiss Citizenship Debate. *Social Anthropology* 16 (2): 187–202.

Zinn, Dorothy L. 2011. "Loud and Clear": The G 2 Second Generations Network in Italy. *Journal of Modern Italian Studies* 16 (3): 373–85.

6 LIVING IN TRANSNATIONAL SPACES

Azorean Portuguese Descendants in Quebec

Josiane Le Gall and Ana Gherghel

Monica's parents immigrated to Canada as children in the 1960s with their own parents. Most of her kin are also migrants settled in Canada—the provinces of Quebec and Ontario—and the United States. Only one of her grandmother's sisters, her son, and the grandchildren remained in the Azores. Her parents have always lived in a Portuguese neighborhood in Montreal and participated in community activities and festivities that are also considered family events. Monica's grandparents and parents, mostly her mother, have preserved connections with family members spread across national boundaries. Monica remembers that during her childhood, they exchanged letters and greeting cards on special occasions like Christmas or New Year's Eve. Monica first visited the Azores islands a year ago, at twenty-three years old, when she accompanied an aunt and her maternal grandmother. During that visit, a maternal cousin hosted them. Since then, she maintains regular transnational social relations, by phone and e-mails, with her maternal cousins. Although she considers this visit to the Azores determinant in her life, she feels at home in Montreal and has no intention to settle anywhere else.

Monica represents the majority of second- and third-generation Azoreans in Quebec who feel at home where they grew up but also display various ties to their parents' or grandparents' homeland.[1] Data from research on Azorean Portuguese in the province of Quebec show that several second- and third-generation descendants still visit their ancestral homeland during holidays and maintain contact with kin in the country of origin or in other places around the world. They develop various forms of belonging to an Azorean heritage based on selective attachment that can manifest in different domains and change across the life course. These observations contradict critics of transnationalism who often underline the ephemeral character of transnational practices (Portes 1999; Kasinitz et al. 2008). However, respondents' discourses indicate a transformation of home place connection over time, and that descendants maintain different relations to the origin country than in previous generations. The Portuguese in Quebec represent an excellent case study to assess the perpetuation and transformation of transnational ties across generations, as this group has a long history of migration to Quebec and Canada in general—with three generations existing today in migrant-descendant families.

In this chapter we discuss in which ways second- and third-generation descendants of Azorean immigrants living in Quebec engage in transnational practices and hence operate in transnational social spaces. We emphasize that being raised in *a transnational social field* (Glick Schiller et al. 1992; Levitt 2002, 2009) or within a *transnational habitus* (Vertovec 2010) leads to the development of an emotional attachment to an Azorean heritage. This process draws on the presence of an extended family network, dispersed between two or three countries, maintaining ties across national borders and thus favoring cultural intergenerational transmission and a multiple hybrid identity. The chapter is organized in several parts. First, we briefly situate our research and approach with regard to the literature on transnational practices of migrants' descendants. Second, the context of our research and methodological considerations are presented. The analysis and discussion of our results is then divided in two main parts: the first part examines the transnational social field in which Azorean descendants grew up and the second one analyzes the types of transnational activities in which they engage showing how they operate in transnational social spaces.

TRANSNATIONAL ACTIVITIES OF SECOND-GENERATION DESCENDANTS

While some scholars argue that transnational practices may be important for the first generation, but not for their children (Alba and Nee 1997; Portes and Rumbaut 2001; Rumbaut 2002; Zontini 2007; Kasinitz et al. 2008), others suggest that transnationalism will continue over time and across several generations (Levitt and Waters 2002; Smith 2002). When youth grow up in families where individuals, goods, money, ideas, and practices of the origin country circulate on a regular basis, their socialization incorporates norms specific to both the receiving and sending countries. Thus they acquire social contacts and skills that are useful in both settings. In other words, transnational practices of the second generation can depend on their relation to cultural, family, and social norms and values transmitted from previous generations (Levitt and Glick Schiller 2004).

As Vertovec (2004: 21, 2010) points out, the concept of *transnational habitus* describes this "dual disposition or orientation" of some migrant groups to retain references related to both home and host countries. Elements referencing various locations can be incorporated in migrants' everyday practice and activities, in conscious or nonconscious manners, thus creating a complex "bifocal" frame of cultural configurations—with regard to social ties, views, and potential action. Their impact on the second generation is important as it contributes to the formation of multiple identities integrating elements from both cultures. In our case, this dynamic is reinforced by what Landolt (2001: 217) has labeled "circuits of transnational obligations and interests" developed within kinship groups maintaining ties and affiliations in several locations.

Our research on Azorean Portuguese descendants in Quebec reveals particular patterns of transnational connections and hence engagement in transnational space. Maintaining ties with the origin country is based on the desire to preserve family ties and a multiple hybrid identity where Azorean heritage remains a core value, although, as we will see, important differences with the first generation are observed. As Brettell and Nibbs (2009) note, recent research suggests that members of the second generation no longer choose to emphasize one identity over the other; rather, their identities are more fluid and multifaceted. Some studies highlight a link between these multiple identities and connections with the parents' homeland that, in some instances, are a form of "emotional transnationalism" that can exist without even being actively engaged in maintaining transnational social relationships (Wolf 2002: 350; see also Ho Peché in this volume). However, this sense of belonging and attachment can also manifest itself through more direct connections. For instance, Wessendorf (2007) has suggested that such a sense of belonging led several children of Italian migrants in Switzerland to relocate to their parents' place of origin. As we will show in this chapter, for Azorean descendants, return is never a realistic option; the origin country represents mostly a symbolic resource. In a pluralist society such as Quebec and in the context of globalization, involvement in transnational social or family networks and preserving connections to the ancestral homeland favor active knowledge of several languages and different cultures, thus representing an indisputable valuable advantage or resource (Meintel and Khan 2005; Le Gall and Meintel 2014).

AZOREAN MIGRATION TO QUEBEC

Migratory movements from the Azores archipelago, an autonomous region of Portugal, have a long history and were mostly directed to the Americas—Brazil, the United States, Canada, and the islands of Bermuda and Hawaii, by contrast with emigration from mainland Portugal directed toward European countries (France, Switzerland, etc.). Portuguese communities in North America (the United States and Canada) are principally formed by Azoreans, in proportions varying between 50 and 70 percent, depending on locality (Melo 1997; Williams and Fonseca 1999; Brettell 2003; Oliveira and Teixeira 2004). This intensive migration occurred through migration networks that have been described as "networks of contacts" (Anderson 1974: 160) or even "island-centered migration chains" (Williams and Fonseca 1999: 74–75), based on kinship and friendship ties (Anderson and Higgs 1979; Chapin 1989).

Emigration to Canada is the most recent important migratory route for Azoreans. It started in the mid-1950s and reached a peak in the mid-1970s. This phenomenon soon became a family-led migration, based on sponsorship through reunification programs. Portuguese migrants in Canada are mostly concentrated in the provinces of Ontario and Quebec. By 2006 the population of Portuguese origin in Quebec (mostly in the Montreal metropolitan area) was estimated to be 57,445. Among the immigrant population, 64.6 percent arrived in Canada before 1981 and 19.8 percent between 1981 and 1990; a smaller proportion entered the country after 1990 (Gouvernement du Québec 2010). Thus, in Canada today there are three generations of Portuguese immigrants and their descendants. According to the 2006 Canadian census, in Quebec, more than half (57.7 percent) of persons of Portuguese origin, aged fifteen or older, are of the first generation, and 42.3 percent are of the second and third generations.

Studies on Portuguese descendants (Meintel and Le Gall 1995; Noivo 1997; Oliveira and Teixeira 2004; Trindade 2007; Gomes 2008; Da Silva 2011; Sardinha 2010) confirm the preservation of strong family ties and the transmission of culture across generations. They also show how the second generation in Quebec (Meintel 1992) and in Ontario (Sardinha 2010) are developing multiple identities. This is reinforced by the fact that they form cohesive communities in urban centers like Toronto and Montreal metropolitan areas (Teixeira and Rosa 2000; Teixeira 2000; Nunes 2003).[2] Moreover, Quebec's context plays a significant role for cultural and ethnic reproduction. As several researchers have observed, immigrants' native language and other manifestations of ethnic identity within minority groups are preserved in Montreal over longer periods than in other North American regions. This phenomenon is explained by the fact that the province of Quebec and especially Montreal is characterized by bilingualism and a "double majority"—Francophone and Anglophone—while the other Canadian provinces are predominantly Anglophone (Anctil 1984; Meintel 2000).[3] To understand the complexity of this phenomenon, one should evoke the multiethnic character of Quebec, especially Montreal. Among all Canadian provinces, Quebec is distinguished by greater diversity of immigrants' origin countries (Germain and Trinh 2011). This diversity results from successive migratory waves from various geographic regions. Until the mid-1970s immigrants were mainly from European countries, such as Portugal or Italy. Since the late 1970s, a diversification of immigrants' origin countries is observed. As a result, an important proportion of Quebec's population is today formed of immigrant populations (born outside Canada). Moreover, the province of Quebec is also distinguished by its politics of selection and integration of immigrants, defined as *interculturalism* and emphasizing the sociocultural, educational, and economic insertion of newcomers into the Quebec's Francophone majority. This politics, introduced in the 1970s, differentiates in important ways the climate of Quebec compared to other Canadian provinces.

Several studies of Portuguese migrants who settled in European countries—France, Switzerland, and so on—demonstrate the existence of transnational ties associated with various practices, like return visits, participation in hometown celebrations, or building houses in the origin villages (Charbit et al. 1997; Klimt 2006; Marques and Gois 2008; Dos Santos 2010; Leal 2011). The existence of social networks across frontiers and hence the maintenance of strong ties with the homeland have also been observed in the case of Portuguese migrants to North America (Anderson 1974; Anderson and Higgs 1979; Chapin 1989; Williams and Fonseca 1999; Brettell 2003). Such observations in the United States led Brettell (2003: 50) to the conclusion that studies of transnationalism and transnational families can benefit from in-depth analysis of the Portuguese case because "maintaining links with the homeland and sustaining the idea of return for as long as one is abroad is deeply rooted in Portuguese history and culture." Our study brings new data that sustain this observation emphasizing the creation and transformation over time of transnational spaces created by Portuguese Azorean migrants in the province of Quebec and their families in different sites around the world. This case study also introduces location-related considerations to the debate on the perpetuation of transnational practices over time. As we will see in the following sections, the contexts specific to the receiving and sending countries influence the present configuration of these transnational spaces.

METHODOLOGY

This chapter is based on multisited research investigating the transnational practices of Portuguese migrants from the Azores archipelago who reside in the province of Quebec, Canada.[4] The research has been conducted simultaneously in the homeland of the Azores and in the receiving community of Quebec using both structured biographical interviews (in French, English, and Portuguese) and *in situ* observations.[5] Interviews with 127 members of about forty kinship groups across at least three generations have been completed. This sample includes twenty-six Azorean migrants and fifty-four descendants of the 1.5, second, and third generations in Quebec (mostly in the Montreal metropolitan area), as well as thirty-four return migrants and thirteen nonmigrant relatives in the Azores (São Miguel Island). In order to select an equal number of respondents by categories, various strategies of recruitment were deployed in each location: informal contacts, institutional references (obtained from ethnic community organizations and administrative institutions), and snowball sampling (family reference to other kin, key informants' references, etc.).

Respondents selected at one site were systematically invited to refer us to other potential participants among members of their kinship group living in Quebec or in the Azores. Researchers contacted the referred persons inviting them to answer an interview, according to their availability. In this way, several members (up to seven) have been interviewed in each family in order to include various categories of respondents in each unit investigated. Diversification of the sample according to gender, age, migration trajectory, and position in the family was also pursued. The discussion presented in this chapter is based on analysis of thirty-two interviews with members of the second (seventeen) and third (fifteen) generations that were conducted in Quebec. This part of the sample includes men and women, with ages varying between the twenties and late thirties. Interviews were centered on issues related to family networks (local and at a distance): migration history of the family, configuration and composition of the family network, its evolution in time, transnational connections, intergenerational transmission of cultural and family values, and practices and behaviors. The following sections present results of our research based on a thematic content analysis of Azorean descendants' narratives.

TRANSNATIONAL SPACES OF CHILDHOOD

What are the entrance points of the second and third generations into transnational spaces? Connection to the ancestral homeland established by their parents' and grandparents' generations plays a pivotal role in maintaining the Azores as a reference point in descendants' lives. If for the family members in Montreal region tight-knit relations are favored by geographic proximity—all living in close neighborhoods, regularly socializing during family events or community celebrations, helping each other in difficult moments, and so on—the feeling of emotional proximity with Azorean kin is based on long-lasting transnational ties created by first-generation migrants. During childhood, members of the second and third generations participated in many ways in transnational family activities, such as visits to the Azores and family reunions (in several countries where family members live) organized on the occasion of life-cycle events involving rituals.

Our interviews show that return visits during summer holidays were quite common in the past, especially for the second generation. The frequency of holiday visits to the Azores was higher for families who had a house (secondary residence) in their native village. These return visits to the Azores during childhood or adolescence were motivated by family reasons—to participate in family gatherings and life-cycle rituals (weddings, funerals, anniversaries, etc.), to present children to the family, or to take care of the house or land that the family owned. Such visits were not only an important opportunity for Azorean descendants to establish their own connections with people living in the Azores, but they also strengthened their transnational bond to this location.

Unlike Monica, who visited the islands only once in her twenties, several respondents had opportunities to visit the islands more frequently during their childhood and thus developed a closer, stronger, and lifelong bond to this location and to people there. For instance, Marie (thirty-three years old, second generation) developed a friendship with her cousins during her summer holiday visits dating back to childhood and continues to keep in touch with them: "Every time we went in Portugal, when I was younger, we all stayed with the other uncle. He has three children, and we are three children in the family also. We write to each other, we e-mail. So there was this link that we continued. . . . When we were children, we went there during the summer for about a month, in their house." For his part, Roberto (thirty years old, second generation) remembers about his numerous visits in the Azores during his childhood and people he met over there on these occasions: "You get there, then people tell you: 'this is your cousin, and this one too is your cousin and him too.' All of them, they are all your cousins. I have met a lot of people this way." During these visits, the family was hosted by a cousin of Roberto's grandmother, with whom they maintained closer ties and who also visited Montreal for the first time a few years ago.

A few respondents also described tentative return experiences to the Azores during their childhood when their parents decided to relocate their homes in the islands. For all of them this period of return, which lasted between six months and two years, was never positively experienced, as these families faced limited economic conditions and other difficulties in their everyday lives. These families definitively returned to Quebec. However following their sojourn in the Azores, they reported an increased frequency of contact with family members residing in the islands. For instance, Eduarda (thirty-five years old, second generation) describes such an experience. In the 1980s, her parents decided to move back to the islands with their three children to work in a family enterprise and return to the origin village that they always missed. A few years later they returned to Montreal, but they continued to visit their kin living in the Azores for about a month over the years and regularly spent their holidays there, being hosted by an uncle.

Migrants also maintained over time various ties at a distance with kin left behind in the Azores. While nowadays communications by phone are predominant, in the past migrants mostly communicated by letter in order to keep in touch with family members dispersed in various locations, especially with those in the Azores. They exchanged news about family events and various services. Material exchanges were also reported by most respondents. Sending money and goods was a common practice, especially before traditional holidays, like Christmas or for the organization of the *festas*. Even parents and grandparents of interviewees who never returned to the Azores after migration have preserved connections at a distance with family members in the Azores, the United States, or other Canadian provinces (Ontario, British Columbia), on a more or less regular basis.

For second- and third-generation Azorean descendants, these different kinds of links perpetuated by their parents or grandparents—omnipresent during their childhood—have become the foundation on which they have built their own ties to the Azores as adults. The most extensive and strongest transnational practices are found among those who had been involved in transnational space during their childhood through frequent visits to the islands, family gatherings to celebrate life events, intensive material and informational exchanges at a distance, and so on. These are the individuals raised with a transnational habitus that endures into adulthood. For instance, descendants who spent a part of their childhood in the islands following their parents' relocation or those frequently participating in return visits have more chances to be actively involved in transnational networks. However all respondents indicated that they grew up in transnational spaces even if their families never or rarely visited the island. Our data show that insertion in multigenerational kinship networks and maintaining transnational connections and cultural practices in family and community spheres to enhance intergenerational transmission represent the other instances that facilitate the engagement in transnational spaces on the part of members of descendant generations.

MULTIGENERATIONAL KINSHIP NETWORKS

A feeling of embeddedness within a kinship network represents one of the essential factors that explain the persistence of the second and third generations' involvement in transnational spaces. Regular links with the origin community maintained during their childhood helps descendants to preserve knowledge about the family network at a distance. Our respondents are included in multigenerational family networks that preserve various active ties, locally and at a distance (with family members living in other Canadian provinces or other countries), although changes over time are equally reported. All the respondents insisted on the importance of these networks during their childhood, but also at present. For emigrant families settled in the Montreal region, family ties are essential considering the importance of chain migration, which explains the considerable size of the networks registered and the high density of relations within it. Indeed, many of the kinship groups included in this study count more than one hundred persons living in various countries. For several interviewees, numerous family members are still present in their everyday life, even if particular events or conflicts can sometimes disrupt the links with some of them. All the respondents grew up surrounded by a large family, grandparents, uncles, aunts, cousins, and so on, on both the maternal and paternal sides. The situation of Alberto (thirty years old, second generation) is a typical example. His paternal grandmother and uncles and his father (who was sixteen at the time) settled in Montreal at the end of 1960s. They joined the grandfather who had already been settled in Canada for several years. Nowadays, Alberto's paternal uncles and aunts have relocated to other Canadian provinces. Alberto's mother also moved to Montreal at age sixteen with her mother and sisters to join the father who had already been living there for several years. Presently, Alberto's kinship group also includes a paternal uncle returnee and several other more distant relatives in the Azores. When asked about his family relatives in Montreal, he reported strong ties on the maternal side due to geographic proximity, since they all live in the same neighborhood: "Because . . . they all live next door, the next house . . . because my grandfather when he decided to buy a house, actually he bought two." In the same spirit, Beatriz (thirty years old, third generation) describes how the migration chain initiated by her grandparents regrouped an important part of her kinship group in the same neighborhood: "So they gathered a big gang; they bought almost all the street because everybody lived in the houses in the same street." This geographic regrouping provided a context of socialization and constant interaction and exchanges in everyday life.

When kinship networks are more dispersed between various locations, contacts can be less intense, but ties are not completely loosened. Even when individuals are not living in close proximity, their kinship networks remain active, with members meeting or having exchanges regularly or more exceptionally on occasions like religious festivals or important family events,[6] and ceremonies such as baptisms, weddings, and funerals that gather migrants and nonmigrants together in Montreal or elsewhere in Canada or the United States. Most nonmigrant and returnee interviewees also reported such family events as reasons to visit their migrant siblings in Canada. Participating to these events offers occasions to preserve a sense of family cohesion and to develop ties with family members of the same age, from the same locality or elsewhere. These gatherings also represent important occasions for descendants to meet their relatives living in other regions and countries. Later on, they develop their own relations at a distance with cousins, aunts, and uncles. Therefore, these family events as well as the visits are essential for the perpetuation of transnational connections. Many of our interviewees emphasized the importance of these family ties and gatherings and talked about family in a positive light. Irene (thirty-six years old, second generation) indicates that her parents always insisted on the importance of knowing the entire kinship group: "You know, every time we went in the United States or in Toronto to meet family, my father tried to find out more about our kin. Then we went to visit them. It was very important for him to tell us, me and my brother: 'this is your cousin from your granddad.'" These considerations indicate a view of family and kinship centered on solidarity and cohesion, and the maintenance of family commitments and engagements, all of which generated a strong feeling of belonging to a definite group. Even in these cases of dispersed networks where contacts are diffuse or indirect, at some point in life descendants demonstrate their intention of and interest in renewing or reactivating transnational attachment.

Engaging in transnational space is thus built on the foundation of kinship networks. It is important to bear in mind that descendants' experiences within transnational spaces created by Azorean migrants and their families are also shaped by various cultural manifestations of Portuguese ethnic belonging perpetuated in Quebec (in family and community spheres). Circulating within this transnational space enhances understanding among younger generations of the culturally specific traits of their grandparents or parents that were maintained and transmitted in various ways during decades after settling in the receiving country.

INTERGENERATIONAL CULTURAL TRANSMISSION

Insertion in active multigenerational family networks (local/transnational) not only has an impact on maintaining transnational connections or developing new ones. It is also important for the intergenerational transmission of cultural elements, which in turn can reinforce the feeling of attachment to the origin country and the transnational practices of those of the second and third generation, once they have become adults. All our respondents were exposed during childhood to several distinctive elements of Portuguese culture that constitute an important basis on which to construct their identities and life plans. Significant differences are noted however between second- and third-generation descendants because the latter often are only indirectly exposed to these cultural settings.[7] Most immigrant parents are determined to transmit to their children knowledge of the language, religion, cultural traditions, and food. As Carolina (twenty-six years old, third generation) observed: "The connections I have from my Portuguese heritage, it's because of my parents. It's because they wanted, for me, to be exposed to it."

Several migrants' descendants, even among the third generation, are fluently trilingual (French, English, and Portuguese), a situation rather usual in Montreal among migrants' descendants across a range of national origins (Lamarre and Lamarre 2009). They learned the Portuguese language at home with their parents and grandparents and have spoken it fluently since childhood. Portuguese is often the main language spoken with grandparents, as they do not always speak French very well. As a child, Ramira (third generation, twenty-four years old) spoke only French and English with her parents, immigrant descendants themselves. She learned Portuguese with her grandparents who took care of her for several years: "in my childhood, I spoke [Portuguese] a lot with my grandparents because I stayed with them." Other descendants participated in Portuguese Saturday classes.

The majority of our interviewees also declare that their parents and grandparents emphasized religious practices during their childhood, that is, attending Sunday mass every week, following catechesis, and participating in religious festivals. Many also participated in various activities organized by Portuguese associations—music groups, folklore dance groups, sports club, and so on—as well as in the celebrations of traditional festivals specific to migrants' origin villages. In this way, descendants grew up in a transnational social space where elements of the origin culture country were present not only in parental homes but also in social, religious, and community ethnic contexts.[8] Participating in these spaces familiarized them with Portuguese culture since their early childhood and allowed socialization in diverse Luso-Canadian settings. Like many other parents, Carolina's father encouraged the participation of his children in community feasts: "My dad had us all very involved. If there was a Portuguese party nearby or at the Portuguese clubs that are in other regions [neighborhoods] my dad would always go and take me and my sister with him. . . . When I grew older, he sent me to the folklore."

For some respondents, cultural retention was enhanced by the fact that, during their childhood, they resided in the "Little Portugal" district or other neighborhoods of the Montreal metropolitan region (Anjou, Sainte-Thérèse, etc.) with a high density of Portuguese households. For some, living in a Portuguese neighborhood is highly important, especially as this enhances a feeling of belonging. Return visits to the Azores during childhood represent a strategy that the first generation often used to ensure the preservation of a Portuguese identity. As we show below, second- and third-generation descendants continue this practice themselves, although to a lesser extent, in order to raise their own children with an awareness of Portuguese culture. These intergenerational dynamics reinforce the capacity of living at least mentally in a transnational space for second and third generations.

CURRENT TRANSNATIONAL ACTIVITIES

As adults who are well integrated into Montreal life, Azorean descendants continue to participate in transnational spaces. They develop a wide range of ties to the Azores, albeit at varying levels. From the total, twenty-two of our respondents maintain direct ties with friends and relatives of the same generation and similar age living in the Azores. The scope of these ties is limited to elective relations, with people sharing affinities, long-lasting friendships, or particular experiences. Compared to their parents or grandparents who preserved contacts with the extended kinship group, these descendants are involved in a limited number of contacts with fewer family members. Repeated encounters during holidays and spending time and doing activities together either in Quebec, in the Azores, or elsewhere represent the most frequent contexts for sharing common experiences. These are at the basis of transnational continued ties. Despite the obvious impact of geographic distance on physical contact, for many these transnational relations have as much importance as local ones. For instance, some respondents said that they communicate several times per week, and sometimes even on a daily basis. For five respondents, mainly third-generation descendants, contacts with extended family are indirect, being exclusively mediated by their parents or grandparents. In these cases, parents and grandparents maintain contacts and share news and information about the larger kinship group with younger members of the family. For example, Claudio (thirty years old), a third-generation descendant, his mother being Portuguese and his father French Canadian, knows about his Azorean maternal relatives only through his mother, who is principally involved in communication at a distance with the family living in the islands. Two respondents occasionally travel to the Azores, even if no family member is still living in the island. Finally, three respondents don't maintain any active ties with their ancestral homeland.

The transnational practices of the second and third generations in Quebec include not only ties maintained with kin living in the Azores, but also ties with siblings settled in other countries, mostly the United States, but also Brazil and elsewhere. Even those families that don't have ties with kinship in the Azores maintain more or less regular contacts with kin and friends of the same ethnic origin living in the United States or in other countries. Translocal ties with family members living in Toronto and other locations in the province of Ontario, Vancouver, and other locations in the province of British Columbia can juxtapose transnational ties, thereby situating everyone within a wider multilocated, multigenerational kinship network. Many of our interviewees stressed that their families are dispersed in various parts of the world. For example, Carlos (thirty years old, third generation) describes a kinship network composed of individuals dispersed mostly between the United States, Canada, and the Azores, but also a few distant relatives in Brazil (descendants of a grandfather's brother who emigrated a long time ago, at the same time as his grandparents).

To maintain contact at a distance with their kin, descendants seem to be more prone to use Internet communications (e-mails, chat, Skype, Facebook) than phone calls and letters, especially if they know their interlocutors personally. Marie (thirty-three years old, second generation), for example, regularly exchanges news with her uncle and his family living in the Azores, in addition to maintaining close contacts with her family settled in Quebec. She definitely prefers the rapid and spontaneous character of e-mail and text messages and appreciates the possibility to communicate at any time of day. Phone calls seem to her more complex because of the time difference (four hours) between the two localities. She explains the differences between her generation and her parents' like this: "With the new communication technology nowadays, the means to communicate changed a lot. It helps and facilitates, especially for the younger ones. For the elderly, it's more difficult. My aunt doesn't send e-mails or text messages. She only knows how to use her cell phone." In the same vein, Monica (twenty-four years, third generation) points out this intergenerational difference: "My mother mostly uses the phone. Even my aunt, my grandmother, the eldest in the family are more prone to use the phone. But we [young people] really use Internet most of the time." The use of information and communications technologies (ICTs) contributed to intensification of transnational contacts and facilitated descendants' involvement in transnational ties, developing their own contacts with same age/same generation siblings but also through delegation; that is, parents who are not familiar with the new technologies pass on to their children some of the tasks related to transnational exchanges, like sending photos and updates (Gherghel and Le Gall 2012).

Lately, using Facebook has become the most widespread modality to communicate at a distance as it favors maintaining regular contacts between visits or gatherings and the preservation of ties, especially when family members are dispersed in various countries and localities. The frequency of contacts between Beatriz (thirty years old, third generation) and her uncle living in the Azores increased since they became Facebook users. Through this social media, she has also recently established contacts with kin living in Brazil although they have never met in person. These contacts can be added to the intense ties maintained with numerous family members in Quebec and Ontario.

If the strength of transnational ties depends partly on the ability to use Internet social networking technology, the main factor influencing Azorean descendants' ties with those left behind in the origin community or in other countries is the importance of relations. Contacts are more frequent when descendants and their nonmigrant counterparts know each other personally, as in the case of Monica (twenty-four years old) who communicates with her cousins every day, even becoming confidantes. This Azorean descendant of the third generation explains: "When we met the first time, I didn't think I would attach so much. But when they came here, it was really tough to see them leaving. Then, even when I returned from my trip to the Azores last year, I really had the blues for a long time. I cried all the time during the trip back, and it took me about two months to recover from that."

Proximity with her cousins was enhanced by the fact that her maternal grandmother in Montreal maintained over decades close and regular contacts with her only sister, who remained on the island. However, the situation is quite different with other siblings living in the United States and Toronto that Monica feels are more distant because they communicate less frequently. This case highlights once more the selective character of ties at a distance and how holiday visits in the Azores and elsewhere or visits of relatives (migrant and nonmigrant) in Montreal represent important occasions to establish new contacts or to revive and reinforce already existent transnational connections.

In general, most Azorean descendants reported being involved in one or several of the following transnational practices: holiday visits, secondary residences, cultural exchanges (with folkloric music or dance groups), personal and informational exchanges, and emotional support. In addition to contacts at a distance maintained with kin living in the Azores, traveling to the islands during holidays is one of the most important ways to maintain contacts with the homeland. For those who still have relatives in the Azores, family obligations determine the activities during these visits—to spend time with all siblings, to stay several days in their houses, to share their meals, organize trips or social gatherings and so on. During her childhood, Amelia (twenty-six years old, third generation) had the chance to visit the Azores several times. She continues to return frequently as she can stay in her grandmother's house in the origin village, a site of important family gatherings: "This summer when I went there, I did not go alone. I went with my godparents and my cousins. We all stayed at the house." Like other migrants, Amelia's grandmother preserved their house and land proprieties in the islands although most family members today live in North America. The house remains available to the family even though a cousin was allowed to inhabit it occasionally when no visitors from abroad needed it: "My grandmother gave him permission to live in the house, but she also told him that when the aunts or anyone else in the family wants to vacation there, he has to promise that he will let them stay there—to live there! Because it is out of the question that they go to a hotel. They must stay at the family home." As visits mostly occur during summer holidays, descendants often have the occasion to observe local traditional religious festivals (festas) that take place especially from May to September in all the villages of the islands. These occasions offer the opportunity to better understand the rural background and origin culture of their ancestors, as well as the context of traditions and celebrations perpetuated in their community life in Quebec and that they experienced during their childhood.

Unlike results from previous research on remittances in the transnational social field, material and financial exchanges are exceptional and were rarely reported by our respondents. If sending remittances (money and goods like clothes, food products, or domestic equipment) back home was an intensive practice of Azorean migrants in the past, this kind of exchange diminished significantly during the late 1990s and is very rare nowadays. However, giving and receiving gifts is still intensively practiced especially during visits, by both migrants and their nonmigrant counterparts. Gifts particularly include products that are not available or only rarely accessible in the other location. In the case of migrants or descendants, gifts received from Azorean kin—mostly handicraft and decorative objects, liqueurs, and various traditional food products like pastries—have a symbolic significance rather than an instrumental one. Upon their visits in the islands, migrants bring various gifts mostly with intended utilitarian purpose like clothing, food items (coffee, chocolates, etc.), and other products that are generally cheaper in Quebec.

Consistent with other scholarship (Levitt 2002; Lee 2008), our study suggests that transnational activities do not remain constant across the life course. Events such as marriage, having children, or changing jobs affect the ways in which people engage in transnational activities. Indeed, respondents who were are at different stages of life reported different ways in which they engaged in transnational activities. Some of our respondents noted a recent and constant diminution of their family network following the deaths of several older kin in the Azores. For others, becoming a parent modified their relation to the origin culture and incited them to revive their relation to Portuguese heritage and stimulated their interest in knowing more about the islands.

Although most Azorean descendants born in Quebec evolve in transnational spaces punctuated by Portuguese culture, they generally do not imagine their future in Portugal. Moreover, contrary to what is observed in several studies on other ethnic groups (Lievens 1999; Santelli 2001; Morawska 2003; Strassburger 2004; Beck-Gernsheim 2007; Levitt 2009), Azorean descendants are rarely in the situation to choose a life partner in the origin country or to return to work or live there, although a few exceptions can be noted. It is important to note that engaging in transnational activities is neither an indication of a failure of professional insertion in Quebec or the result of experiencing socioeconomic exclusion. According to our interviewees, the quality of life in their parents' homeland would not be better than in Quebec. For example, some explained that they couldn't imagine moving elsewhere, because the Canadian environment offers many opportunities and a more favorable standard of living. As Carolina (twenty-six years old, third generation) explains: "I have no reason to go back. I see it more as a place to get away, you know. It's like a second home, there." Similarly, Julie (eighteen years old, third generation) points out that she would like to maintain her ties to the Azores, have a secondary residence, and spend holidays abroad, but would never envision returning for longer periods because of the isolation and lack of opportunities that she feels characterize the region.

> *A:* I think I will never live in the Azores an entire year because I'm a modern girl who regularly follows the news, the politics. I'm in tune with the actualities, I love to go to museums, to keep up with the cultural and urban life. The Azores, when I talk to people I realize it, it's a much [more] closed environment. Like it or not, it's an island, and people, anyhow the majority of adolescents and youth, are not aware of international debates, news, and stakes in general; they have never traveled. For me, it's very important to keep up with the news and actualities. So I don't think I will live [in the Azores] for a long time, but I have plans to buy a house for holidays. I'd like to keep in touch, to stay connected with this place. . . .
>
> *Q:* The visit to Azores helped you to understand the choice your grandparents made?
>
> *A:* I understand very well the decision my grandparents made to go to Canada because . . . I spent two months in the Azores and I wish to return to Canada; I want something else. Meaning that I'm very well here on holidays, people are kind, I love the culture, I love being here, it's splendid, but I understand [my grandparents] left because I would do just the same. For me, it's because the environment is too closed and isolated."

By contrast with their children or grandchildren, members of the first generation sometimes expressed their desire to return to the Azores upon retirement. Indeed, some immigrants who are already retired have set up transnational living arrangements, spending several months each year in the islands, in their secondary residences. Also, several other respondents decided to return to the Azores and relocated their homes in the islands either upon retirement or as adult families with children in order to take over a family business or to create an enterprise.

THE MIGRANTS' ANCESTRAL HOMELAND AS A SYMBOLIC RESOURCE FOR DESCENDANTS

If they do not plan to return to Portugal, how do descendants perceive these connections with their parents' or grandparents' homeland and the gains from the relationships they share in these transnational spaces? Even though their sense of inclusion within Quebec society is explicit, most of the descendants interviewed in our study express strong attachments to their ancestral homeland that are shaped by their experiences within transnational spaces created by Azorean migrants and their families. They self-identify as Canadian or Quebecois, yet also as Azorean or Portuguese. As has been observed in other studies of the second generation in Quebec (Meintel 1992; Meintel and Le Gall 1995), the majority of our respondents consider these multiple identities as an advantage. The account of Roberto (thirty years old, second generation) expresses well this idea: "I'm privileged to have parents who are not Quebecois because . . . yes, I consider myself a Quebecois, but I also consider I have something more. You know, I have a bonus, all that Azorean culture."

According to our respondents, developing these multiple affiliations means having a richer life experience. Further, speaking several languages, retaining dual citizenship, acknowledging other cultural aspects (folklore, music, painting, etc.) appear to be conceived as advantages that open up opportunities in a globalized world. As Carolina (twenty-six years old, third generation) stated: "I think just of opportunities. . . . Jobs, of course. I think job is a big one. But also, the way of life, technologies, just being more aware of what is going on in the world. I find we have more connections over the world." The majority also insists on the benefits of speaking several languages: "I think it's an asset, something more that you have. Also, it's pleasant to speak Portuguese." Beatriz (thirty years old, third generation) has a similar view: "It's one more language you know. I think that more languages you know, the more you can achieve in life." All these considerations motivate descendants to pursue or develop their own engagements in transnational spaces, but in different ways than their parents or grandparents.

If for second-generation descendants cultural transmission mostly occurred in a context where constraints, obligations, and impositions by parents were predominant, the process is differently perceived for the third generation. Many respondents expressed the desire to provide grounding in Portuguese culture and language for their children. However for many in the second generation, socialization into a predominantly Portuguese environment was imposed by their parents. Thus in late adolescence, they distanced themselves from these practices. As parents, those of the second generation wish to instill in their children an interest in and feeling of belonging to their Azorean heritage mediated through their own experience, selecting some elements considered as advantages and bringing new significance and interpretation to traditional cultural elements. In the same vein, knowledge of the Portuguese language is perceived as a rich asset for the children. Regardless of their level of knowledge of Portuguese, all respondents manifested the intention to teach the language to their own descendants. Irene (forty-six years old, second generation) grew up in a Portuguese family that regularly celebrated Azorean traditions and emphasized family values. Asked about the relation she expects her own children to have with the Azores, she doesn't hesitate to affirm "*that they perpetuate it.*" Irene taught Portuguese language to her children and, like many other in the second generation, brought them to the Azores several times, as her own parents did during her childhood. A similar disposition is manifested by Marie (thirty-three years old, second generation). She points out that she feels grateful to her father, who required his children to speak only Portuguese at home. Nowadays, she is married to a Portuguese and insists that she will do the same with her own children. It thus appears that the process of constructing multiple Luso-Canadian identities continues over time through cultural reproduction strategies of socialization like in the cases quoted above. This process can also be enhanced by third-generation descendants who revisit forms of engagement in transnational spaces that may have diminished over time among some of their parents' generation. For example, Vanessa (thirty-four years old, third generation) has never visited her grandparents' homeland. But she considers it important for her children to develop a feeling of belonging to the Azores and thus she feels obliged to transmit as much information and knowledge about the country as she can. She tries to expose her children to cultural symbolic events, such as folklore and music, without the obligation to follow classes. She intends to organize trips to the Azores for her children and teaches them the Portuguese language. At the same time, she sees these initiatives as occasions that open up opportunities in general, which are of high importance in her opinion. Similarly, Monica (twenty-four years old, third generation) is delighted to speak Portuguese and stresses the importance of transmitting the language to her own children: "I am truly very happy to be able to speak, to express myself in Portuguese. So, it will be important for me one day to transmit this language to my children."

Julie (eighteen years old, third generation) grew up in the cosmopolitan environment of Montreal and in a multiethnic home with an Azorean-descendant father and a Francophone Canadian mother. She didn't learn Portuguese as a child and participated only sporadically in community activities. She visited the Azores on a few occasions with her family during summer holidays, living in her paternal grandfather's house. Over time, the links with the origin community loosened, particularly as her grandparents aged and only some of their friends remained behind in the Azores. As a young adult, Julie decided to renew her relation with the homeland of her father's family and her Portuguese heritage. She traveled alone to the Azores during a summer holiday to attend Portuguese classes and to visit the island. This experience made her more aware that she had grown up in an environment impregnated by Azorean Portuguese culture—something she sees as a legacy of her grandparents. Her evolving relation with her Portuguese heritage illustrates how Azorean descendants are constructing multiple identities and acknowledging gradually over time their multiple affiliations. Julie also wishes to transmit Portuguese to her children:

> *A:* I don't want to do the same mistake as my father did with me, I will speak Portuguese to my children.
>
> *Q:* Yes? So for you, it's very important?

A: Yes, I wish to continue this. And I also want to learn much more about the food and cooking from this culture in order to inculcate it to my children. I want to learn this because I think one has to learn from several cultures and retain the best of each one in order to better form as a person. It's perfect to give the chance to the child from birth to immerse in two or three cultures because with this knowledge the child could later construct his own personality for a more interesting life. Actually it's important to know your past, and then knowing a language is also an advantage.

Parents (of both the second and third generations) who consider insufficient their knowledge of Portuguese turn to other sources, like the Portuguese school.[9] Some of them also count on their parents or grandparents to cover this task. For instance, Carolina (twenty-six years old, third generation) wished her parents had sent her to a Portuguese school in her childhood. As a parent, she encourages grandparents to talk in Portuguese with her children. She also plans to send her children to the Azores so that they will come to understand their origins: "I feel like I don't have what it takes. You know, like, that's why I tell my father, 'I will want to leave my kids with you for a summer, and take them to Portugal.' You know, like, show them around."

As suggested with the examples above, the lives of members of the second and third generations are shaped by values and practices specific to Portuguese Azorean tradition. However, participants in this research developed over time a particular relation to the culture of their parents' ancestral homeland that they also consider as cultural patrimony and symbolic resource, in contrast with first-generation migrants who mostly express attachment and intention to perpetuate "Portuguese culture" as they knew it in the origin country. For instance, Roberto has participated since his childhood in the numerous festivities celebrated in Azorean communities in the metropolitan region of Montreal. More recently he has become involved in a folk group and also teaches music classes to youth. He explains the reason for his involvement in religious events as follows: "You know, I don't go to church anymore. I'm not a believer. But I think these feasts are something very important . . . simply because it's something so . . . central in the Azorean culture. . . . If this disappears, nothing will survive [of this culture]." Unlike his parents, who attached importance to the religious character of the feast, Roberto mostly considers its cultural dimensions, emphasizing the symbolic meaning of these traditions and their preservation. Vanessa (thirty-four years old, third generation) participates in the most important religious festivals to accompany her family. She says motivations to participate in these ceremonies are variable: for older people, it is to "pay a promise to God" or "to meet people." For her, like for many other Azorean descendants, it is to "eat the Portuguese sandwich" and to maintain family ties. Several respondents also reported that in their adolescence or adulthood, they ceased to participate in activities organized by various Portuguese/Azorean associations, like folklore groups, but several preferred to be involved in activities organized within the larger local community such as media production, organization of cultural events like the Portuguese week, or students' associations.

Living in transnational spaces is thus seen as an enriching asset for second and third generations because it allows the practice of another language, knowledge of and openness to other cultures, and occasions to participate in various cultural activities. All the respondents emphasize the need to pursue transnational ties and visits during holidays and their importance. Many of those who traveled to the Azores during their holidays reported that they wished "to discover" or "rediscover their origin country," which has changed importantly during the past few decades. They appreciate seeing the place where their grandparents and sometimes their parents were born and grew up. Carlos (thirty years old, third generation) repeatedly identifies himself as a Quebecois during the interview and at the same time feels a constant attraction to the Azores. Since his first visit, he tries to repeat the experience despite the expensive cost of the travel: "The first time when I went to Portugal I was sixteen years old, . . . then [the] more I discovered of my country, of my origin country, [the] more I wanted to go back. It was like it echoed so much with myself." In fact, tourist reasons motivate the visits of members of the second and third generations more often than the familial motivations characteristic of first-generation respondents. Analysis of respondents' discourse suggests that for the second and third generations, the Azores is a place of memory in positive terms. They particularly appreciate the beautiful scenery of the islands, and the spectacular natural landscapes. This viewpoint contrasts with the predominant views of their predecessors expressed through the reports and stories gathered from their parents or grandparents, who often describe the Azores as a "land of misery and poverty."

There are also third-generation descendants who decide at some point in their lives to reacquaint themselves with their Portuguese ancestry, an action that is distinct from their parents (of the second generation), who distanced themselves from it. For instance, several respondents have recently taken steps to obtain Portuguese citizenship and visit the islands, while others, like Julie, started to learn Portuguese. Such initiatives demonstrate that the ancestral homeland can gain importance over time. These examples show that growing up in transnational spaces where Portuguese culture is present represents a strong foundation to build on and can lead descendants to develop of their own ties with the ancestral homeland. This intergenerational dynamic is one indication of how participation to transnational spaces can change over time, be activated at some significant moments and loosen at others, and in some cases be perpetuated across generations.

CONCLUSION

This chapter, based on interviews with second- and third-generation Azorean descendants in Quebec, offers an account of the perpetuation and transformation of transnational spaces across generations. We have shown that transnational spaces can persist long beyond the first generation and that descendants of immigrants can be as involved in these spaces as the original emigrating generation, although there are important differences from one individual to another. For some, transnational practices are regular, while for others, they are occasional and sporadic. However, as we have seen, the level of engagement in transnational activities can vary across the life span.

Our study supports Levitt's observations that growing up in a transnational family offers a partial explanation for the transnational practices of the second generation. As we noted, parents' or grandparents' involvement in transnational connections with their homeland and other geographic locations have profound effects on their children and grandchildren. Some of them are raised to a *transnational habitus*, thus maintaining active practices with explicit transnational orientation similar to their parents'—recurrent visits in the origin country, regular contacts at a distance with kin and friends, material and other types of exchanges. Others are raised in families characterized by active long-distance ties with kin or friends of the same ethnic origin scattered around the world but no return visits to the Azores, while a minority is raised in multiethnic, multigenerational families with transnational connections that loosen over time—trips to homeland are rare and contacts at a distance only occasional. As Leal (2011: 49–50) demonstrated in the case of Luso-American communities, transnational practice is unevenly distributed among individuals and various institutions of the community, some maintaining transnational orientations while others manifesting a 'long-distance regionalism' without actual transnational connection.

As our respondents emphasize, the transnational social field in which they grew up is created by practices of multigenerational, both local and transnational, kinship networks, favoring cultural transmission and promoting links between the local emigrant community in Quebec, the homeland, and other emigrant communities (in other Canadian provinces, the United States, or elsewhere). Parents develop strategies for maintaining a transnational dimension to their children's lives mainly through cultural maintenance within the family and participating in religious, cultural, social, or community events and celebrations where aspects of Portuguese culture are displayed. Some also maintain the centrality of their country of origin through frequent holiday visits, having a secondary residence in their hometown, or practicing intensive *kinwork* (with regular annual rituals, gatherings, meetings, or communications at distance). Family socialization strategies also include participation to various community and family social activities and religious practices, thus reinforcing this cultural intergenerational transmission that explains attachment to the country of origin and the development of multiple identities, which in turn can support the development of transnational activities and engagement in transnational spaces. It is worth noting that the ways in which these descendants engage with their parents' and grandparents' homeland are shaped at the same time by characteristics of the emigrant group itself (and its migration history in Canada favoring the presence of large kinship groups established at various locations or dispersed in the North American context) and the characteristics of the receiving society, Quebec (facilitating cultural, linguistic, and ethnic retention through its focus on the double majority).

Obviously, Azorean descendants' transnational ties and practices have different forms than those observed among their parents or grandparents. While the first generation mostly focused on material exchanges, preservation of traditions, and strong family ties, maintaining family bonds becomes secondary among the descendants' generation, and only selective connections are preserved. Transnational spaces based on family links are thus transformed into larger *spaces of identity* where cultural and symbolic reference to the Azores as ancestral homeland is predominant, incorporating traditions and family practices of Portuguese origin with those that express Canadian belonging. Transnational connections and practices can shape the process of identity construction. At the same time, feelings of belonging and attachment also turn out to be crucial for the conservation of ties with their parents' origin country.

The transnational experiences of second- and third-generation Azorean descendants in Quebec that we explored in this chapter have several policy implications. First, we observed complex identity constructions and projects in the case of these individuals who are completely inserted in Quebec's economic, political, and social life. These considerations indicate that ideas about integration that are promoted and socially accepted should encompass more flexibility in order to acknowledge the fact that multiple cultural and ethnic belongings or affiliations can be maintained at the same time. As underlined by Goulbourne et al. (2010), the singularity of belongingness required by nationalist ideology may have to be yet again delayed or abandoned, and multiple identities, shared identities, and long-distance identities accepted as normal. Second, we suggest policy makers should explore further the richness of this type of cultural and social capital where various affiliations can be juxtaposed in different life domains. Developing cultural and social programs that acknowledge the multitude of cultural heritages that compose Quebec society nowadays could benefit the larger community as it embodies its current cosmopolitan character.

NOTES

1. Second generation means a person who was born in Canada whose parents have immigrated to Canada, while the third generation is defined as having both parents born inside Canada (Rumbaut 2004). The third generation are children of the second generation, so their grandparents are of foreign descent. In this research, second- and third-generation Azorean descendants refer to Canadians having at least a parent or respectively a grandparent of Azorean origin.

2. In these cities, Portuguese populations are concentrated in neighborhoods at high density of occupation (Teixeira and Rosa 2000) and have a high level of "institutional completeness," as they developed in time a significant number of social, cultural, and religious institutions, as well as media (television, radio, and newspapers) in Portuguese language.

3. The term "double majority" refers to ethnic and linguistic characteristic of the Montreal region's population that is composed by descendants of the two founding peoples, the French and the British, in similar proportions.

4. The research was made possible by Portuguese national funds from the Fund for Science and Technology (Fundaça para a Ciência e Tecnologia FCT) and from Migration et Ethnicité dans les Interventions en Santé et en Services sociaux (METISS), Centre de santé et services sociaux (CSSS de la Montagne).

5. About twenty observations were also conducted in various contexts that are public spaces where migrants and nonmigrants gather on various occasions: religious and popular festivals, community celebrations and feasts, neighborhoods, churches, and Portuguese associations of various types (cultural, religious, etc.).

6. Some respondents reported organization of festivities for Espirito Santo (traditional community religious festival celebrated in the Azorean islands) as an important occasion to gather all the kinship either in the Azores or in the migrant community.

7. Many third-generation descendants are raised in mixed families with one parent of Portuguese origin, as opposed to the first and second generations, raised in endogamous households.

8. We note that our respondents grew up during decades 1980s and 1990s, when owing to multiculturalism policies, ethnic communities could develop an intensive social and cultural life. During this period, many Portuguese associations, some of them Azorean based, were formed and displayed an intensive activity. Thus many community settings existed during that period offering spaces for ethnic conationals to gather, spend time together, and celebrate traditions, rituals, cultural events, and so on. Even if in the last years the number of these associations diminished, their activity created a wider community dynamic in the past.

9. There are three Portuguese schools organized by community associations in different locations of the Montreal region. Portuguese-language courses are available in the public education system as well.

REFERENCES

Alba, Richard, and Victor, Nee. 1997. Rethinking Assimilation Theory for a New Era of Immigration. *International Migration Review* 31 (4): 826–74.

Anctil, Pierre. 1984. Double Majorité et Multiplicité Ethnique à Montréal. *Recherches Sociographiques* 25 (3): 441–56.

Anderson, Grace M. 1974. *Networks of Contact: The Portuguese and Toronto*. Waterloo, Ontario: Wilfrid Laurier University Press.

Anderson, Grace M., and David Higgs. 1979. *L'Héritage du Futur: Les Communautés Portugaises au Canada*. Paris: Le Cercle du Livre de France.

Attias-Donfut, Claudine. 2008. Les grands-parents en Europe: De nouveaux soutiens de famille. *Informations Sociales* 5 (149): 54–67.

Attias-Donfut, Claudine, and François Charles Wolff. 2009. *Le Destin des Enfants d'Immigrés: Un Désenchaînement des Générations*; Éditions Stock. Paris: Revue de presse, 2009.

Beck-Gernsheim, Elizabeth. 2007. Transnational Lives, Transnational Marriages: A Review of the Evidence from Migrant Communities in Europe. *Global Networks* 7 (3): 271–88.

Brettell, Caroline B. 2003. *Anthropology and Migration: Essays on Transnationalism, Ethnicity, and Identity*. Walnut Creek, CA: AltaMira Press, 2003.

Brettell, Caroline B., and Faith G. Nibbs. 2009. Lived Hybridity: Second-Generation Identity Construction through College Festival. *Identities: Global Studies in Culture and Power* 16 (6): 678–99.

Chapin, Frances White. 1989. *Tides of Migration: A Study of Migration Decision-Making and Social Progress in São Miguel, Azores*. New York: AMS Press.

Charbit, Yves, Marie-Antoinette Hily, Michel Poinard, and Véronique Petit. 1997. *Le Va-et-Vient Identitaire Migrants Portugais et Villages d'Origine*. Paris: Presses Universitaires de France, Institut National d'études Démographiques.

Da Silva, Emanuel A. 2011. *Sociolinguistic (Re)Constructions of Diaspora Portugueseness: Portuguese-Canadian Youth in Toronto*. PhD diss., University of Toronto.

Dos Santos, Irène. 2010. *Les 'Brumes de la Mémoire': Expérience Migratoire et Quête Identitaire de Descendants de Portugais de France*. PhD diss., École des Hautes Études en Sciences Sociales.

Germain, Annick, and Tuyet Trinh. 2011. Immigration in Quebec: Profile and Players. In *Immigration and Inclusion of Newcomers Minorities across Canada*, John Biles, Beyer Burstein, James Frideres, Erin Tolley, and Rob Vineberg, eds., pp. 247–75. Montreal: McGill-Queen's University Press.

Gherghel, Ana, and Josiane Le Gall. 2012. Maintaining Transnational Ties in Time: Intergenerational Differences among Luso-Canadians of Azorean Origin in Quebec (Canada). Draft paper, IMISCOE annual conference, Amsterdam, August 28–29.

Glick Schiller, Nina, Linda Basch, and Cristina Blanc-Szanton (eds.). 1992. *Towards a Transnational Perspective on Migration: Race, Class, Ethnicity and Nationalism Reconsidered*. New York: New York Academy of Science.

Glick Schiller, Nina, and Georges Fouron. 2004. Transnational Lives and National Identities: The Identity Politics of Haitian Immigrants. In *Transnationalism from Below*, Michael Peter Smith and Luis Eduardo Guarnizo, eds., pp. 130–61. New Brunswick, NJ: Transaction.

Gomes, Frederica. 2008. *Selective Expressions of Portugueseness: Notions of Portugueseness among Second-Generation Portuguese-Canadian Youth in Toronto*. M.A. thesis, Ryerson University.

Goulbourne, Harry, Tracey Reynolds, John Solomos, and Elisabetta Zontini. 2010. *Transnational Families: Ethnicities, Identities and Social Capital*. New York: Routledge.

Gouvernement du Québec. 2010. *Portrait Statistique de la Population d'Origine Ethnique Portugaise Recensée au Québec en 2006.* Québec: Immigration et communautés culturelles.

Haller, William, and Patricia Landolt. 2005. The Transnational Dimensions of Identity Formation: Adult Children of Immigrants in Miami. *Ethnic and Racial Studies* 28 (6): 1182–213.

Kasinitz, Philip, John H. Mollenkopf, Mary C. Waters, and Jennifer Holdaway. 2008. *Inheriting the City: The Children of Immigrants Come of Age.* Boston: Harvard University Press.

Klimt, Andrea. 2006. Divergent Trajectories: Identity and Community among Portuguese in Germany and the United States. *Portuguese Studies Review* 14 (2): 211–40.

Lamarre, Patricia, and Stéphanie Lamarre. 2009. Montréal "on the move": Pour une approche ethnographique non-statique des pratiques langagières des jeunes multi-lingues." In *Formes and Normes Sociolinguistiques: Ségrégations et Discriminations Urbaines*, T. Bulot, ed., pp. 105–34. Paris: L'Harmattan.

Landolt, Patricia. 2001. Salvadoran Economic Transnationalism: Embedded Strategies for Household Maintenance, Immigrant Incorporation and Entrepreneurial Expansion. *Global Networks* 1 (3): 21–41.

Leal Joao. 2011. *Azorean Identity in Brazil and the United States: Arguments about History, Culture and Transnational Connections.* Dartmouth, MA: Tagus.

Lee, Helen. 2008. Second Generation Transnationalism. In *Ties to the Homeland: Second Generation Transnationalism*, Helen Lee, ed., pp. 1–32. Newcastle: Cambridge Scholars Publishing.

Le Gall, Josiane, and Deirdre Meintel. 2014. *Quand la Famille Vient d'ici et d'Ailleurs: Transmission Culturelle et Identitaire.* Montréal: Presses de l'Université Laval.

Levitt, Peggy. 2002. The Ties That Change: Relations to the Ancestral Home over the Life Cycle. In *The Changing Face of Home: The Transnational Lives of the Second Generation*, Peggy Levitt and Mary C. Waters, eds., pp. 123–44. New York: Russell Sage Foundation.

———. 2009. Routes and Roots: Understanding the Lives of the Second Generation Transnationally. *Journal of Ethnic and Migration Studies* 35 (7): 1225–42.

Levitt, Peggy, and Nina Glick Schiller. 2004. Conceptualizing Simultaneity: A Trans-national Social Field Perspective on Society. *International Migration Review* 38 (3): 1002–39.

Levitt, Peggy, and Mary C. Waters (eds.). 2002. *The Changing Face of Home: The Trans-national Lives of the Second Generation.* New York: Russell Sage Foundation.

Lievens, John. 1999. Family-Forming Migration from Turkey and Morocco to Belgium: The Demand for Marriage Partners from the Countries of Origin. *International Migration Review* 33 (3): 717–44.

Marques, Jose Carlos, and Pedro Gois. 2008. Pratiques transnationales des capverdiens au Portugal et des portugais en Suisse. *Revue Européenne des Migrations Internationales* 24 (2): 147–65.

Meintel, Deirdre. 1992. L'identité ethnique chez de jeunes montréalais d'origine immigrée. *Sociologie et Sociétés* 25: 441–50.

———. 2000. "Identity Issues among Young Adults of Immigrant Background in Montreal. *Horizonte* 14 (1): 13–38.

———. 2002. Transmitting Pluralism: Mixed Unions in Montreal. *Canadian Ethnic Studies* 34 (3): 99–122.

Meintel, Deirdre, and Emanuel Kahn. 2005. De génération en génération: Identités et projets identitaires des montréalais de la "deuxième génération." *Ethnologies* 27 (1): 131–65.

Meintel, Deirdre, and Josiane Le Gall. 1995. *Les Jeunes d'Origine Immigrées: Rapports Familiaux et les Transitions de Vie—Le Cas des Jeunes Chiliens, Grecs, Portugais, Salvadoriens et Vietnamiens.* Collection Études Et Recherches. Québec: Gouvernement du Québec.

Melo, Pedro M. 1997. *The Life History of Portuguese Return Migrants: A Canadian-Azorean Case Study*, M.A. thesis, York University.

Morawska, Ewa. T. 2003. Immigrant Transnationalism and Assimilation: A Variety of Combinations and the Analytic Strategy It Suggests. In *Toward Assimilation and Citizenship: Immigrants in Liberal Nation-States*, Christian Joppke and Ewa T. Morawska, eds., pp. 133–76. Basingstoke: Palgrave Macmillan.

Noivo, Edith A. 1997. *Inside Ethnic Families: Three Generations of Portuguese-Canadians.* Montreal: McGill-Queen's University Press.

Nunes, Fernando. 2003. Marginalisation, Social Reproduction and Academic Under-achievement: The Case of the Portuguese Community in Canada. In *The Education of Portuguese Children in Britain: Insight from Research and Practice in England and Oversea.* Guida de Abreu, Tony Cline, and Hannah Lambert, eds., pp. 122–58. Luton: University of Luton.

Oliveira, Manuel Armando, and Carlos Teixeira. 2004. *Jovens Portugueses e Luso-Descendentes No Canadá.* Oeiras: Celta.

Portes, Alejandro, and Rubén G. Rumbaut. 2001. *Legacies: The Story of the Immigrant Second Generation.* Berkeley: University of California Press.

Portes, Alejandro. 1999. Conclusion: Towards a New World. The Origins and Effects of Transnational Activities. *Ethnic and Racial Studies* 22 (2): 463–77.

Rumbaut, Rubén G. 2002. Severed or Sustained Attachments? Language, Identity, and Imagined Communities in the Post-immigrant Generation. In *The Changing Face of Home: The Transnational Lives of the Second Generation*, Peggy Levitt and Mary C. Waters, eds., pp. 43–95. New York: Russell Sage Foundation.

———. 2004. Ages, Life Stages, and Generational Cohort: Decomposing the Immigrant First and Second Generations in the United States. *International Migration Review* 38 (3): 1160–205.

Santelli, Emmanuelle. 2001. *La Mobilité Sociale dans l'Immigration: Itinéraires de la Réussite des Enfants D'Origine Algérienne.* Toulouse: Presses de l'Université de Toulouse-Le-Mirail.

Sardinha, João. 2010. Integration, Identity and Gender: Portuguese-Canadian and Portuguese-French Second-Generation Emigrant Women Narrate Return to Portugal." In *Working Paper Cemri*. 7th Annual IMISCOE Conference, Workshop: Gender-Age-Generations: Exploring Intersectionality, Liege, Belgium, September 13–14.

Smith, Robert C. 2002. Life Course, Generation, and Social Location as Factors Shaping Second Generation Transnational Life. In *The Changing Face of Home: The Transnational Lives of the Second Generation*, Peggy Levitt and Mary. C. Waters, eds., pp. 145–67. New York: Russell Sage Foundation.

Smith, Robert Courtney. 2005. *Mexican New York: Transnational Lives of New Immigrants*. Berkeley: University of California Press.

Strassburger, Gaby. 2004. Transnational Ties of the Second Generation: Marriages of Turks in Germany. In *Transnational Social Spaces: Agents, Networks, and Institutions*, Thomas Faist and Eyup Ozveren, eds., pp. 211–32. Burlington, VT: Ashgate.

Teixeira, Carlos, and Victor Pereira da Rosa. 2000. Introduction: A Historical and Geographical Perspective. In *The Portuguese in Canada: From the Sea to the City*, Carlos Teixeira and Victor Pereira da Rosa, eds., pp. 3–14. Toronto: University of Toronto Press, 2000.

Trindade, Jani. 2007. *Identity and Belonging Formations of Second Generation Portuguese*. MA thesis, Ryerson University.

Vertovec, Steven. 2004. Trends and Impact of Migrant Transnationalism. Working Paper 3, Oxford: Centre on Migration, Policy and Society.

———. 2010. *Transnationalism*. London: Routledge.

Wessendorf, Susanne. 2007. "Roots-Migrants": Transnationalism and "Return" among Second Generation Italians in Switzerland. *Journal of Ethnic and Migration Studies* 33 (7): 1083–102.

Williams, Allan, and Monica Lucinda Fonseca. 1999. The Azores: Between Europe and North America. In *Small Worlds, Global Lives: Islands and Migration*. Russell King and John Connell, eds., pp. 55–76. London: Cromwell.

Wolf, Diane. 2002. There Is No Place Like 'Home': Emotional Transnationalism and the Struggles of Second-Generation Filipinos. In *The Changing Face of Home: The Transnational Lives of the Second Generation*, Peggy Levitt and Mary C. Waters, eds., pp. 255–94. New York: Russell Sage Foundation.

Zontini, Elisabetta. 2007. Continuity and Change in Transnational Italian Families: The Caring Practices of Second-Generation Women. *Journal of Ethnic and Migration Studies* 33 (7): 1103–19.

7 RELIGIOUS SPACES

"Boat People" Legacies and the Vietnamese American 1.5 and Second Generation

Linda Ho Peché

This chapter explores the multiple ways in which a repurposed former refugee camp in Galang, Indonesia, has come to function as a meaningful and instructive religious space for different generations of diasporic Vietnamese. Through the narrated experiences of a select number of participants of an international group tour, I reveal how families fulfilled burial rites for relatives that perished at the camps, and how the group collectively acknowledged and paid tribute to the local communities that presumably helped the refugees in their time of need.[1] By visiting key sites on the tour, the group discursively reinscribed an alternative history to the official nationalist discourses, both in Vietnam and in the United States, that overlook and misrepresent their experiences as "boat people." Whereas this former refugee camp was once the site of displacement—literally the liminal space between civic and economic uncertainty and newfound citizenship—it has become for some, the object of a returning pilgrimage to a site of reconnection and rebirth. Through the performative act of appeasing their ancestral spirits, these returning pilgrims created a new narrative centered around the trope of "rebirth," one that is located through a diasporic identity whose future perpetuation hinges on the acquiescence, if not substantiation of a particular legacy inherited by the 1.5 and second generation.

AFTERWARD

In 1975, after the end of the war in Vietnam and a North Vietnamese victory, nearly one million South Vietnamese left the country. The exodus to a number of countries, including Australia, the United States, and France, included refugees from Laos and Cambodia, as well as Vietnam. In the United States, this resulted in the resettlement of the single largest group of refugees in American history (Chan 2006). Hundreds of thousands fled by boat throughout the 1980s in the midst of a difficult economic restructuring of the country and the increasing hostility and discrimination faced by civil servants or party members of the ousted government, the educated class, artists, religious leaders, and ethnic Chinese and other minorities (Chan 2006: 65).

In the countries of reception, these "new" immigrants experienced the psychological traumas of displacement and the social "problems" of adaptation, including the differences in worldviews between the first and second generations (Starr and Roberts 1982; Freeman 1995; Kibria 1995; Nguyne 1998; Zhou and Bankston 1999; Do 2002; Collet and Selden 2003; Dang 2011; Lieu 2011; Brettell and Reed-Danahay 2012).[2]

In the following case study, I offer one way in which to contextualize the 1.5- and second-generation experience—by exploring the materialized, grounded, and traditionalized manifestation of a particular "sacroscape" that, in this case, creates an intergenerational diasporic legacy through the performative act of civic pilgrimage and through the discursive reframing of a collective narrative.[3]

VỀ BẾN TỰ DO: RETURN TO A PLACE OF FREEDOM

Officially, Vietnam seems to have overcome the gruesome civil war of over thirty years ago, but Mai Lan Gustafsson (2009) points out that "Vietnam is haunted by the War. It is everywhere, manifested in bomb craters and amputated limbs, in daily television reports listing those still missing from the war, in soap operas dramatizing love among the trenches, on the radio in songs about soldiers longing for their mothers, in family altars in nearly every house bearing photographs of some long-gone child or spouse or parent" (2009: 56).

In private, many have not been permitted to forget the war because of an unforgiving presence in their lives—the angry ghosts of the past who are believed to have borne them illness and ill luck. Many Vietnamese living overseas experience a different kind of haunting, located in a very different kind of place—the refugee camps where relatives were buried and left unattended by the appropriate funerary or filial rites during those crucial days or months when families fled Vietnam by the thousands. By returning to these places of liminality and constructing a different sense of home, a number of diasporic Vietnamese are engaged in a very different kind of communal narrative of self, spirit, and community—which also has had to bear the physical, mental, social, and spiritual consequences of the Vietnam War.

In August of 2011, I disembarked from a ferry and landed in Indonesia. I was on a guided tour to visit Pulau Galang, the site of a former United Nations refugee camp where over 145,000 Southeast Asians, mostly Vietnamese, were temporarily housed beginning in 1979. At that time, many fled by sea to escape political persecution and economic hardship following the war in Vietnam. Thousands were processed at refugee camps and were granted asylum by Canada, Australia, and the United States, among other nations (Pathoni 2005). Between 1979 and 1996, the Pulau Galang refugee camp (run by the United Nation's High Commission for Refugees), resettled these asylum seekers in other countries until the last few thousand Vietnamese remaining on the island were involuntarily repatriated in 1996. Today, groups of Vietnamese living abroad organize annual tours to visit these former refugee camps across Southeast Asia, including those in Malaysia, the Philippines, and Indonesia. For some tour participants, it is their first visit to Galang Island since their departure as asylum seekers more than thirty years ago. Other tour participants return year after year, bringing with them their spouses and children to visit the camps. Organizers often narrate the group tours as a chance for Vietnamese living overseas to return to a symbolically potent place in their diasporic history.

It may be useful to situate group tours like these in the context of other similar pilgrimages among Vietnamese nationals and in the diaspora. Apart from the much-advertised group tours to refugee camps, there has been a recent resurgence of pilgrimages in Vietnam proper, such as those dedicated to the Lady of the Realm in the southeastern corner of Vietnam (Taylor 2004). For the diasporic community in the United States, the religious celebration of the Marian Days is observed annually in the tiny town of Carthage, Missouri, where (some participants report) over eighty thousand Vietnamese Catholics converge each August. It is common to hear radio and television advertisements about other pilgrimages to religious temples or shrines in places like Texas or France. It is worth noting that these pilgrimage opportunities have arguably emerged in a time of transition, of economic change in Vietnam, and of the emergence of an overseas-born generation elsewhere. It is fair to say that these pilgrimages address these social, economic, religious, and cultural reconfigurations. In fact, the popularity of pilgrimages throughout Vietnam presently has lead Philip Taylor (2004) to conclude that "pilgrimages are characteristic of societies in transition: marked by changing relationships to landscape, social structural dynamism, expanding cultural pluralism, and transitory forms of subjectivity" (2004: 16).

The tour in which I participated was called Về Bến Tự Do, translated as "a return to destination freedom." The Archives of Vietnamese Boat People (AVBP), a nonprofit organization with offices in Australia and the United States, organized it. The organization's mission is "to record as many meaningful details of the Vietnamese Boat People as possible, the event[s] which happened from 1975 to the time when the last Vietnamese Boat People from refugee camps have been resettled in a third country."[4] Organizing group trips to former refugee camps is one way in which the organization fulfills this educative mission. Unlike other refugee campsites that have fallen into disrepair in Malaysia and the Philippines,[5] Pulau Galang has been developed into a heritage site and tourist destination that has revitalized the local economy. The two-hundred-acre refugee camp complex is currently managed by the Batam Industrial Development Authority and boasts newly built asphalt roads leading into the area and renovated historical structures including a small museum, Catholic church, and Buddhist temple (Carruthers and Huynh-Beatty 2011). For the former refugee camp residents who arrived on the island in small fishing boats, the return journey stood in stark contrast—all of us arrived in the most modern modes of transportation, including transcontinental flights and air-conditioned taxis and travel buses. While this type of travel may be accessible only to those with a newly acquired class-based mobility, the information and personal stories about the tours circulate to a much wider Vietnamese population through various ethnic media outlets globally, including Vietnamese-language radio and newspapers and the AVBP Internet website and blog. This has allowed for organizers to coordinate this kind of travel experience for participants coming from different parts of the world and to communicate their mission (and appeal to a sense of collective solidarity) with the broader diasporic community that cannot physically or financially make the journey. Word of mouth also plays an important part in disseminating information. I learned of the tour through my volunteer involvement with another nonprofit organization called the Vietnamese American Heritage Foundation, based in Austin, Texas.

Non-Vietnamese tourists come mostly from nearby Singapore. However, there is some ambivalence among the overseas Vietnamese community about marketing the site as "dark tourism for non-purposeful tourists" devoid of any historical connection to the war (Carruthers and Huynh-Beattie 2011). The concern is that the camp could be presented to tourists merely as a generic site of human suffering, trauma, and death—or worse, a gimmicky site for ghost hunters and stories of hauntings. Not all tour members would self-identify as "purposeful" tourists; for some it was another stop on their vacation itinerary to visit other tourist sites. Nevertheless, the first-generation and 1.5-generation former camp residents overwhelmingly responded that the tour offered an opportunity to reminisce about the refugee experience, and to reflect on the fate of those who temporarily called Pulau Galang home. For the younger generation of participants, the tour offered an opportunity to accompany their parents on a meaningful personal journey in their parents' lives. However, as I will show, by the end of the trip, the second- and 1.5-generation participants began to "own" the experience much more and to develop ideas about how they fit into a larger collective narrative based on a diasporic identity.

I began my journey as a "purposeful" researcher, tourist, and second-generation Vietnamese American. I eagerly met up with the tour group at a hotel in Singapore's Geylang district. It was a forty-five-minute ferry ride across the waters of the Singapore Strait—a very different kind of arrival than that experienced by the weary asylum seekers over thirty-five years ago. It was in these moments of transport that a unique kind of community developed between members of our tour group. When we disembarked the ferry, we boarded a tour bus, and during this bus ride, the organizers asked us participants to identify ourselves and our motives for joining the tour. Our group of twenty-three tour group members included former refugee camp occupants, former residents at other camps, and those who were accompanying their siblings, spouses, or parents. About one-fourth of our group consisted of 1.5- or second-generation Vietnamese, including Linda, a second-generation Vietnamese American in her midtwenties from San Francisco, who was studying cosmetology at the time. David also joined us, a 1.5-generation participant also from San Francisco in his thirties, a father of two young children who remained in the United States. Two of us were PhD candidates, also in our thirties at that time, conducting research, both with young daughters waiting for us at home. Melissa, a 1.5-generation participant who is ethnically Chinese and was born in Vietnam, joined us from Australia. She brought along her two second-generation Australian-born children, a nine-year-old daughter and fourteen-year-old son.

A local Indonesian tour guide and security guard, Abu, also joined us on the tour bus. At the time he was in his late thirties and had moved near the Galang refugee camp as a youth when his mother was hired as a cook. As a result, he is a fluent Vietnamese speaker and beloved by the Vietnamese tour groups that come year after year. So here we were, Abu and I, two people who straddled the line between outsiders and insiders: Abu, an Indonesian who speaks Vietnamese, and myself, a second-generation half Vietnamese half Mexican American who needed translation assistance throughout the tour. Melissa dubbed us two "funny Vietnamese." As I reflected on these playful but teasing moments, I came to realize that, indeed, much of this trip was about delineating the contours of what constitutes "being" Vietnamese. Perhaps my presence as a multiracial American-born Vietnamese is as much a statement about the complexities of what it means to be Vietnamese today as Abu's ability to speak Vietnamese as an Indonesian reminds us that war and exile leave an indelible mark on people and landscapes beyond what we can imagine. As I will show, throughout the trip, our past experiences provided roles for us—for example, as former refugee residents with firsthand eyewitness experience of camp life, or as survivors of a harrowing sea journey and thus "boat people," or as second-generation tour participants with a legacy to inherit. The stories we shared with the group about our reasons for being there, however diverse, cemented us as a collective with a common legacy despite our differences.

Some participants find this tour so meaningful, they join up year after year. Melissa is one of these participants; she joined the tour for the third year. When asked why she returns to this place so frequently, she stated, "Why do I come back? I come back because this is where my life started. My life started in Galang. I want my children to know that."

Even so, Melissa admitted that she had never fully relayed the story of her childhood escape from Vietnam to her children. And so, my prying questions into her past and the bus ride to our next tour stop offered the opportunity for her to recount her journey. Her children and I sat together and listened intently to her memories of living in Saigon's Chinatown district, her escape journey, arrival at the camp, and the sights, sounds, and smells of life on the island. The children had heard bits and pieces of the stories from their mother before, but never in full. This was very much like the fragmentary memories I heard from my own father, which were often interrupted by the exigencies of daily life. Yet, on this trip, and especially during the transitory times between tour stops, I heard many a life story recounted, political rants, and fond nostalgic memories of camp life—all of which became an important part of the tour experience.

Our tour group learned that two families, both from San Francisco, California, had joined us in order to find relatives' tombs. They sought to find the respective grave sites to pay their respects and take care of the logistics of proper burial and to consider possible disinterment. The first family was represented by Mai (Linda's aunt), who introduced herself to the group, tearfully revealing that she hoped to find her father's grave site. She was accompanied by her elder sister Ly, Linda's mother. Mai was fifteen years old when she fled Vietnam with her father (Linda's maternal grandfather) in 1983. The decision to leave the country was similar to many others'—her father's disillusionment with the government, frustration from an impoverished existence, and little hope for a brighter future pushed the family to choose to leave Vietnam. Part of the family, including Ly, had already arrived safely to the United States. It was common for families to split up relatives and attempt to leave on separate boats because of the overwhelming odds against successful escapes: escapees could be (and often were) caught by Vietnamese government officials before crossing into international waters. There loomed the possibility of being turned away from countries already suffering "compassion fatigue" (Chan 2006) or worse, and there was a very real danger of being stranded at sea and not surviving the journey. After a weeklong journey on a small fishing boat that ran out of supplies, Mai and her father landed on an Indonesian island called KuKu before being resettled in the Pulau Galang refugee camp. They had been living in the camp in a wooden longhouse a little less than a year before her father, only forty-four at the time, grew ill and passed away; she was left alone to await reunification with her sister in the United States. She remembers the deep sadness, and calling on her neighbors, some living in makeshift campsites, to ask for prayers for her father's spirit. They laid him to rest in the camp cemetery in a Catholic burial ceremony, alongside others whose journeys ended on that island. A few weeks later, she was granted documentation to immigrate to the United States and met her older sister at the San Francisco airport; it was a bittersweet reunion. Over twenty-five years later, Mai, Ly, and Linda have set out on a journey back to find his tomb, to pay their respects, and to attain a sense of closure.

The second family was represented by another fellow traveler, Dang (David's uncle), who related his story to me on one of our bus rides. He was sixteen when he left Vietnam in 1984 with his sister Nhan's mother-in-law, Den (David's paternal grandmother). After only a few days, the fishing boat's motor gave out, and the group was relegated to suffering the whims of the unpredictable current. A passing oil tanker sheltered the stranded passengers for a few days. During this time, Den recognized her niece's husband among the crew, a young Filipino youth named Herminio, who was also a mechanic. She negotiated with the fishing boat's captain to allow Herminio to try to fix their broken motor. He was successful, after which the international Red Cross was hailed, and they were steered toward KuKu island before being resettled in the camp. It is said that everyone owed their lives to Den and to Herminio. Unfortunately, after only a few short months on Pulau Galang, Den suffered a serious head injury from a bad fall and died shortly thereafter. Sixteen-year-old Dang, as the only surviving relative in the camp, was charged with organizing the appropriate funerary arrangements. With no resources, he himself chiseled her name and birth and death dates on the tombstone. A Buddhist monk presided over a funerary ceremony and burned incense and paper votive money at the grave site to ensure that her spirit moved on to her next life. Twenty-five years later, Dang was joined on this tour by his sister Nhan (David's mother), her husband, Kiem (David's father and Den's son), and David. The three of them had their own escape story; they fled Vietnam on a different boat in a weeklong journey that claimed the lives of a number of people. David was six years old at the time, and Nhan was pregnant with her second child. They landed in Bidong, Malaysia, and sought refuge in that camp, where their daughter was born, before immigrating to San Francisco. On this trip Dang, Kiem, Nhan, and David made the journey back to Pulau Galang from half a world away to search for the tomb of the family matriarch and to fulfill filial obligations.

It is a common Vietnamese folk belief that spirits can linger for years if they are not given proper burial rites, and tombs should be kept clean so as to not engender the wrath of the dead. In fact, in many Vietnamese families, the ancestral spirits and the living coexist in a relationship nurtured by a sense of reciprocal obligations. The living often ask for luck or blessings from their ancestors, and ancestors often demand repayment or proper respect in return (Gustafsson 2009). Thus, both the tour and the organization's mission serve to situate things—tombs or spirits, for example—in their proper place. The following section will address the importance of fulfilling filial duties associated with the respect for the spirits of the dead, on an individual level, as a family, and last, as a community.

APPEASING THE SPIRITS OF AN IMMINENT PAST

Dang related to me that soon after Den's death, he was offered a passage to France, where his half-sister resided but, in his self-described youthful insolence, decided that "France had done nothing to create this mess" and that it was "the obligation of the United States to take me in."[6] Thus, Dang remained at the camp for over three years waiting for his opportunity to immigrate to the United States. He was beginning to lose hope for leaving the refugee camp when one night Den visited him in his dreams. In this nightmare, she chased him around his room while he asked incredulously, "How can you be chasing me?" He remembers saying, "You are dead, and you want to take me with you!" She then asked, "What do you want?" To this he responded, "To go to the United States with my brother." She then commanded him, "Then, you will place balloons on my gravesite." Whether she asked this because of his benign neglect of her gravesite is unclear to him, but with no balloons available on the island, he resorted to inflating condoms and placing them on her gravesite in order to comply with her request. ("It was an island!" he stated emphatically. "Where would she expect me to find balloons?") One week after he fulfilled this obligation, he was called to immigrate to the United States. Indeed, in Vietnam as well as in the diaspora, spirits can appear in dreams to warn their relatives of impending doom or offer preemptive advice. They can negotiate social friction between family members, offer solutions to complex situations, and comfort the living. Through these different ways of communicating with ancestors, people learn what they need to do to assuage the *con ma* or angry ghosts, and if they've suffered physical ailments due to this bad spirit, properly following orders could restore their health (Gustaffson 2009: 68).

Linda (Mai's niece and a second-generation Vietnamese American) confided her own anxieties about paying proper respects to her grandfather. On the first night of our trip, she had woken up in the middle of the night with an eerie anticipation; she stayed awake for hours, afraid that their trip would be in vain and that they would not find her grandfather's grave. She explained that on a previous trip to visit relatives in Vietnam, she unintentionally approached her family's ancestral altar without bowing or lighting incense. She merely looked over the images of her grandfather and her grandmother, admiring the flowers and the ornate carvings of the furniture. Later that night, she had a nightmare that someone grabbed her feet and attempted to drag her out of bed. Shaken, she related the story to her mother in the morning, who merely disregarded the account until Linda's younger brother, only five or six years old at the time, asked, "Is your friend visiting us again? The one that slept between us?" Linda's mother, Ly, promptly called a local Catholic priest to bless the house. That experience happened once again on her last birthday, and Linda now makes sure to pay her respects properly in front of the family altar by bowing and lighting three sticks of incense.

In fact, an improper gaze or direct stare into the image of an ancestor or a deity is often thought to be an act of disrespect and can garner magical infelicity for the perpetrator, whether purposeful or not. Kendall (2010: 7) offers this explanation of a caretaker's experience of maintaining a shrine dedicated to the Mother Goddess in Vietnam: "A temple keeper should not stare at the Mother Goddess images in his or her keeping. Although he had tended them for many years, [the caretaker] claimed, 'I don't dare to really get a good look at the images. They are frightening!'" Linda thinks that perhaps this journey to find the grave site of her grandfather will finally appease his spirit and amend this infraction. These two anecdotes point to the interrelationships between individuals and ancestors, and the importance of maintaining healthy affective relationships with them through the fulfillment of filial duties.

Immediately upon our arrival in Batam, we made haste to a local market in order to find the material offerings appropriate for a visit to the cemetery—incense,

incense holders, fresh flowers, vases, paper money (often burned at burial sites), and brightly colored and crispy fresh fruits. Neither family knew whether they would find the graves—it had been years since any of them had returned to the site. The families chose their offerings carefully, and a feeling of anticipation and anxiety made this supposed quick trip into a lengthy hour-long endeavor. Before we set out to the cemetery, the tour bus stopped at two significant sites. Our first full stop took us to the pier where boat people arrived and left the island. An old, battered, and graying boat is still anchored, remaining as a testament to numerous tearful and joyful arrivals and departures. As we walked along the pier, former camp residents recalled that a particular song was played each time someone left the island. As we listened to the stories of former camp residents, both first- and second-generation participants were brought to tears as we stood on that pier, a place that encapsulated so many complex emotions of the time—hope and hopelessness, community and isolation, fear and joy.

We rode the tour bus to Ngha Trang Cemetery in the early afternoon. Luckily, the grave sites of each of the ancestors were found, to the relief of the families. The first order of business was to clean the graves and uproot weeds among both of the grave sites. A Catholic priest, who was among the group tour participants and a former refugee himself, led prayers and sprinkled holy water on Linda's grandfather's grave. Her mother and aunt coordinated with Abu to upgrade the grave; they ordered his name and birth and death dates chiseled on the tomb (because the paint was fading), and concrete was to be poured into the tomb to seal it. Later, a priest, a fellow tour participant, performed a Catholic mass in an old musky Catholic church built by the refugees over thirty years ago.

David's parents, Kiem and Dang, commissioned a Buddhist monk to prepare an altar at the cemetery site, where incense was offered by all in attendance in order to coax Den's spirit to follow them to the temple. Kiem, a first-generation participant and eldest son, laid out a small cloth at the tombstone of his mother. Incense was placed in an urn and surrounded by fruits and flowers; he burned paper votive money and placed it on the tomb. He bowed three times on his knees, with incense in his hands. He rose up tearful and relieved, while his wife, Nhan, and then (1.5-generation participant) David followed his lead. Dang, David's uncle, said he preferred to pay respects privately. Neither family decided to disinter the remains. The tombs were in an auspicious location, against a backdrop of a beautiful Indonesian forest, and it was well maintained as a park by the Indonesian government. Future generations would have to travel to Pulau Galang to pay respects to these ancestors.

There were also roles for the rest of us to fulfill. The whole group, including the 1.5- and second-generation participants, helped burn paper votive money and spread it across the cemetery among the 503 grave sites to help appease those spirits that died without relatives. It was a stirring site. Meanwhile, some of us were recruited to photograph each and every tombstone to post online for families still searching for relatives, and for those who could not make the trip. A few minutes later, we followed the altar, which was placed in the back of a pickup truck and sent to a Buddhist temple, which was under construction. The whole group was happy and talkative on the way back to our hotel in Batam. There was a palpable sense of relief.

On an individual and familial level, the process of "situating the spirits" provided a resolution and sense of closure. David, a 1.5-generation participant, eloquently summed up his reflections through e-mail correspondence soon after he returned to San Francisco:

> Being alongside my grandmother's grave completed one of the big journeys in life
> for my father [Kiem]. I think seeing the grave was a big relief for him, as he was able
> to release thirty years of pent-up emotions and anxiety in his own quiet way. I know
> it eased his mind considerably knowing that the grave is in a good state (I mean the
> site is now a national park and the backdrop is the Indonesian rainforest, what more
> can you ask for? And the spirits were given passage to that unfinished temple that we
> visited). I was also touched to see Linda's family share a similar experience. I recall
> that I almost broke down and cried myself when her aunt introduced herself and
> the tears came pouring down her eyes as she recounted that her father passed away
> in Galang over twenty years prior. I was moved by everyone's gesture in burning the
> extra incense and placing them in the neighboring graves. Seeing my uncle [Dang]
> smile (but really emoting underneath) as he sat on the grave that he built and poured
> cement onto thirty years ago was amazing to witness. It was great to see him take it
> all in, as I took it all in myself.

While David understood the emotional weight of the moment for his father in particular, he had originally begun the journey feeling like an objective observer. On the first day of the tour he commented, "This is their trip. I am here to experience this with them." Yet it became clear throughout the trip that those of us who are second-generation descendants were inheriting much more than an insight into the first generation's experience, rather inheriting a legacy. He went on to write,

> I felt that in a way, this closure also meant that our ancestors (especially my grand-
> mother) was reminding us of our own passage or rites, to start our own new
> journeys, to go out and discover and/or rediscover. I believe it has changed all of
> us quite a bit, and for the better. For example, I've sensed more closeness between
> me and my father, though our relationship wasn't bad before. I feel that there is
> some work to be done, to look into the past and rediscover my roots and tradition,
> and embrace all of it, for what it means for the future and what I can pass down
> to my children.

For Linda, a quiet and introspective second-generation participant, the emotions of the visit were summed up by a simple but poignant statement after finding her grandfather's burial site: "I feel so relieved." Thus, while these experiences ful-filled certain motives on an individual level (for example, Linda's desire to make amends with her grandfather's spirit), and on a familial level (by fulfilling burial rites and obligations), there were also roles designated by the coordinators for the rest of the participants that unified us, and encouraged us to think of ourselves as part of a community, both as tour group participants and as representatives of the Vietnamese diaspora. This was accomplished in our collective burning of paper money at the grave sites, and as I discuss next, paying homage to shrines that cap-tured the imagination of the Vietnamese diaspora.

Like many tourists to this park, we stopped at Miếu Ba Cô, or the Shrine for the Three Ladies. Based on various retellings that I compiled from the tour, it is said that two (or three) young girls were raped at sea by pirates that accosted their small boat, and once they landed in Galang, they faced shame, scrutiny, and taunt-ing from some members of the community. To make things worse, their emigration status was declined because of an incident where one of the boat members stole something of value from an immigration officer, who, not knowing who the per-petrator was, decided to decline everyone's chances of leaving the island. Hopeless and ashamed, the girls hung themselves from a grove of coconut trees. Soon after, a shrine was erected at that site and newly arrived refugees began to light incense, pray, and ask the spirits of these young women for help with their plights and attempts to find a host country that would accept them. A park pamphlet dubbed it the "bodhi tree," while a sign nearby reads, "body tree." The interesting play on the words *bodhi*, meaning "enlightenment" in the Buddhist sense, and *body* refer-ring to the bodies once hanging from the trees, points to the multiple frames of meaning that the space has engendered.

According to Vietnamese mortuary conceptions, dying a grievous death will cause the soul to remain trapped in mortal agony, reliving the violent circumstances of death repeatedly (Endres 2008: 758). It is possible that in the case of an innocent child or a virgin girl dying during an auspicious hour (*giờ thiêng*), or an untimely, violent, or voluntary heroic death, their souls may be admitted into heaven; in exceptional cases they may even transform into a deity (Gustafsson 2009). Under other circumstances, the death of a young person may be thought to be of parti-cular sacred potency. These hungry ghosts are thought to have similar needs to those of the living, and thus require the care of the living (through offerings and prayer) in order to sustain themselves. In these situations, reciprocal relationships are cul-tivated with these spirits, who are considered efficacious, or able to answer prayers (Jellema 2007: 488). It is not uncommon for Vietnamese practitioners to perceive spiritual efficacy in a range of spirits, "even those of thieves, beggars, prostitutes, night soil collectors, and others whose moral qualities are dubious"; it is all depen-dent on whether they prove themselves to be responsive to the appeals of attentive practitioners (Endres 2008: 758). Interestingly, the spirits who have earned repu-tations for being the most responsive tend to have been people who were in some way marginal in life—women, people from the social periphery, victims, and those who died untimely deaths (Taylor 2004). As virgins, sexless mothers, or women who have died young or badly (as in this case), they could be seen as a form of self-containment—an indication that there are few options for women but to embrace a conditional (and peripheral) status as a means to social integration and cultural validation (Taylor 2004).

Regional tourists are often drawn to this particular shrine for its numerous claims of ghost hauntings. Others see it as a sacred site and light incense and petition the spirits of the women for luck or health. Local Indonesians claim they sometimes see the spirits of the young women walk among the trees. For the group organizers, the visit to the site was a matter of religious obligation to set these spirits to rest. Hence, they collected money to appropriately care for the tormented spirits. Dong, one of the organizers stated: "It's not safe for spirits to stay in a place of nowhere; it's better to be in a temple so they can rest in peace. We bring spirits to the temple and wish that they rest in peace. The purpose is to bring the spirit to the temple. But the spirit will not enter the temple unless it is invited by the monk. It's not cheap. We paid fifteen hundred Indonesian dollars." Our tour group organizer arranged for a priest and Buddhist monk to meet us at the site and to fulfill the Buddhist rites and then to successfully coax their spirits to a local temple. The presiding Buddhist monk chanted the corresponding liturgical texts and performed symbolic acts of purification. The burning of votive paper offerings at the cemetery marked the end of the ritual. The overall aim of the Mahayana Buddhist rite *lễ mông sơn* is to appease the lost souls (*cô hồn*) and invoke Buddha, bodhisattvas, and saints to lead them onto the path of religion and facilitate their salvation (Endres 2008: 760). A priest, in the case that any of the spirits were Roman Catholics in their lifetimes, also recited Catholic prayers. However, interpretations and understandings of these rites vary widely. For example, Kirsten Endres (2008) discusses how in Vietnam, the souls of the war dead are considered to be in a perpetual hell, and so this rite liberates them so that they may enjoy the food and votive offerings offered by the living. Instead of facilitating their reincarnation, this rite would transform them into benevolent deities. Some participants whispered that these spirits would never be at peace, because it was only their true relatives that would be able to coax them out of their misery. Although our tour group leader acted as their representative, he was not related by blood, and some participants suggested that the spirits might not heed his call to follow the altar they erected for this occasion. We all watched as the temporary altar was mounted on the back of a pickup, to be placed in the Buddhist temple so that the monks could petition the spirit world for official recognition of these tormented souls.

So, why return for the spirits if they may not follow? I argue that by acknowledging these three spirits, and, in the process, negotiating for their return to a spiritually safer place, this Vietnamese group is claiming the "Body/Bodhi Tree" narrative and staking an ownership of the space. At a time when different groups are vying for differing stories—tourists, locals, the Indonesian and even Vietnamese government—it has become a sacroscape that serves as a didactic device for former Vietnamese refugees and their children to individually and collectively craft a mnemonic experience and a new mode of cultural production with a particular purpose. This ritual process (and the tour in general) made participants of those of us that may have started as observers and crafted roles for each of us, whether we were former camp residents or not—as journalists, researchers, first-, 1.5-, or second-generation participants, tour guides, volunteers, or tourists. We had parts to play in a much larger narrative of rebirth and reempowerment, with broader ramifications, which is the focus of the next section.

"WE ARE ALL BOAT PEOPLE" AND THE CULTURAL POLITICS OF GRATITUDE

The Pulau Galang refugee camp is more than a tourist destination; I suggest that Vietnamese group tour participants return to be spiritually, socially, and ideologically transformed by the lessons that emerge from a common "heritagized" experience. Many on this tour, whether of the first, 1.5, or second generation, described their experience at the camp as a "rebirth," and the beginning of a new life and history. As Duc, another fellow first-generation passenger proclaimed, "99 percent of me died in my escape, but I was reborn after that experience. This trip is spiritual. Some come for vacation, but I come here to learn. And there are so many people to pray for."

While these trips and journeys are especially significant for families with filial obligations to fulfill, these trips are narrated to the participants and the broader Vietnamese diasporic community in the discursive rhetoric of "sacrifice and freedom." For example, in addition to organizing visits to refugee camps, the majority of the AVBP organization's efforts include fundraising to restore the many grave sites that dot the shores across Southeast Asia, and to erect memorials that commemorate the "boat people" experience with text such as this one erected in Galang in 2005: "In commemoration of the hundreds of thousands of Vietnamese people who perished on the way to Freedom (1975–1996). Though they died of hunger or thirst, of being raped, of exhaustion or of any other cause, we pray that they may now have lasting peace. Their sacrifice will never be forgotten."

Memorials have been commissioned by AVBP in each of these sites in Malaysia and Indonesia, with the financial help of thousands of dollars from overseas Vietnamese from all over the world. Other memorials have since been erected; three in Germany, two in the United States (in California), one each in France, Switzerland, and Belgium, and two in Australia (in Melbourne and Sydney).[7] This memorial in Galang and the one in Bidong, Malaysia, were demolished by the local Indonesian and Malaysian governments later in 2005 owing to mounting pressure from Hanoi (Carruthers and Huynh-Beattie 2011). This has provided another rallying cry for the organization's mission, which encourages a sense of duty to make public the cost for "freedom." Paradoxically, there has been an effort by the Vietnamese government to officially entice back overseas Vietnamese through the rhetoric of "national loyalty" and framing ancestral veneration as a national as well as a filial duty (Jellema 2007). Nevertheless, overseas Vietnamese are keenly aware that any public activities they engage in are still under the official gaze of the Vietnamese government. For example, many are aware that the revitalization of the Lady of the Realm pilgrimage in southern Vietnam, while a meaningful and spiritually fruitful experience for many, still operates under the guidance of local Vietnamese officials (Taylor 2004).

Overseas Vietnamese, however, are also aware of their enormous influence, in large part supported by the ability to organize and fundraise globally through diasporic networks. As a result, Vietnamese living overseas have been able to exert an enormous influence on the emergence of religious development practiced by Vietnamese in the diaspora and even in Vietnam itself. Some scholars credit them for the Buddhist revival, spirit possession, Catholicism, and the presence of a number of nongovernmental organizations in Vietnam (Taylor 2008). However, the Vietnamese government continues to actively thwart efforts to memorialize, record, or document South Vietnamese narratives of trauma. Escapees have been maligned in official and popular discourses as either deserters or troublemakers. Physical reminders of opposition to communist Vietnam—such as South Vietnamese mass grave markers—are razed and strategically forgotten. Indeed, in Vietnam and elsewhere, the experiences of overseas Vietnamese remain conspicuously absent from national discourses. Hence, the recasting and renarrating of sites such as the Pulau Galang refugee camp is part of the Vietnamese diaspora's struggle to combat the (Vietnam) state's interventions in renarrating the circumstances of their exile.

The struggle extends to the United States as well, where the issue is not so much about counteracting a hegemonic narrative of national loyalty (as it is in Vietnam), as it is a struggle for visibility and credibility. In the United States, while the images of refugees being rescued by US fleets once functioned to reinforce a national narrative of US benevolence, these discourses were quickly replaced in the US popular press with the rhetoric of national healing for American soldiers through the erection of memorials that strategically omitted South Vietnamese participation. According to Espiritu (2005), to the extent that Vietnamese refugees are visible and intelligible at all to Americans, it is only because of their arguable successful assimilation as model minorities, which has set them in antagonistic opposition to other communities of color to uphold the virtues of America as the "land of freedom." Thus, in the United States, the Vietnamese, who make up the largest group of resettled asylum seekers in our nation's history, have been the centerpieces of an interesting paradox—simultaneously characterized as honest (and a model minority) as well as "sneaky" or untrustworthy—views that are rooted in the racist cultural narrative of "Asian duplicity"(Christopher 1995: 6). Each of these stereotypes has worked to estrange and exclude them from the American body politic, and as racialized "others," even the second generation continue to be cast as perpetual foreigners outside of the nation's citizenry (Lowe 1996).

Thus, coordination of these group tours, the collective efforts to erect memorials, and the website appeals are attempts by overseas Vietnamese to reinscribe themselves into the popular memory of a war that overlooks their participation on both sides of the diasporic experience. It is an attempt to reclaim a new narrative of perseverance, honor, and power instead of the more ubiquitous, hegemonic, and fundamentally victimizing narrative of the Vietnamese as passive. At the crux of this mission are the efforts to educate the second generation about this history and to encourage this generation to embrace the refugee legacy, despite having no first-hand experience.

One of the most effective nodes of these efforts involves the politically motivated and highly symbolic adoption of an identifying label that had once been used to oppress, and was now being taken back to empower: the "boat people" trope. As Dong Tran, one of the tour organizers, described, "we started calling ourselves Boat People. It's more romantic than the term *refugee*, and more poetic." The term itself came into contemporary use when, in the late 1970s, images of small fishing boats overfilled with famished and exhausted asylum seekers captured the attention of a worldwide audience. It was not long before they became the twentieth century's most publicly narrated and celebrated "boat people"—a term that the *Oxford English Dictionary* (2012) defines as "refugees who have left a country by sea, esp. the Vietnamese people who fled in small boats to Hong Kong, Australia, and elsewhere after the conquest of South Vietnam by North Vietnam in 1975." As often happens after an international crisis of this magnitude, an outpouring of initial concern allowed for many refugees to be granted asylum in a number of participating countries. As more and more boat people landed on the shores of Hong Kong, Malaysia, and Indonesia, however, public support turned to irritation, and many boat escapees were pushed offshore when they attempted to land or were repatriated back to Vietnam. Refugee camps were filled to capacity, and many resorted to living there for years before being relocated (Chan 2006).

Reclaiming the "boat people" narrative has meant reappropriating the term and expanding its reach. Dong Tran claims all overseas Vietnamese in his statement, "we're all boat people, whether by walking, by plane, or some other way, but we all have that experience." Perhaps more significantly, the second generation is cast as inheritors of this legacy, and thus much of the tour and the efforts of AVBP are specifically targeting future generations of Vietnamese, as I will address in the next section. Thus, the Pulau Galang group tour, marketed and narrated as a return to the "destination of freedom," symbolically acknowledges a different kind of history than that perpetuated by either Vietnam or the United States. While at first glance the boat people identity seems to reproduce the same dominant discursive models that cast them as victims in the popular and academic imagination, a closer examination reveals a more complex negotiation at work, an act of what Marita Sturken calls "cultural memory" (1997: 1).

To define memory as cultural is, in effect, to enter into a debate about what memory means. This process does not efface the individual but rather involves the interaction of individuals in the creation of cultural meaning. Cultural memory is a field of cultural negotiation through which different stories vie for a place in history (Sturken 1997: 1). Invoking a boat people identity is both an act of empowerment and potential subversion. Indeed, I argue that for the first, 1.5, and second generations, this process of self-making is fundamentally empowering, transforming, and grounding a new and unique concept of home, place, reclamation, and spiritual rest. But rather than romanticize the reappropriation of the concept, it is important to note that in the United States for example, identifying as boat people instead of immigrants is set squarely within the highly volatile political disputes defining citizenship and legality and determining who is deserving of the nation's acceptance at the expense of others (Ngai 2004). I assert that it is because of the (mis) characterizations of the Vietnamese and their children—as racialized foreigners (despite being American born, for example), psychologized victims, "good" noble model minorities, or possible threats—that the sites like the Pulau Galang refugee camp have come to take on new meaning. It is significant that it is in these refugee camps—which over thirty years ago were depicted and experienced as the liminal space between political and economic uncertainty and newfound citizenship—that the diasporic community has found a significant space of identity to own and appropriate. It explains why many would choose to revisit spaces that seem at first to reinforce narratives of dislocation, liminality, and nostalgic longing. In response to being characterized as racialized subjects of their new nations—either stereotyped as model Asian minorities or pathologized as victimized refugees—the community has forged a diasporic identity, circulating narratives of collective survival and subsequent success, actively narrating a common heritage. One way in which these efforts are manifest and materialized are through virtual and performative displays of gratitude that are directed at a broad global audience through the complex and problematic discourses of "freedom" (M. Nguyen 2012). There is also an encouragement, or demand rather, of gratitude from the second generation, which is the focus of the following section. While the experience and discourses about exile and rebirth are articulated by the first generation, 1.5- and second-generation participants are continually addressed and incorporated as viable participants of this "boat people" experience and thus actively engaged to embody and perform this narrative of gratitude, freedom, and belonging as their own.

The rhetoric of gratitude was a trope that emerged throughout the group tour and a major initiative for organizations like the Archive of Vietnamese Boat

People. For example, the opposite side of the (now razed) plaque described above read: "In appreciation of the efforts of UNHCR, the Red Cross and the Indonesian Red Crescent Society and other world relief organizations, the Indonesian government and people, as well as all countries of first asylum and resettlement. We also express our gratitude to the thousands of individuals who worked hard in helping the Vietnamese refugees."

OVERSEAS VIETNAMESE COMMUNITIES 2005

At the crux of these efforts is a conscious reclaiming of the proverbial boat people narrative from a trope of shame, secrecy, rape, violence, illegality, and displacement to one of pride, connection, dignity, legacy, and home. Similar to how victims of the Holocaust were enlisted for the development of the Holocaust Museum on the National Mall, there is an urgency to, "make their deaths public, instructive deaths" to future generations (Linenthal 2001: xiii). There are also efforts by the first generation to carefully instruct the second generation in properly acknowledging the sacrifices of their parents. The AVBP website makes the appeal:

> Where do I come from? Why I am here? Life is completely meaningless! I want! I want! I want!
>
> NO! To understand the roots and the values of the living, it is necessary for the future generations to know the undeniable true facts that their parent's generations had to pay an expensive price for Freedom. For every single one who reached it there was one who had to lie down forever, and [what they wanted was] completely simple, but still they could not have it easily.

Narratives like these reveal the anxieties and fears of the first generation that their children will forget their diasporic legacy, exemplified through the common parental complaint that their children are becoming, "too American" to appreciate their parents. On one of the last nights of the tour, I was introduced to one of the ways in which this acknowledgement of gratitude was performatively encouraged and promoted. During an entertaining dinner where certain tour participants sang improvised versions of *cải lương*,[8] the organizers collected donations from everyone on the group tour. The organizers explained that this financial donation was to be presented to a local Indonesian grade school in gratitude for the benevolence shown by the locals and the Indonesian government for the refugees years ago. To my trepidation, I was chosen to make a speech to the classroom of children and their teachers. "Why me?" I asked anyone that would listen. "Because you're a professor," someone said. "And you are young. The children will like you," someone else commented. "What do you want me to say?" I asked. All I received for advice was, "We trust you." On the bus ride home that night and on the way to the village the next morning, I asked my tour companions why we were donating money to a local school. I jotted down their answers, including Duc's reply, which previously mentioned being given the chance to be "reborn" on the island. "Now, I repay," he said. "I share with everyone. I give money to everyone, the temple, the coconut [vendor], that [Indonesian] family with the sick child [we met on a tour stop]." The overwhelming answer that I received was that "we should all be thankful for them taking us in." In this response it is important to note that "we" has narratively come to signify all of us as "the boat people" and "them" came to represent "the Indonesian peoples" on the island and the government. I was not a refugee at the Galang camp myself, nor was my father, who was processed at the Guam refugee camp. But nevertheless, that was how it came to be that one of the "funny" Vietnamese was chosen (grudgingly) as a representative of all the refugees that were processed on that island. I was uncomfortable in this position, not least because it thrust me into a role I was not prepared to fulfill as an ethnographer. In fact, I am personally ambivalent about the rhetoric of gratitude deployed by diasporic Vietnamese, agreeing with Mimi Thi Nguyen (2012) that our complicity as "grateful refugees" is imaginable only in the context of justifying and upholding the values of US Empire.[9] But I spoke nevertheless. Through a translator, I explained to the students that their parents and grandparents on that island accepted the Vietnamese refugees when they needed refuge, and that was why we were thanking them that day. Without a clue about the conditions and possibilities for educational opportunities in that village, I shared my hopes that they would continue to study. I felt inadequate and unsure of myself, but the children eagerly received my short speech, clapped enthusiastically, hugged me, and shared their aspirations to become doctors and teachers in the future. I believe that to them, I came to symbolize the possibility of their dreams. Then, Duc lined up the students and gave them each a crisp bill, insuring that the students themselves would benefit from our group's donation. I received positive feedback from my fellow tour companions, and I felt that I emerged as an insider to our tour group after that experience.

Perhaps this experience can reveal how complex issues of "identity" and "community" really are, and why spaces of spiritual commemoration become so central to activating ideas of collective solidarity. While particular diasporic narratives are seemingly carefully constructed and deployed by the refugee generation, those of us who are second generation construct for ourselves the meanings that will continue to tie us to these sacroscapes. For Linda, visiting her grandfather's grave offered an opportunity to reconcile her relationship to her ancestor. David was inspired by the beautiful landscape and religious significance of the site, compelling him to promise to visit his grandmother's grave again with his own children. Both of Melissa's children were finally privy to their mother's life story in full—and as their third time to visit, have become familiar and comfortable in Pulau Galang, the place where their mother's (new) life began. In my moment of conflict as a representative of the group, I used the opportunity to tell the local children about how important I thought an education is, and that I believed in them. The lesson I learned was that this expression of gratitude, while deployed as a collective act, can also be an intimately personal and introspective experience as well. For example, throughout the trip, Melissa attempted to locate a Chinese storekeeper who gave her a job running errands delivering goods across the refugee camp when she was a child. It was one of the few jobs on the island, and it became essential to the livelihood of her entire family. She had heard rumors that he relocated his shop to a Chinatown district in the nearby city, but as we searched for him and asked the locals about his whereabouts, they proved to be unfounded. She hopes one day to find him to thank him for his compassion. So, for many of us, the trip was, although in some ways transformative, also "unfinished" and evocative, both on a personal and communal level. As David reflected,

> Maybe it is the people, or the atmosphere, or the memory of sharing a meaningful experience, but I feel like I left a piece of myself in Indonesia during this trip, and I'm looking for a way to make myself whole again. I think the boat people feel that they must return because this was a very emotional and powerful place for them. It was a springboard, a gateway to a potentially better place and life. It was a place where some of their loved ones passed away. It was the place where they risked their lives to get to. It was the end of a life that they once knew.

Upon reflection of this particular pilgrimage experience—both personally and collectively—I recognize that it is neither possible, nor perhaps even desirable, to capture a complete picture of the Vietnamese American experience across generations as well as sociopolitical boundaries. Rather, it has been my goal to clarify and illuminate the multiple ways in which this particular sacroscape and the journey (as a collective experience) served to activate and encourage a certain "structure of feeling" among the heritage participants who traveled there. Thus, rather than pose the first or second generation as a monolithic community, or a demographic variable to consider, I move toward an understanding of how selves and communities are negotiated and defined, or even redefined in particular spaces. It is ultimately, I would argue, a creative, complex, and contradictory process through which immigrants and their children situate, displace, and constantly reconstruct both individual and collective narratives of belonging and identity across time and space—physically through travel and through the narrativization and materialization of an always-changing diasporic imaginary. This process is particularly acute, I argue, among the American-born second generation of Vietnamese.

Over fifteen years after the opening of global relations and trade with Vietnam that has allowed ex-patriots to visit the homeland, there is a growing American-born Vietnamese second generation who can, virtually and physically through travel, explore what it means to be diasporic Vietnamese by returning to their families' places of origin and transition. In their own homeland, the US second-generation Vietnamese also find themselves struggling to create a sense of belonging and identity in a paradoxical environment in which their parents worry that they may be losing their culture by becoming "too American," and "Americans" refuse to let them forget that they are racially, ethnically, and religiously "other" (Maira 2002). The question for this population then, is how to understand the meaning of this kind of pilgrimage experience and the recirculation of a narrative of war and an identity as "boat people" that it supports, for those who never experienced either one. I suggest that the starting point for this process begins with a rearticulation of a shared legacy of war, racism, and violence that have produced such circumstances in the first place. Such a narrative makes imaginable a place of rebirth and spiritual rest on an Indonesian island and traces collective roots tracing roots back to a narrative of displacement and dislocation—all in an attempt to reinscribe a sense of dignity and visibility from official erasures of people's very existence.

This is one example—occurring in the "ethnographic present" of August of 2011—of how a particular diasporic community of participants healed and moved beyond a time of conflict and violence. Far from being passive victims, or a homogenous mass of trauma-ridden refugees, these participants envisioned themselves as having successfully emerged from the postwar era. The meanings ascribed to this site may change in time and across generations, but for now, Pulau Galang carries the solemn weight of a spiritually imbued diasporic narrative that has been inherited and adapted by the Vietnamese 1.5 and second generation.

NOTES

1. This chapter is based on semistructured interviews with twenty-three tour participants.
2. Scholarly definitions of 1.5 and second generations vary, and most acknowledge that these classifications according to age are somewhat arbitrary. Sucheng Chan (2006: xiv) defines the 1.5 generation as immigrants who arrive at a young age and thus associate with American-born peers, yet retain their ability to speak their native language, as well as retain the values and norms of their immigrant parents. Thus, it is more important to acknowledge that these terms are fluid and negotiable, a starting point from which to examine different spheres of cultural and social dynamics.
3. By using "traditionalize," I call attention to what Hymes described as a process (1975). In other words, by using the term *tradition* as verb as well as noun, we can call attention to the ways in which people invest objects and practices with meaning, sometimes "inventing" traditions that become a meaningful component of establishing solidarity. I borrow from Thomas Tweed (2008: 61) the term "sacroscapes," which "attend to the multiple ways that religious flows have left traces, transforming peoples and places, the social arena and the natural terrain."

4. Original text from the organization's website *www.vnbp.org/* states: *Đề án này nhằm ghi lại càng nhiều càng tốt những chi tiết có ý nghĩa chung quanh biến cố đã xảy ra trong khoảng tháng 4–1975 cho đến khi Thuyền nhân Việt nam cuối cùng ở trại tỵ nạn được định cư ở quốc gia thứ ba cùng các chi tiết về những thế hệ đầu tiên của biến cố này.* The Archive of Vietnamese Boat People has also published a website under *www.traitynan.com* and was established as a nonprofit in 2004.

5. The AVBP has undertaken major campaigns to revitalize other former refugee camps, for example, the refugee camp in Bidong Malaysia has been marketed as a tourist destination since 2004 and has seen a fair amount of refugee and non-refugee tourists, though not on the same scale as in Galang.

6. Opinions about US involvement in the war are varied among the overseas Vietnamese community, and, as scholar Thuy Vo Dang (2011) has aptly described, the rhetoric of anticommunism often blurs the line between politics and culture.

7. Personal communication with Dong Tran, director of the Archive of Vietnamese Boat People.

8. A form of contemporary Vietnamese folk opera.

9. Nguyen (2012) makes a poignant argument about the emergence and deployment of what she calls the "gift of freedom," which produces always-indebted subjectivities like the grateful refugee.

REFERENCES

Brettell, Caroline B., and Deborah Reed-Danahay. 2012. *Civic Engagements: The Citizenship Practices of Indian and Vietnamese Immigrants*. Stanford, CA: Stanford University Press.

Carruthers, Ashley, and Boitran Huynh-Beattie. 2011. Dark Tourism, Diasporic Memory and Disappeared History. In *The Chinese/Vietnamese Diaspora: Revisiting the Boat People*, Yuk Wah Chan, ed., pp. 147–60. London: Routledge.

Chan, Sucheng. 2006. *The Vietnamese American 1.5 Generation: Stories of War, Revolution, Flight, and New Beginnings*. Philadelphia: Temple University Press.

Christopher, Renny. 1995. *The Viet Nam War/The American War: Images and Representations in Euro-American and Vietnamese Exile Narratives*. Amherst: University of Massachusetts Press.

Collet, Christian, and Nadine Selden. 2003. Separate Ways . . . Worlds Apart? The "Generation Gap" in Vietnamese America as Seen through the San Jose *Mercury News*. Poll. *Amerasia Journal* 29 (1): 199–217.

Dang, Thuy Vo. 2011. *Anticommunism as Cultural Praxis: South Vietnam, War, and Refugee Memories in the Vietnamese American Community*. PhD diss., University of California at San Diego: ProQuest, UMI Dissertation Publishing.

Do, Kiem Van. 2002. Between Two Cultures: Struggles of Vietnamese-American Adolescents. *Review of Vietnamese Studies* 2 (1): 1–18.

Endres, Kirsten W. 2008. "Engaging the Spirits of the Dead: Soul-Calling Rituals and the Performative Construction of Efficacy." *Journal of the Royal Anthropological Institute* 14 (4): 755–73.

Espiritu, Yen Le. 2005. Thirty Years Afterward: The Endings That Are Not Over. *Amerasia Journal* 31 (2) xiii–xxiii.

Freeman, James M. 1995. *Changing Identities: Vietnamese Americans, 1975–1995*. New Immigrants Series. Boston: Allyn and Bacon.

Gustafsson, Mai Lan. 2009. *War and Shadows: The Haunting of Vietnam*. Cornell Paperbacks. Ithaca, NY: Cornell University Press.

Hymes, Dell. 1975. Folklore's Nature and the Sun's Myth. *Journal of American Folklore* 88 (350): 345–69.

Jellema, Kate. 2007. "Everywhere Incense Burning: Remembering Ancestors in Đổi Mớ'i Vietnam." *Journal of Southeast Asian Studies* 38 (3): 467–92.

Kendall, Laurel. 2010. "Beautiful and Efficacious Statues: Magic, Commodities, Agency and the Production of Sacred Object in Popular Religion in Vietnam." *Material Religion: The Journal of Objects, Art and Belief* 6 (1): 60–85.

Kibria, Nazli. 1995. *Family Tightrope: The Changing Lives of Vietnamese Americans*. Princeton, NJ: Princeton University Press.

Lieu, Nhi T. 2011. *The American Dream in Vietnamese*. Minneapolis: University of Minnesota Press.

Linenthal, Edward T. 2001. *Preserving Memory: The Struggle to Create America's Holocaust Museum*. New York: Columbia University Press.

Lowe, Lisa. 1996. *Immigrant Acts: On Asian American Cultural Politics*. Durham, NC: Duke University Press.

Maira, Sunaina Marr. 2002. *Desis in the House: Indian American Youth Culture in New York City*. Philadelphia: Temple University Press.

Ngai, Mae M. 2004. *Impossible Subjects: Illegal Aliens and the Making of Modern America*. Politics and Society in Twentieth-Century America. Princeton, NJ: Princeton University Press.

Nguyen, Ly Thi. 1998. To Date or Not to Date a Vietnamese: Perceptions and Expectations of Vietnamese American College Students. *Amerasia Journal* 24 (1): 143–69.

Nguyen, Mimi Thi. 2012. *The Gift of Freedom: War, Debt, and Other Refugee Passages*. Durham, NC: Duke University Press.

Oxford Dictionaries. 2012. Boat People. *Oxford Mini Dictionary and Thesaurus*. New York: Oxford University Press.

Pathoni, Ahmad. 2005. Tears and Joy as Ex-Vietnamese Boat People Revisit Camp. *L'Agence France-Presse*, April 3. *www.thingsasian.com/stories-photos/3263*.

Starr, Paul D., and Alden E. Roberts. 1982. Community Structure and Vietnamese Refugee Adaptation: The Significance of Context. *International Migration Review* 16 (3): 595–618.

Sturken, Marita. 1997. *Tangled Memories: The Vietnam War, the AIDS Epidemic, and the Politics of Remembering*. Berkeley: University of California Press.

Taylor, Philip. 2004. *Goddess on the Rise: Pilgrimage and Popular Religion in Vietnam.* Honolulu: University of Hawaii Press.

Taylor, Philip, ed. 2008. *Modernity and Re-enchantment: Religion in Post-revolutionary Vietnam.* Singapore: Institute of Southeast Asian Studies.

Tweed, Thomas A. 2008. *Crossing and Dwelling: A Theory of Religion.* Cambridge, MA: Harvard University Press.

Zhou, Min, and Carl L. Bankston. 1999. *Growing Up American: How Vietnamese Children Adapt to Life in the United States.* New York: Russell Sage Foundation.

8 HEALTH SPACES

Representations of French Immigrant Youth in Mental Health Care

Stéphanie Larchanché

In this chapter I explore the *representations* of so-called children of immigrants as they are articulated through the language of school referrals to "specialized" mental health care centers in Paris (Sargent and Larchanché 2009). My contribution thus draws attention to how schools and health institutions both act as sites that define the terms of cultural belonging. While it does not address how children of immigrants *experience* these institutional representations, it contributes to our understanding of how institutions act as sites of social control that may become barriers to belonging for these children. The stories of the three French-born children of immigrants presented here—Salif, Moussa, and Bacari—emerge through the narratives of institutional actors, which put in evidence the local "cultural field" (Nibbs and Brettell, this volume; Hall 2002) second-generation children must negotiate when facing the French educational and health systems. This perspective is ultimately key to understanding the context of identity formation and addresses one of this volume's main objectives; that is, the analysis of the link between social spaces and the politics of identity. I refer to "specialized" mental health care centers as structures that provide culturally sensitive mental health services to immigrants specifically (Sargent and Larchanché 2009). My analysis is based on an eighteen-month-long doctoral field research,[1] during which I carried out participant observation in three different centers, and conducted interviews with both clinicians and referring institutional actors. The general objective of this research was to understand the articulation of what in the French context would be referred to as "cultural difference," both in the institutional discourse of mental health care structures catering to immigrants in France, and in the interactions of the various social actors who meet there.

In school referrals to specialized mental health care centers, the identification of immigrant children's behavioral problems or learning disabilities—and these two often problematically overlap—is frequently accompanied by discussions on immigrant families' socialization model (in reference to French standards) and on what constitutes abnormal behavior/disability. I argue that, more broadly, such discussions shed light on the very categorization of these children as "children of immigrants," and therefore problematize the issue of citizenship and cultural belonging. In a context in which schools have become the sites, in recent years, at once for the policing of urban violence in France—too often associated with children of immigrants—and for the promotion of "equal opportunity programs"—also specifically targeting children of immigrants in marginalized neighborhoods—school referrals to "specialized" mental health care centers offer a lens through which the terms of belonging and the context of identity formation in France can be analyzed.

THE POLITICS OF BELONGING IN FRENCH SCHOOLS

Children of immigrants are particularly vulnerable to regulative discourse and are the object of scrutiny through institutions' efforts to manage immigrant families (Terrio 2009). French schools play a particularly important role as an institution of integration and as a "public socializing agent" (Bowen 2007: 12), training children to become ideal French citizens. Education, in the broad sense of the term, tends to reproduce unequal social relations and cultural representations that symbolically reinforce such inequalities (Bourdieu and Passeron 1977). Thus, I would argue that modes of representations of immigrant children by French institutional actors act as the "mirror function" (Sayad 1999), revealing how France approaches the "integration" of its immigrant populations.

The very categorization of these children as children of immigrants, or as "immigrant youth," is politically meaningful. Noiriel has pointed out that the children of Italian, Polish, or Armenian immigrants in France were never categorized in that way (2001: 224). According to the French historian, we must question that category as stigmatizing in itself, and as participating in a form of racial uniformization of "visible" Others (namely, "blacks" and "Arabs"). Noiriel hypothesizes that the category is in fact the product of the popularization of state "social support" policies (*l'aide sociale*), as a way to at once define, diagnose, and solve social ills. This may explain why it is rarely acknowledged in its racial dimension, especially in schools (Van Zanten 2009), where mechanisms of discrimination have received limited sociological attention (notable exceptions include: Payet 1995; Dubet and Martucelli 1996; Van Zanten 2001; Felouzis, Favre-Perroton, and Liot 2005), unlike in other countries.[2] This form of uniformization of immigrants or children of immigrants as a generic category is also inherent to the French republican ideology that universalist tenets have produced "cultural anxieties" about naming or acknowledging particularisms, such as cultural belonging (Larchanché 2010). This "difficulty with naming," to borrow Didier Fassin's expression (2006), has its history and its present justifications. At times, such difficulty hides racist intentions (Fassin 2006)—a form of racism without race. Encounters around school referrals in specialized mental health care centers, I argue, bring these issues to the fore, as the latter act as experts in mediating between immigrant families and cultural representations of French norms.

First, it is important to underline how schools have become the sites, in recent years, for the policing of urban violence—too often associated with children of immigrants. The Base-Elève project (Student Basic Information Project) for example, established in 2007, required that information on all children enrolled in kindergarten and primary schools be recorded in a central filing system, accessible only to heads of schools and city mayors. Its official intention was to facilitate the general management of schools. The project was highly contested for several reasons, the first being that it initially requested detailed information on children's family members, such as nationality, year of arrival in France, native language, and culture of origin. In the summer of 2008, Xavier Darcos, then minister of education, was pressured to remove such data. Today, the files contain limited contact information, such as a family reference for emergency cases, and a phone number. The project was also designed in the aftermath of the urban riots of 2005 and 2007, which had triggered a national discussion, not so much on the socioeconomic inequalities that were the root cause of such violence, but focusing on the management of early delinquency patterns among urban youth.

The discussion about delinquency, in fact, had been initiated well before the riots and had most likely fueled discontent among disadvantaged suburban youth. It had been spurred by the Ministry of Interior, then led by Nicolas Sarkozy, and had resulted in the adoption of a law in 2003 on "interior security."[3] In that context, the government created a parliamentary study group, called the prevention commission on interior security. The group was headed by moderate right politician Jacques-Alain Bénisti and was highly criticized by French intellectuals and school representatives, as it established a clear parallel between bilingualism among children of immigrants, and the risk for delinquency.[4] This claim was corrected in 2005, as the group released another version of their report, and stated that bilingualism was in fact a great opportunity for children.

A few years later, in 2007, the adoption of a law related to delinquency made schools privileged partners in the institutional detection and prevention of delinquency.[5] On the basis of equations between education and police surveillance, some school directors chose to oppose their school's participation in the Base-Elève project. Other privileged partners in the *detection* and *prevention* of delinquency were mental health professionals, especially psychiatrists. In the Bénisti report, a section was devoted to psychiatrists' collaboration with schools:

At the level of kindergarten, it would be useful to design a culture of dialogue with pediatric psychiatrists and teachers, so as to detect very early on any behavior or attitude that could develop into violent behavior, or lead the child to fail at school.

Pediatric psychiatrists must be sensitized to the school environment, and, alternatively, kindergarten assistants must be sensitized to pediatric psychiatry, so that together they may detect and diagnose children's troubles [*maux*], before making a referral and establishing a broader plan of action [*dispositif*] for prevention around the child. The network of interdistrict psychiatry functions well and could be centralized at the departmental level, with the establishing of a coordinator.

Children with *difficulties* deserve more attention than others, as early as kindergarten. Therefore it is important to facilitate pediatric psychiatrists' access to schools, so that they can carry out proximity work [*faire un travail de proximité*]. The family physician must also pay an important role in the group of referral actors intervening around the child, because he/she is knowledgeable about the family, and has their trust. (my translation, 2004: 16)

This had inspired then minister of the interior Sarkozy to include a mental health component to his law on delinquency, but under the pressure of the psychiatry community, he was forced to remove it.

This political and legal background underlines how, in the detection of behavioral disorders or disability among children of immigrants, one must be aware of the interaction between political ideology and the policing of individual behavior through health and educational policies in particular. It is this problematic interaction that the shifting line between caring and regulating in specialized mental health care school referrals emphasizes.

In the following sections, I analyze school dynamics in the detection of behavioral disorders or disability among children of immigrants. I pay particular attention to ways the recently updated law on disability—theoretically intended to improve care and school environment for disabled children—triggers situations of conflict with immigrant parents. I then turn to how specialized mental health care centers manage school referrals on the basis of behavioral disorder or disability. I examine how these centers are caught in a double bind where their institutional positioning and the very nature of their expertise places them in a position to both amend and contest the dynamics of referrals.

STARTING AT SCHOOL: LOCATING "DIFFICULTIES," NAMING DISORDERS AND DISABILITIES

"Difficulty," as a term of reference in the language of the French education system, is fraught with ambivalence. To start with, the term is very vague and could theoretically encompass references to problems in various domains. Generally, school actors use difficulty to refer to the fact that a given child is failing at school (*en échec scolaire*). In fact the term "student in difficulty" deliberately replaced the term "student failing" in the 1980s, in the National Education system's effort to counteract previous segregating practices leading to early and arbitrary orientations to special aid schools (Monfroy 2002: 33–34). Yet again, difficulty remains—ambiguous, as it can potentially refer to several different gradients of severity in the definition of failure. Consequently, difficulty is used as a generic term, as concerns are initially raised with regards to a given child's problematic school progress, before specific causes are identified, through psychological and medical assessments, for example. Since it remains undefined, both in National Education official texts and in the professional literature, its naming and identifying makes it a social process worth assessing (Monfroy 2002: 34).

The analysis of school referrals reveals a use of the concept in reference to children of immigrants in schools, as being both difficult in the context of the classroom (read: either disruptive or absentminded), and as presenting a higher incidence of learning difficulties (for which various diagnoses are later provided). Indeed, discussions of the identification of the nature of such difficulties often convey stigmatizing representations of immigrants' unusual family structures, lifestyles, and childrearing practices more specifically. More often than not, these are perceived as negatively impacting children's learning abilities, as well as proper behavior—however schools define it. Therefore, the connotations of the use of the word in reference to immigrants and their children, as well as the racial prejudices and moral comments it circulates, require careful attention in the making and naming of school diagnoses, namely learning disabilities and behavioral disorders.

IMMIGRANT DESCENT AS THE BASIS OF "DIFFICULTIES"?

In his discursive analysis of the construction of a disabled learning student, Mehan (1996: 254) focuses on "the competition over the meaning of ambiguous events" as a variety of social actors gather in schools and "try to decide whether a child is 'normal' or 'deviant,' belong in a 'regular educational program' or in a 'special education program.'" In France, the classification of disabilities has become increasingly formalized through state legislation and related institutional reorganization. The goal has been to give the family more agency over the future of their child and over school decision-making, while at the same time allowing disabled youth to remain in the least restrictive school environment possible. However, the administrative management of disabilities at school, from diagnosis to placement, has become increasingly complex and burdensome—despite its intention to improve attendance of disabled children and increase checkups in the diagnostic process. The language of this new system, with its plethora of acronyms (for which the French seem to have a peculiar inclination), is also difficult to process. School actors, whom

I encountered during preclinical consultations or whom I interviewed, themselves complained that they had trouble keeping up, especially considering the system's rules evolved constantly.

Seeing one's child diagnosed with a learning disability is a stressful experience for any parent. But with the new legislation, parents' responsibility in taking charge of managing the disability report has burdened them further. Primarily because of the language barrier, and because of existing tensions with the school as a state institution, immigrant parents may find themselves in extremely anxiety-ridden situations, during which they understand the future of their child may be at stake, but based on a rationale they may not understand or with which they may disagree. Conflicts between immigrant parents and school officials thus recurrently occur around the disability diagnosis and the special-aid school orientation. Such conflicts—rather than the diagnosis per se—form the basis of school referrals to specialized mental health care centers. But before I turn to the analysis of how specialized mental health care centers manage such conflicts, I first examine how the disability diagnosis and referral system is organized in schools.

DISABILITY REPRESENTATIONS: THE STORY OF SALIF

During fieldwork, I had the opportunity to meet Murielle, a school psychologist working at a primary school in an eastern suburb of Paris. This suburb hosts a large Malian community, and it had been the site of violent riots in both 2005 and 2007. Recently, it has received a lot of attention in the context of new politics of urban planning to improve life in the suburbs. Degrading high-rise buildings are being torn down, and slowly replaced by low-rise apartment complexes. As I followed Murielle in her professional activities, I met Salif, an eight-year-old child born in France of Malian parents. At the time of our encounter, Salif was still enrolled in kindergarten. Four years earlier, he had been diagnosed with autism, but conflicts between the school and Salif's family had prevented him from integrating in educational institute specialized in disabilities.

Autism is a particularly tricky diagnosis, considering there are no medical tests for it. A diagnosis must be based on observation of the individual's communication, behavior, and developmental levels. To complicate things further, many of the behaviors associated with autism are shared by other disorders, such as developmental delays, behavioral disorder, or hearing disability. Therefore, detecting autism can take time. As far as Salif was concerned, Murielle explained to me, he would rarely make eye contact with people, had an extremely limited vocabulary and mostly articulated sounds, and would isolate himself, as if drawn into his own world. At the end of Salif's first year in kindergarten, the Diarra family was called to school by the director, so as to discuss an alternative school project for Salif. The school incorporated a part-time class for children with disabilities (CLIS), which Salif was eligible to attend. Following the law of February 2005, the conditions of schooling for disabled children must be adapted in order to see educational and therapeutic needs complemented. The organization of schooling is presumably done within the framework of a partnership between the family, the school, and the service of care; a personalized project of schooling is then defined on the basis of a precise evaluation of the needs for the child. The project is then regularly readjusted. Generally, the child is accommodated with part-time school, alternating with specialized care.

Unfortunately, at the time Salif's case was discussed, the class had reached its maximum of pupils enrolled. The school's director was therefore approaching the Diarras with the possibility of their son being sent to a medical structure outside of school (IME).[6] Salif's father was opposed to the idea. His son was "special," he told the school director, but certainly not disabled. He was cast a spell on (*marabouté*) the day he was born. His mind was governed by a spirit (*jinn*), who would not let go of him. Salif's father was of the opinion that, one day, his son would come back to his own self, being freed from the spirit in his head, and that things would resume to being normal. In fact, Murielle explained to me, the parents had consulted with a multitude of diviners (*marabouts*) in Paris, with the hope of finding the right "cure" for their son.

Almost four years had elapsed between the first meeting between the Diarras and the school director, without the two parties being able to reach an agreement on Salif's schooling orientation. During that time, Murielle had acted as a mediator between the school administration and the parents. At several instances, the school director had threatened the Diarras with a lawsuit for child maltreatment. Murielle had successfully bought more time from her at each threat, convincing her that the Diarras needed more time and space to come to terms with the situation, and that it was in Salif's best interest to let his parents be part of the decision-making. Outside of meetings with Mr. Diarra to deal with the administrative conundrum Salif's case had become, Murielle would also see Mrs. Diarra on a regular basis. She suspected the latter suffered from a severe postpartum depression following Salif's birth. She had shared with Murielle's difficulties relating to her son, and confessed she often simply left him sitting in front of the TV, where he would be so absorbed by images that she would not have to deal with him.

A few months before my visit at Murielle's school, the situation had shifted. That morning, Murielle was receiving Mr. Diarra to discuss the family transformations, along with Salif's progress, and the father's decision to finally sign on to the Personalized School Project adopted by the MDPH for Salif. The appointment had been difficult to schedule, Mr. Diarra working long, ever-changing shifts as a janitor at Charles de Gaulle airport, also a long commute from his residence. When Mr. Diarra arrived, Murielle asked him permission for me to attend their meeting, to which he agreed. He was eager to tell Murielle about the trip his whole family had undertaken to Mali, with Salif and their other newborn child. It was his and his

wife's first time back home since they had come to France. The trip was transformative for the family at many levels, one of which was Salif's behavior. Mr. Diarra had
taken Salif to "the bush" (*la brousse*), where they visited a renowned ritual specialist.
The latter had prescribed a variety of different herbal remedies, some to be mixed
with food and liquids, others to be mixed with Salif's bath water. Every night, Salif
was administered a ritual bath, and within a week, Salif seemed to display significant behavioral changes, making efforts at uttering complete sentences, and making
eye contact more regularly. Mr. Diarra commented:

> I think the *jinn* has left, finally. You know, when I think about all the money I
> invested in those marabouts [ritual specialists] here in France . . . I know people
> say they're all charlatans, but when you're in our situation, you try everything.
> [Turning to me] You know, if it was not for Murielle, I don't know what would
> have happened with Salif. I know people at school mean well for him, but as
> his parents, don't we know best? People have been so mean to us at times. Only
> Murielle took the time to listen to us, me and my wife also. She understands.
> [Turning back to Murielle] Thank you, really.

After Mr. Diarra leaves, Murielle takes advantage of recess to take me to the kindergarten section of school and meet Salif. When I see him, he is playing ball
with one of the school assistants. Although he seems to lack in agility and coordination, he appears very engaged in the game itself (they simply throw the ball
at each other, although Salif does not always seem to intend to throw the ball
back at the assistant). Murielle interrupts them to take Salif to a reading room,
where she observes him play with a variety of plastic objects. She then has him sit
between the two of us, and we flip the pages of a children's book, paying attention to how he engages with the contents. At one point, he stops and points at the
drawing of a mountain and, aloud, articulates "*Montagne!*" (Mountain!) Murielle
turns to me with a look of amazement. "See, he never ceases to amaze me. He
appears to have such a limited vocabulary, and yet he regularly comes with these
words out of nowhere."

Disability diagnoses may sometimes be very difficult to establish. It may be
related to the very nature of the disability, as with autism in Salif's case. In schools,
it is not the existence of the disability that is so much problematic—be it related to
mental, auditory, visual, or motor skills. Rather, it is the severity of the disability
and how to deal with it that becomes more complicated. As Salif's case illustrates,
the difficulty also resides in communicating the disability to immigrant parents,
and negotiating the potentially divergent explanations the latter may have on the
disability and its origins. Schools may not always be willing to take time and accept
such negotiations. Were it not for Murielle's personal engagement with the Diarras
and her sensibility to their conflict with the school, Salif's parents would have been

brought to a justice court, and Salif most likely placed in foster care by child services. A referral to a specialized mental health care center would have certainly taken place.

What Salif's case highlights is the rigidity that institutional actors often readily display with immigrants and/or their children, which ineluctably creates conflicting situations, where there should not be any—or at least where they could easily be avoided. The Diarra family was fortunate to find someone like Murielle to mediate for them. Her willingness to listen and to show the family hospitality were essential in unlocking this situation, and avoiding a referral to a specialized mental health care center, where the same dispositions—listening, tolerance, and hospitality—would have been offered. Communicating acted as a substitute for referring (and potentially suing).

FROM SCHOOLS TO SPECIALIZED MENTAL HEALTH CARE CENTERS: CASES OF BEHAVIORAL DISORDERS

Specialized mental health care centers thus become involved in the negotiation of disorder/disability diagnoses for children of immigrants. On what basis is their professional expertise involved? What is their position vis-à-vis schools' decisions? How do they apprehend the relation between cultural difference and the presence/development of a disorder/disability among children of immigrants?

Sandra, one of the school psychologists affiliated with one of the three specialized mental health care centers where I carried out fieldwork, is the referring psychologist for several schools in a northeastern suburb of Paris. This means that "problematic cases" are signaled to her by schoolteachers or administrators and that upon assessment of the situation she decides whether to refer the child and his family to the specialized mental health care center for consultation or not. The referral is organized in several stages. With respect to the "child in difficulty," Sandra first evaluates the situation at work by meeting with the child and his family. It sometimes happens (as I witnessed once following her to another school site) that she responds to her colleagues' referrals, who also have her meet with the child and family, to assess a given situation. She thus has built a network of professional relations who may rely on her as a special expert or consultant for cases related to children of immigrants.

I accompanied Sandra to an education team meeting in a school in one commune in a northeastern suburb of Paris. Such meetings occur when a pupil is identified as being in difficulty. The team's goal is to discuss the nature of the difficulty, and assess whether it stems from a disorder or a disability, in which case the school is obligated to inform the child's family and organize, in coordination with the Departmental Office for the Disabled (MDPH), a Personalized School Project for the newly labeled disabled child. Sandra is not affiliated with this school in particular, but she participates in the Special Aid Network for Students with Difficulties

(RASED). It is important to note here that Sandra was invited to attend this meeting—concerning the child of Malian immigrants—because the school psychologist knew of her work, and called her as an expert in the possibility that cultural elements arise in this family's case.

THE STORY OF MOUSSA

As we walked to the room where the meeting would take place, Sandra explained to me that the education team had not formally identified any disability with Moussa yet. Moussa was the son of a Malian single mother, who also had a daughter in kindergarten. Sandra informed me that there had already been a meeting during which Moussa and his mother were present. The meeting had lasted three hours, and Moussa had appeared extremely calm to Sandra. He displayed constructive and controlled drawing skills, which, to Sandra, seemed to contradict the schoolteacher's report, according to which Moussa had problems with motor skills. Sandra warned me that the RASED team had suspicions concerning the teacher's report, that they were questioning whether the latter lacked a positive perspective on Moussa, and whether the problem at stake was a reactionary problem on behalf of the teacher, rather than some type of disability with the child. Sandra added that were some kind of disability identified by the team and reported to the school administration, Moussa's mother would have four months to fill out the disability declaration paperwork and submit it to the district's MDPH. Should she fail to do so, the school could threaten her with a lawsuit.

As we entered the room, we were met by the school's psychologist, the Maître E (in charge of learning disabilities), the Maître G (in charge of relational disabilities), and Moussa's schoolteacher. Moussa's mother had been informed of the meeting and was expected by the team, but she ended up not coming.

The meeting started with a discussion of last month's meeting with Moussa's mother. The schoolteachers struck me as looking extremely uncomfortable during the discussion, especially as Sandra reiterated her observations that Moussa had not appeared to have any of the motor skills deficiencies he had been reported to have. Before Sandra had finished speaking, the schoolteacher stood up and nervously went through a folder filled with children's drawings. She was shaking. The team members exchanged looks of concern, until the school psychologist, in a reassuring voice, invited the teacher to join the circle again and sit down:

> *School psychologist (SP):* We are not saying that your observations are wrong. We are simply trying to assess the situation at this point, and determine how serious those motor skills problems you mentioned are. If Moussa appears normally stimulated outside of the classroom, we may wonder what constraints he feels when he is in the classroom. Perhaps his behavior is reactionary to something yet to be determined.

Sandra: Hasn't there been a medical diagnostic yet? I thought Moussa was to be tested for a potential neurological disorder.

Maître E: There hasn't been a diagnostic yet.

Teacher: Well, I'm worried about Moussa. Do we have to wait for a diagnosis? [Looking overwhelmed and teary eyed] My problem is that Moussa won't stay still on his chair, and he keeps disturbing his schoolmates. He's always provocative with them. I can't always punish him! Honestly, I'm tired. It's difficult enough to manage a classroom. I can't just focus all my attention on him constantly.

Maître E: He has incorporated all the learning skills he should have acquired by now though. He just doesn't show them in the classroom. Perhaps we can obtain permission from the school superintendent to have him repeat his CE2 [third grade], even though he's already repeated a grade before . . .

Teacher: The problem is that Moussa does not benefit from a listening structure at home. Let's not fool ourselves here. *It's not a disease or a disability issue* [emphasis mine].

Sandra: She's right. The school has only helped Moussa's existing problem emerge. The trouble is, Moussa's family won't understand his behavior the same way we do. Although they did agree to have the medical tests carried out. But I have to tell you, there will necessarily be a confrontation issue between our perspective on Moussa's disability—if disability there is—and the family's cultural understanding of the situation. Not mentioning that this situation is very confusing and scary for Moussa.

A discussion followed concerning the family's living conditions and the mother's situation. After she left her husband (no mention of the reasons why she did so), she and her children sought shelter at what is commonly named "the 115," a program for homeless people, established by the City of Paris, and coordinated by the Social Service branch of SAMU (Service d'Aide Médicale Urgente or Emergency Medical Assistance Service).[7] For weeks, the family traveled from one shelter to another, until they found housing in a structure welcoming single mothers and their children.[8] The school psychologist explained that Moussa's mother had been feeling depressed and vulnerable. She often expressed fears of her children being in danger, especially since she had found a job and had to leave her children on their own more often than she liked. The situation worsened when her daughter, accompanied by Moussa on her way to kindergarten, was hit by a car near school. Fortunately, she suffered no injuries. Shortly thereafter, the mother's "companion" left her without notice. This triggered a long discussion on the sincerity of the companion's feelings for Moussa's mother, considering he was an illegal immigrant, and was most likely interested in a romance that would lead him to obtain legal paperwork:

Sandra: I wonder how she interprets all of this. The fact that she didn't show up this morning may mean that she's not doing well, that she's isolating herself.

Teacher:—You know, I must say that when I pay attention to him specifically, Moussa behaves really well. Everything is fine. I think he's looking for a privileged relationship.

Sandra:—And he surely can't find that at home either. His mother raises them like in Africa, with everybody else . . .

At that point, a bell rang, indicating it was time for recess, and everyone had to resume their regular activities. A meeting was scheduled again for the following month.

This case started with an ambiguous situation. First, the teacher's report on Moussa's motor skills disability appeared to be contradicted outside of the classroom context, as verified by Sandra during the first Pedagogical Team meeting, and by Maître E, who presumably met with Moussa outside of class to assess his learning abilities in general. Soon after hearing those expert counterassessments, the teacher suggested that Moussa might merely be seeking attention, and that "he's looking for a privileged relationship." Her willingness to try and situate Moussa's contradictory behavior was facilitated by Sandra's intervention. This is where, I believe, Sandra's expertise came in as relevant. As she herself put it, her role is more that of a conflict mediator between immigrant families and school institutions, rather than of a "specialized" psychologist (very much echoing Murielle's description). She attempted to show where and why different interpretations of Moussa's behavior may emerge. By allowing the possibility for Moussa's mother to be interpreting the situation differently than the school ("Moussa's family won't understand his behavior the same way we do" or "I wonder how she will interpret all of this"), as well as initiating a discussion on Moussa's family environment (unstable living conditions and their impact on child care), Sandra successfully led the teacher to feel less defensive about her response to Moussa's behavior, and be more receptive about apprehending him differently in the classroom. The communication Sandra's presence encouraged ultimately prevented Moussa's case from being referred outside of the school, to a specialized mental health care center.

One may nonetheless find Sandra's approach problematic through the stigmatizing representations of immigrant families it indirectly reinforces. Indeed, themes discussed—notably comments on unusual family structures, childrearing practices, and precarious social environments—do disseminate moral judgments (especially in the discussion of Moussa's mother's relationship) and indirectly comment on how immigrants deviate from a "standard" socialization model and "normal" behavior. Surely, Sandra's approach is not intended to reinforce such commonplace stereotypical judgments on immigrants' lifestyles and their suspected impact on their children's problematic behavior. However, this is the risk her specialized mental health care expertise itself produces. Moussa's teacher may be willing to concede that there is no actual disability at stake here, but she may very well conclude from the discussion on generic ways of raising children in Africa that it is Moussa's culturally different background that make him behave abnormally in the classroom. Sandra's closing comments ("His mother raises them like in Africa, with everybody else . . .") seemingly validate this conclusion. In other words, Sandra's intervention may have unlocked the conflict between Moussa and his teacher (and potentially with the family), but it simultaneously may have encouraged the discussion of problematic behavior in culturally stigmatizing terms, using the same line of argumentation that so often makes the behavioral disorder diagnosis particularly problematic for children of immigrants.

THE STORY OF BACARI

Later that day, it was precisely the use of this culturally stigmatizing rhetoric that Sandra and I witnessed during a departmental MDPH meeting, where Sandra was replacing her sick colleague.[9] The meeting gathered specialized teachers, social workers, the MDPH doctor, an academic/pedagogical advisor, the department's school superintendent, and Sandra as the referring school psychologist. The cases presented that afternoon all concerned children who had already been transferred from regular schools to specialized therapeutic institutes.[10] Their eligibility for another transfer to an institute where they could receive professional training (SEGPA) was discussed.[11] Each child's learning difficulties were assessed from both educational and psychological perspectives.

I was struck (and so was Sandra, as she later told me) by the discussion of one case concerning Bacari, the twelve-year-old son of a polygamous family from West Africa. The father had two wives, living in two separate apartments, but on the same floor of a building, and fifteen children. The social worker appointed to the case had reported that the all children in the family displayed educational deficiencies. A legal educational measure had in fact been implemented by the youth justice services on the family.[12] Bacari's school psychologist recommended for Bacari to be sent to a SEGPA boarding school, but the school was far from the family's apartment, and therefore transportation issues were raised. At this point Sandra interjected:

> *Sandra:* What exactly does Bacari's family understand of this Personalized School Project?
>
> *School Psychologist:* Not much. What they don't understand is how disturbing for the child it is to go from his father's apartment to his mother's.
>
> *Sandra:* Well, there are a lot of fragmented families in which children don't have any adaptation issues.

SP: It's not the family structure per se that we question. It is simply the psycho-logical state of the child we are concerned about.

MDPH Doctor: We have great difficulties communicating with the father, but the family is very cooperative in general.

Sandra: In the written report, in the educational deficiencies box, there are refer-ences to Bacari's "improper clothing" and "bodily hygiene issues." How relevant are those?

SP: Uh . . . not sure. This was written by the schoolteacher.

[Each written report consists of a double-sided sheet of paper, with relatively succinct comments on it. It usually is filled out by the child's teacher.]

Superintendent: I suggest we hold making a decision for now. It's not clear yet whether there will be a spot available in a SEGPA class, and the transportation issue needs to be dealt with.

Very quickly, the team switched to another case, but in private Sandra showed me another note on Bacari's report, stating the following: "susceptible to delinquent tendencies."

Although it would be improper to bear judgment here on the accuracy of the diagnosis for Bacari, given the limited information revealed about the context in which a diagnosis was made, it is interesting to note how, once again, discussions of Bacari's deficiency relate to his family's unusual living arrangement. In fact, no one raises questions concerning the evaluation establishing Bacari's deficiency itself. An underlying moral discourse on the practice of polygamy, and its indirect rela-tionship to delinquent "tendencies," are seemingly meant to reinforce the MDPH's expertise (Smardon 2008). One may very well imagine, however, that the issue of a potentially unstable family structure and visible signs of a lack of hygiene in a child may raise red flags in the psychological evaluation of any child, whether of immi-grant parents or not. Interestingly, it is Sandra here who objects to a potentially culturally stigmatizing reading of the polygamous family structure as psychologi-cally damaging to children, by establishing a parallel to other forms of "fragmented families" (single-headed households, blended families, etc.) in the "general" popu-lation, and by simultaneously contesting the arbitrary relationship between family structure and child pathological behavior.

IDENTIFYING STIGMA FOR SECOND-GENERATION IMMIGRANT CHILDREN: THE CONFLATION OF CULTURE AND CLASS IN THE FRENCH CONTEXT

The overlap between differentiating representations of children of immigrants and judgments on their mental well-being (and by extension, their families') thus appears to be quite complex, as it is often difficult to clearly identify the share of stigmatizing cultural representations that may inform school referrals from benevolent concerns with problematic family environments. I suggest that in fact, it is this complex overlap that informs ambiguous referrals, especially those calling for behavioral disorders, as they depend more on subjective assessments than disabilities do.

In that context, the stigmatizing projections that may shape teachers' categorization of children of immigrants as difficult children, bound to become children in difficulty, reflect a mix between generic representations of culture/race and representations linked to class. In fact, culture may be used as a proxy to address class differences and social inequalities, and vice versa, depending on the context. This dynamic is particularly inherent to the French context in which the ideology of republican universalism constantly creates tensions with acknowledgments of cultural difference. As a result, in public discourse, people favor talking about social inequalities even when it refers to cultural/racial stigmatization. Likewise, the tension is reflected in how France considers its immigrant populations both in their humanity following universalist ideals, as well as radically foreign in terms of national and legal rights (Larchanché 2011). As immigrants are particularly vulnerable to social inequalities and discrimination, immigrants embody the overlap between the "social issue" and "the racial issue," and French scholars have clearly shown how both are in fact interconnected (De Rudder et al. 2000; Fassin and Fassin 2006).

Although it did not focus on cultural/racial stigmatization in relation to children of immigrants at school, Monfroy's study on the definition of students in difficulty in Priority Education Zones (also known as ZEPs in the French context—*Zones d'Education Prioritaire*) found that "students from lower social classes are frequently perceived [by their teachers] through very generic representations, massively resorting to images of deprivation and social misery, as well as to explanations framed in terms of 'sociocultural disability'" (2002: 35). Teachers' representations thus focus on students' behavior and attitude—rather than academic performance strictly, with a strong propensity to psychologize problems (Monfroy 2002: 35). These attributions, which are external to the school context, lead teachers to commonly categorize students in difficulty in two broad categories: withdrawal (*figure "du retrait"*) or resistance (*figure "de la résistance"*) (Monfroy 2002: 36). Parallel qualifications are used with children of immigrants. Monfroy also shows how such external attributions lead teachers to "consider children's difficulties as being unrelated to pedagogy and/or school, but rather from a lack of will, of interest, or of motivation, sometimes a pathological problem (paralysis—*"un blocage"*), on which they cannot act because they would be related to these students' personal characteristics and/or their families" (Monfroy 2002: 37). Again, one may easily understand how, in addition, stigmatizing stereotypes about immigrants' unusual family structures and lifestyles—and the dangerous youth they breed—would make children of immigrants particularly vulnerable to such categorizations. Monfroy concludes that teachers' suffering and professional burnout weigh significantly in the subjective assessment of such students, and the consequences that derive from such assessment (responsibility withdrawal, special aid orientation request, etc.) (2002: 39). All these reasons make referrals for children of immigrants particularly problematic.

In the case studies reported here, it becomes apparent that the conflation of cultural stigma and concerns with pathology-producing structural factors is encouraged by the intervention of specialized mental health experts themselves. As apparent in Sandra's position on Moussa's case, specialized mental health care professionals often become caught in a double-bind between disputing the stigmatizing basis on which some of the referrals are made on the one hand, and preserving their professional positioning (and indirectly that of the center they work at) by catering to the demand for cultural expertise on the other.

Therefore, where their intervention may simply be perceived as one among other institutional resources in helping with seemingly unsolvable situations, specialized mental health care experts may be the ones feeling the need to justify their intervention and institutional use by eliciting a cultural interpretation of the situations at stake.

CONCLUSION

In the analysis of these school referrals, it becomes readily apparent how the conflation of cultural stigma and concerns with pathology-producing structural factors is encouraged by the intervention of specialized mental health experts themselves. As apparent in Sandra's position on Moussa's case, specialized mental health care professionals often become caught in a double bind between disputing the stigmatizing basis on which some of the referrals are made on the one hand, and preserving their professional positioning (and indirectly that of the center they work at) by catering to the demand for cultural expertise on the other.

Meanwhile, the very categorization of children as children of immigrants, or as immigrant youth, goes undisputed. For that reason, the analysis of the language used in specialized mental health discourse, as well as in related institutional interactions, is paramount. The conceptualization of otherness in relation to suffering is at stake. The discourse of referring actors reveals unscripted perspectives, which in turn offer a mirror into a collective reflection on identity, cultural difference, and the differential treatment deemed necessary for certain populations. This discourse reveals a perspective in which cultural difference is perceived as creating social difficulties, which in turn produce pathological situations. Such discourse is not necessarily articulated as being stigmatizing, but rather as translating a benevolent attitude toward immigrants, a desire to help with their difficulties.

Regardless, discussions on the identification of the nature of such difficulties thus often convey stigmatizing representations of immigrants' unusual family structures, lifestyles, and child-rearing practices more specifically. More often than not, these are perceived as negatively impacting children's learning abilities, as well as proper behavior—however schools define it. Therefore, the connotations of the use of the word in reference to immigrants and their children, as well as the racial prejudices and moral comments it circulates, require careful attention in the making and naming of school diagnoses, namely learning disabilities and behavioral disorders.

The analysis of clinical referrals thus provides an analytical window into observing the strategic manipulation of euphemisms that dissimulate direct references to cultural differences behind the register of suffering. Bourdieu (1991) has argued that substituting one word for another can be equated to changing the vision of the social order, hence the "illocutionary force" of speech. Through schools referrals, we may evaluate situational mechanisms of cultural differentialism. In such a context, I would argue that the repertoires of "difficulty" and "suffering" used in referrals perform what Michele Lamont calls "boundary work" (2000: 3). They provide culturally meaningful and socially acceptable repertoires of evaluation used to make judgments about various social domains and to discuss the terms of belonging to local identity norms. While such repertoires of evaluation have been show to target first-generation immigrants, in the context of humanitarian practices and immigration politics in particular (Ticktin 2011), this research shows how relevant they continue to be in defining second-generation experiences and in shaping the background for identity formation in the French context.

NOTES

1. This doctoral research was supported by the National Science Foundation and the Wenner-Gren Foundation.
2. As pointed out in the Introduction to this book, the sociological literature on mechanisms of discrimination in schools is particularly significant in Great Britain and the United States.
3. Law of March 18, 2003, on national security (LSI or Loi Sarkozy II). Text available on the National database for legal documents (*Légifrance*): *www.legifrance.gouv.fr/ affichTexte.do?cidTexte=LEGITEXT000005634107&dateTexte=vig.*
4. Assemblée Nationale, XIIᵉ Législature. 2004. Rapport préliminaire de la commission prévention du groupe d'études parlementaire sur la sécurité intérieure. *www.afrik.com/ IMG/pdf/rapport_BENISTI_prevention.pdf.*
5. Law of March 5, 2005, on the prevention of delinquency, available on the French Department of Home Affairs website: Loi du 5 mars 2005 relative à la prévention de la délinquance: *www.interieur.gouv.fr/sections/a_la_une/toute_1 _actualite/archives-actualites/archives-securite/loi-delinquance-5-mars-2007/downloadFile/attachedFile/mise_ en_page_5_web.pdf?nocache=1178545944.26.*
6. Institut Médico-Educatif or Medical and Educational Institute.
7. This program was initially established in 1993. This organization assists homeless people to find a bed in an emergency shelter, mainly through a toll-free telephone number (115). These shelters are usually run by independent private charitable organizations having an agreement with the SAMU social. The SAMU social also has minibuses

collecting homeless from the street to bring them to these shelters. Homeless people needing medical care are referred by the SAMU to public hospitals or day care centers. In emergency shelters, homeless peoples are offered a bed, dinner, and breakfast for three consecutive days.

8. These shelter structures vary according to the location, and some target specific populations, such as women victims of conjugal violence.

9. Each school district appoints a school psychologist to represent his/her colleagues' work at MDPH meetings.

10. ITEPs (Therapeutic, Educational, and Pedagogical Institutes).

11. SEGPAs (Adapted Professional Education Sections).

12. Educational measures are implemented by the judicial system. They make take several forms, depending on the nature of the family's problem (socioeconomic precarity, child abuse, conjugal violence, child delinquency, etc.), ranging from part-time surveillance and assistance at home, to foster care placements. A definition and typology for such measures are provided by the French Department of Justice on their website: *www.justice.gouv.fr/justice-des-mineurs-10042/presentation-10043/les-mesures-les-sanctions-educatives-et-les-peines-www.justice.gouv.fr/index.php?rubrique=10042&ssrubrique=10270&article=11984.*

REFERENCES

Bénisti, Jacques Alain. 2004. Rapport préliminaire de la commission prévention du groupe d'études parlementaire sur la sécurité intérieure—Sur la prévention de la délinquance. Report available on the website of the National Documentation Center (*La Documentation Française*) which compiles official administrative documents: *www.ladocumentationfrancaise.fr/var/storage/rapports-publics/064000294/0000.pdf.*

Bourdieu, Pierre. 1991. *Language and Symbolic Power.* Cambridge, MA: Harvard University Press.

Bourdieu, Pierre, and Jean-Claude Passeron. 1977. *Reproduction in Education, Society and Culture.* Translated from the French by Richard Nice. Beverly Hills, CA: Sage.

Bowen, John. 2007. *Why the French Don't Like Headscarves: Islam, the State, and Public Space.* Princeton, NJ: Princeton University Press.

De Rudder, Véronique, Christian Poiret, and François Vourc'h. 2000. *L'Inégalité Raciste: L'Universalité Républicaine à l'Épreuve.* Paris: Presses Universitaires de France.

Dubet, François. 2004. *L'École des Chances: Qu'est-ce qu'une École Juste?* Paris: Seuil.

Dubet, François, and Danilo Martucelli. 1996. *A l'École: Sociologie de l'Expérience Scolaire.* Paris: Seuil.

Fassin, Didier. 2006. Nommer, Interpréter: Le sens commun de la question raciale. In *De la Question Sociale à la Question Raciale? Représenter la Société Française*, Didier Fassin and Eric Fassin, eds., pp. 27–44. Paris: La Découverte.

Fassin, Didier, and Eric Fassin (eds.). 2006. *De la Question Sociale à la Question Raciale? Représenter la Société Française.* Paris: La Découverte.

Felouzis, Georges, Joëlle Favre-Perroton, and Françoise Liot. 2005. *L'Apartheid Scolaire: Enquête sur la Ségrégation Ethnique dans les Collèges*. Paris: Seuil.

Hall, Kathleen D. 2002. *Lives in Translation: Sikh Youth as British Citizens*. Philadelphia: University of Pennsylvania Press.

Lamont, Michèle. 2000. *The Dignity of Working Men: Morality and the Boundaries of Race, Class, and Immigration*. Cambridge, MA: Harvard University Press.

Larchanché, Stéphanie. 2010. *Cultural Anxieties and Institutional Regulation: "Specialized" Mental Health Care and "Immigrant Suffering" in Paris, France*. PhD diss., Washington University; Paris: EHESS.

———. 2011. Intangible Obstacles: Health Implications of Stigmatization, Structural Violence, and Fear among Undocumented Immigrants in France. *Social Science and Medicine* 74 (6): 858–63.

Mehan, Hugh. 1996. The Construction of an LD Student. In *Natural Histories of Discourse*, M. Silverstein and G. Urban, eds., pp. 253–76. Chicago: University of Chicago Press.

Monfroy, Brigitte. 2002. La définition des élèves en difficulté en ZEP: Le discours des enseignants de l'école primaire. *Revue Française de Pédagogie* 140: 33–40.

Noiriel, Gérard. 2001. Les jeunes "d'origine immigrée" n'existent pas. In *État, Nation et Immigration: Vers une Histoire du Pouvoir*, by Noiriel, pp. 221–29. Paris: Belin.

Payet, Jean-Paul. 1995. *Collèges de Banlieue: Ethnographie d'un Monde Scolaire*. Paris: Meridiens-Klincksieck.

Sargent, Carolyn, and Stéphanie Larchanché. 2009. The Construction of "Cultural Difference" and Its Therapeutic Significance in Immigrant Mental Health Services in France. *Culture, Medicine, and Psychiatry* 33 (1): 2–20.

Sayad, Abdelmalek. 1999. "Costs" and "Benefits" of Immigration. Translated by Priscilla Parkhurst Ferguson et al. In *The Weight of the World: Social Suffering in Contemporary Society*, Pierre Bourdieu et al., eds., pp. 219–21. Stanford, CA: Stanford University Press.

Smardon, Regina. 2008. Broken Brains and Broken Homes: The Meaning of Special Aid Education in an Appalachian Community. *Anthropology and Education Quarterly* 39 (2): 161–80.

Terrio, Susan J. 2009. *Judging Mohammed: Juvenile Delinquency, Immigration, and Exclusion at the Paris Palace of Justice*. Stanford, CA: Stanford University Press.

Ticktin, Miriam I. 2011. *Casualties of Care: Immigration and the Politics of Humanitarianism in France*. Berkeley: University of California Press.

Van Zanten, Agnès. 2001. *L'École de la Périphérie: Scolarité et Ségrégation en Banlieue*. Paris: Presses Universitaires de France.

———. 2009. Une discrimination banalisée? L'évitement de la mixité sociale et raciale dans les établissements scolaires. In *De la Question Sociale à la Question Raciale? Représenter la Société Française*, 2nd ed., Didier Fassin and Eric Fassin, eds., pp. 114–38. Paris: La Découverte/Poche.

9 LEGAL SPACES

Failed Asylum-Seeking Children in the Irish Homeland

Erin Moran

In March 2005, nineteen-year-old Olunkunle Eluhanla was deported from Ireland back to his home county of Nigeria. Labeled a "Failed Asylum Seeker," Eluhanla was returned on the grounds that he did not qualify for asylum in Ireland just months shy of earning his high school diploma. While Eluhanla was awaiting a decision in his asylum case, which took about three years, he remained in the custody of the state and attended Palmerstown Secondary School outside of Dublin. The case caused a national stir when one hundred students and teachers marched on the Parliament building to protest Eluhanla's deportation, calling on the minister of justice, Michael McDowell, to allow Eluhanla to return to Ireland to take his high school exit exam. Plastered across media outlets, the case gripped the attention of the nation for most of that year.

I analyze the story of Eluhanla as entrée into thinking about how migrant children of the 1.5 generation living in Ireland experience shifts in their legal status, how this impacts the ways they perform their identity, and how they are understood in Ireland. There is a growing population of 1.5ers like Eluhanla born abroad to non-Irish parents living in Ireland who were sent abroad alone to seek asylum at a young age. These children grow up in Ireland under the loose supervision of a state trustee and must navigate the many challenges associated with social integration and legal normalization on their own.

I assert that individuals, states, and publics concurrently cocreate representations of 1.5-generation migrant children, and that the various avowals (and, at times, disavowals) of self and other work together to produce overlapping legal and moral spaces through which claims to belong are asserted and contested. Exploring this legal-moral space sheds light on a sense of ambivalence peculiar to modern nation states relative to 1.5-generation children; resident migrant children evoke a contradiction between state legal mandates against foreign encroachment and public moral imperatives regarding the protection of children. Public contests between these forms of authority can make available narratives that tell us much about how people assert belonging and what it means to belong.

The legitimacy of modern nation-states is embedded in the ability to govern and regulate noncitizens (migrants) and limited citizens (children). States are territorialized through their ability control their national boundaries and, by extension, who may or may not be a citizen of the nation. Simultaneously, children (variously defined) are viewed as vulnerable and in need of state protection; the state provision of health, welfare, and education to children is one way in which states spatialize a moral authority to rule. These competing interests in citizenship and childhood can impact on young migrants in unexpected ways, creating tension and even moral paradoxes within state-ordered legal spaces of belonging.

One of the ways states protect their sovereign spaces is by deporting failed asylum seekers, whose presence in the state has been deemed illegitimate. Usually, moral authority and sovereign power are complementary and work together to strengthen and legitimize the legal-moral space of the modern nation-state. When it comes to failed asylum-seeking children, however, these forms of power collide. A failed asylum seeker (whose unauthorized presence constitutes an act of delinquency) activates the state's policing role; when a child is involved, however, the state is often held to a different standard of humanitarian protection. In Ireland, the difficulty of this paradox has emerged to define the ambivalence with which Irish people and the Irish state relate to failed asylum-seeking children of the 1.5 generation, such as Eluhanla.

In this chapter, I explore the ways in which the Irish state, the Irish public, and Eluhanla himself have variously asserted his right to complete an education in Ireland. I ask how multiple social groups (including Eluhanla himself, speaking from Nigeria) mounted a campaign to redefine Eluhanla as a child in need of Irish state care, rather than an adult alien deportee. To answer this question, I conducted an analysis of local and national Irish TV, print media, and online media using qualitative coding and category comparison techniques (Bernard 2008). I also drew on my fieldwork experiences in Dublin (2008–2009), which took place when Eluhanla's case was still regularly in the news. Neither fully first-generation adult migrant nor a child of migrants (second generation), 1.5-generation children emerge in a sort of social and legal limbo that produces a quandary for their incorporation into modern nation-states. I argue that 1.5-generation children, and specifically those who are failed asylum seekers, pose a special challenge to states and the public because they draw together and highlight often-conflicting ethical and coercive forms of governance within a context of shifting social values. In Ireland, failed asylum-seeking children evoke these complexities because childhood and (non)citizenship are salient social categories that exist within ill-defined moral and legal spaces of belonging.

THE CONTEXT

Since the mid-1990s Ireland's boom economy has made it an important destination for migrants and refugees from all over the world. At the height of Ireland's economic prosperity (about 1995–2008), recruitment of Eastern European migrant labor was paralleled by an unprecedented influx of African asylum seekers. Of these migrants, on average about 27 percent are under the age of nineteen (statistical average 2006–2012) (Central Statistics Office 2012). In 2002, Ireland received twelve thousand asylum applications, a dramatic increase over the thirty applications they received less than a decade earlier in 1994 (Quinn 2008). Asylum seekers are migrants who have arrived in Ireland "by unconventional means" (perhaps via clandestine border crossing or by means of a false passport) and whose case is under review by the Refugee Tribunal. While their case is under review, asylum seekers are granted temporary permission to reside in Ireland with restricted rights (for example, asylum seekers in Ireland do not have the right to work and are pressured to reside in state-provided housing). If the individual case is determined to have merit, the individual will be granted refugee status (which confers similar entitlements as to Irish nationals). If the case is determined to be without merit, the individual will be deported.

Nigerians, like Eluhanla, are unlikely to be granted asylum. In 2006 the Irish minster for justice expedited the deportation of Nigerian asylum seekers, asserting that the move was justified because Nigerians have a "reputation for lodging false petitions" (Irish Naturalization and Immigration Services 2005). Nigerians are the largest population of asylum seekers in Ireland—41 percent in 2005. However, less than 7 percent of all asylum applications are granted, and, among Nigerians, the recognition rate is just 0.6 percent (Irish Naturalization and Immigration Service 2005). Since the minister's decision, Nigerians are consistently the top nationality deported from Ireland.

Migrants under the age of eighteen who have arrived to Ireland without a parent are called "unaccompanied minors" and remanded to the care of the state. Unaccompanied minors, such as Eluhanla, often arrive to Ireland through a third party who has been paid to procure transportation and a false passport. Other unaccompanied minors may also be trafficked into Ireland as sex workers or slave labor. At the time of the Eluhanla case, the total number of unaccompanied minors in Ireland had risen from thirty-two in 1999 to forty-two thousand in 2005 (Children's Rights Alliance 2006). The legal rights and access of unaccompanied minors in Ireland is rather ambiguous. As an unaccompanied child is a ward of the state, a government representative decides whether or not to submit an asylum application on behalf of the migrant child. The conditions under which the state decides whether or not to submit an asylum application on behalf of an unaccompanied minor are unclear, although there is an emphasis on factors such as the asylum seeker's country of origin (Irish Naturalization and Immigration Service 2005).

In 2005, just 131 asylum applications were submitted on behalf of unaccompanied minors (Central Statistics Office 2012).

Children who are under review by the Refugee Tribunal are offered housing, education, and welfare until a decision is made in their case. However, during the process they face intense legal and moral scrutiny. Anthropologists have highlighted the difficult experiences of youth in adult-centric asylum systems (Giner 2007; Crawley 2010; Eastmond and Ascher 2011), particularly in social settings like Ireland in which refugees and asylum seekers are viewed with suspicion (Watters 2008). As one young asylum seeker in Dublin put it, "We do not like the asylum process. . . . [I am] worried about being deported when [I] become 18. Our stories are not believed. They try to catch us out and our credibility is questioned. If they do not think our story is credible, then we do not get status, and then they say we lied" (Children's Rights Alliance 2006). The difficulties asylum-seeking children face are exacerbated in the Irish context because the immigration system is still relatively new and evolving, often creating situations of uncertainty and irregularity for these young migrants (Laoire 2011).

Children whose cases are not submitted for asylum review remain in limbo without legal status or social welfare of any kind. While the Ministry for Justice maintains the right to deport these children, it does not usually do so until the child reaches age eighteen (Children's Rights Alliance 2006). Residing within the legal space of the nation, yet not belonging to it, these children's legal future and sense of place in the world is indefinitely suspended. The minister for justice faces a similar quandary in relationship to children whose applications for asylum have been rejected by the Refugee Tribunal before they have reached the age of eighteen, like Eluhanla. Children's applications are commonly rejected, and increasingly so in recent years. In 2005, 57 percent of child applicants were granted refugee status, while in 2008 just 17 percent of applications from children were accepted (Central Statistics Office 2012). Like the child whose case is not submitted for review, the failed asylum-seeking child is subject to deportation but will usually not be deported until legal adulthood. This solution does not definitively answer the question about the legal belonging of these children, nor does it define the moral relationship of the state to these children. However, ignoring these legally unauthorized children allows the state to circumvent the question by generally allowing the child to complete his or her secondary education. (In Ireland, the end of secondary education is very closely associated with the attainment of adulthood, irrespective of the individual's age.) It is estimated that there are about two hundred children in this situation in Ireland at any given time (Children's Rights Alliance 2006).

Cultural notions of personhood, morality, and autonomy, as well as the role of states vis-à-vis children, create varying discourses and practices surrounding youth and adulthood and regimes of protection, as well as power and authority. As people in the process of becoming adults, children embody futurity and possibility, particularly as it pertains to the nation (Cole and Durham 2008). As such, child-citizens represent a source of anxiety and intervention for the modern nation-state, the target of extensive policies, programs, and rhetoric, such as child welfare and development programs (Chatterjee 1993; Coe 2008). Nancy Scheper-Hughes and Carolyn Sargent (1998) have called the ideological, political, and cultural use of children and the concept of "the child" "the cultural politics of childhood." Within the context of international immigration, the politics of childhood take on even more complex dimensions. As a uncertain symbol of a changing world, children of the 1.5 generation are caught between personal and family goals and local and state politics, as well as global human rights regimes, all of which make use of age categories to advance moralistic and ideological positions (Rosen 2007). Following Western norms, the UN Convention on the Rights of the Child (UNCRC) defines "childhood" as beginning at birth and ending at age eighteen, the so-called Straight-18 position (Sheppard 2000; Udombana 2006; UN General Assembly 1989: article 1). As a signatory to the convention, Ireland complies with this legal definition of childhood, although, as I will discuss below, it is clear that the social meaning of childhood (and even its legal boundaries) is malleable and disputed.

At times, the role of the state in upholding the rights of the child conflicts with its responsibility to control immigration; this causes the Irish state and the public to relate to members of the 1.5 generation like Eluhanla with unease. These tensions highlight a central paradox facing modern states regarding these migrant children: whether to protect them as children or apply the law to them as immigrants. These two choices conflict when states are faced with a failed asylum seeker who continues to reside within their borders, such as Olunkunle Eluhanla.

DEBATING DEPORTATION, DEBATING CHILDHOOD: ELUHANLA'S CASE

Eluhanla's case was brought to the attention of the media through public pro-test raised by his classmates and teachers. However, what really captured the Irish public's imagination was that Eluhanla was a student in his secondary education. At the time of his case, a series of similar cases involving child asylum seekers were in the news, and the Irish public was grappling with uncertainty regarding the moral limits of inclusion. For example, major news media covered the case of Nigerian asylum seeker Olivia Agbanlahor and her autistic son, Great, on an ongoing basis between 2005 and 2008. Although they were ultimately deported, there was extensive debate about the morality of sending away a child with special needs. Similarly, Pamela Izevbekhai and her two young daughters fought their asylum case on the grounds that the girls would be subject to female genital cir-cumcision if returned to Nigeria (2005–2011). After a tense public debate about the role of motherhood and the rights of the child, the Izevbekhai family was also eventually denied asylum and deported. Public debates about child protection and state immigration regulation like these were increasingly common in Ireland in the mid-2000s and highlight the fraught political and emotional landscape in which Eluhanla's case emerged.

Nineteen at the time of his deportation, Eluhanla was legally an adult in the eyes of the state. However, a provision within state welfare law allows for a student of secondary education under the age of twenty-one to be legally recognized as a child. Consequently, Eluhanla's student status—and therefore child status—was key to the challenge against his deportation. Multiple actors came together to mount the political challenge to Eluhanla's deportation, including nationally recognizable opposition-party politicians, religious figures, teachers, and students from around the country, as well as Eluhanla himself. These actors had several goals: (1) to highlight Eluhanla's status as a secondary school student; (2) to attempt to link Eluhanla's student status with the state mandate to provide special care to school-age children and; (3) to pressure the state to view this case, not as a law enforcement issue, but as a humanitarian cause.

To make these claims, protestors built on culturally embedded notions of childhood as a legally protected category. Historically, the concept of childhood has been key to advancing the right to self-governance and self-rule in Ireland. The constitution of Ireland asserts that children have a right to a family, home, and education. Although this right is not an explicit and independent constitutional clause, the courts have upheld these rights over the years. Most notably, in a 1990 landmark case, the Irish Supreme Court granted asylum seekers who had given birth to an "Irish-Born Child" (IBC) permission to remain in Ireland to care for their citizen-child under provision 41.1 of the Irish Constitution, which guarantees Irish children the right to the "care and comfort of its parents." Significantly, the Supreme Court reversed this finding on the very same grounds in 2003, asserting while IBCs were entitled to their parents' care, that care need not occur within Ireland (Decision of the Supreme Court, *Lobe and Osayande v. Minister for Justice Equality and Law Reform*, January 23, 2003). This opened up the possibility for the deportation of Irish-born citizen children along with their noncitizen parents. Emphasizing Eluhanla's legal exceptionality as a student, Eluhanla's supporters distributed images of him in his school uniform, and Eluhanla himself emphasized his student status in a radio interview from Lagos, Nigeria, after his deportation. He said,

> What happened was I got a letter from immigration that say a deportation order. . . . And they take me to detention. And they didn't even tell me that they were taking me to Nigeria that very day—from there! . . . So I was locked up and they called me outside and they say, "Ok, you are going to Nigeria now." I was in school in Ireland and I was about to finish my exam, I've already paid for my exam, to make a better life for myself. (RTE News at One 2005a)

Eluhanla went on to describe being taken directly from the schoolyard to the detention center, and then summarily deported without so much as the opportunity to pack his belongings or to change out of his school uniform.

As Eluhanla spoke from Nigeria, his schoolmates and teachers organized a public protest. Using their affectionate nickname for him, "'Kunle," parents, teachers, and Eluhanla's classmates dressed in their school uniforms and carried signs imploring the government to "Bring 'Kunle Home" and to "Stop deporting children from Ireland." Some in the crowd even called a halt to the deportation of all asylum seekers from Ireland. The protestors marched through Dublin to the Parliament building, where teachers, students, and government ministers gave rousing speeches to the crowd.

Opposition party member TD Joe Higgens, a Teachta Dála (i.e., member of the Lower House of Parliament), urged clemency for Eluhanla by evoking the symbol of his school uniform. From the steps of Parliament, the TD painted a picture of a hardworking schoolboy spirited away to a dangerous city. Using the Irish word for school, *iosolde*, TD Higgens explained,

> The manner of [Eluhanla's] deportation was shameful and shocking. He was taken in his school uniform . . . and he was dumped in Lagos with his public school, *iosolde*, uniform still on . . . with nowhere to go in a city which is extremely precarious at the best of times. . . . By the accounts of his teachers, [Olunkunle Eluhanla] was a model student, working very hard towards that goal. (RTE Morning Ireland 2005b)

Similarly, on a morning call-in show, Senator Pat Boat (a member of the Upper House of Parliament) emphasized Eluhanla's vulnerability as schoolboy rather than his legal age. Likening his deportation to child abduction, Senator Boat claimed that Eluhanla was deported directly from school. "It is completely unacceptable to be snatching school children out of the classroom, literally, and onto chartered flights and normal human dignity not to apply" (RTE News at One 2005a).

These varied claims for state compassion are constructed around assumptions about the needs of children. Political claims about the needs of children rely on a model of universal "modern" childhood characterized by domestication, schooling, and a lack of productivity (Stephens 1995). Anthropologists have pointed out that both "the child" and "childhood" have become sacrosanct in the West (Jenks 1996). This has made children central to state politics as an object in need of protection from problems constructed as "dangerous" to children. Jane Helleiner (1998) argues that, in Ireland, "modern childhood" is defined by settlement and education. In her study of the Irish state's assimilation program of its ethnic minority Traveller population (a gypsy population native to Ireland), Helleiner argues that, early in the Republic, Travellers became a target of state intervention because of their differing values of mobility and early marriage for children (which often resulted in minimal formal education). A discourse of Traveller child neglect was used to justify the forced settlement and formal education of Traveller children in Irish schools. Simultaneously, Irish children needed to be protected from Traveller children who were thought to spread disease. Helleiner effectively argues that the state was able to link anti-Traveller discourse to a discourse of child protection because there already existed a widespread acceptance that childhood must be "protected" as a necessary foundation for adult Irish citizenship. Childhoods that deviated from this model were portrayed as both dangerous and endangering. A discourse of child vulnerability was instrumental in bringing about the state-led, church-provided education system that is constitutionally guaranteed to Irish children and of concern in the Eluhanla case.

At the protest over Eluhanla's deportation, Teacher's Union leaders pled for state compassion over the strict application of the law. One union member argued that the state resources that had gone into the education of this young man would be all of naught if Eluhanla were not allowed to take his exit exam. She said, "I know the minister said that resources have been put into [Eluhanla's] education, but we feel that all that is futile if the end result isn't achieved. So we feel that humanitarian considerations should have been of the foremost importance here" (quoted in RTE News at One 2005b) The claimant positions Eluhanla's case in relation to both the state's edict to ethically administer public finances and the state's role as humanitarian leader.

Similarly, Eluhanla's classmates emphasized that, as a student, Eluhanla deserved clemency. Calling on the minister for justice (who maintains complete discretion to reverse individual asylum case decisions) to bring Eluhanla back to Ireland, one student-protester commented, "If we get the minister to see what he's done and to see it as a humane act instead of a legal act, maybe we can bring [Eluhanla] back" (News at One, March 23, 2005).

Soon, the Catholic archbishop of Dublin, Dr. Diarmuid Martin, weighed in on the debate. Bolstering the protestors' claim to Eluhanla's student-child status, the archbishop claimed that the state had a moral obligation to the well-being of children and should, therefore, allow Eluhanla to return to take his high school exam. While taking a hard-line position on the misuse of asylum law, the archbishop nonetheless argued that education is essential to a child's develop and is a young person's human right. The archbishop said,

> I am utterly against the abuse of asylum, and anybody who abuses asylum should face the consequences—even if it means deportation. But in this particular case we recognize that [young] asylum seekers are people and they have rights to their development. And luckily in Ireland they can have access to schools, and they do very well. But if we accept that, how could you possibly deport the young man just a few weeks before he was to do the leaving certificate [high school diploma]?

The education he received will certainly stand him good, but having a certificate is not about having a bit of paper. It would have been about the affirmation a young person gets by sitting in exam with his peers. With the sense of achievement and self esteem that that would have brought. Now, even if the person had to be deported, he would have gone away much more enhanced as a person. (RTE Morning Ireland 2005a)

Likening the status of immigrant youth to that of criminals as individuals with limited rights, the archbishop went on to say, "even in sentencing for criminal cases, judges will allow people to stay to allow people to carry out their leaving certificate [diploma]." In Ireland, 96 percent of public education is provided by the religious denominations, primarily the Roman Catholic Church (Coolahan et al. 2012), and the church is often described as the head of the family of the nation. However, at the time of Eluhanla's case, the Irish Catholic Church had been rocked by salacious accounts of child sexual and physical abuse, which severely diminished the moral authority of the church. Parents, who had entrusted the church with the education of their children, now railed against the church as a corrupt institution. Popular accounts described the once-full pews as empty as the church's moral authority. Consequently, the archbishop's comments were well timed to reassert the church as the spiritual leader of the nation. Once more, ethical claims about children and childhood emerged at the center of this social struggle.

Teachers, parents, students, politicians, and religious leaders, and even Olunkunle himself worked together to reframe the Eluhanla case as a humanitarian issue by highlighting his student-status and, by extension, his need for state protection as a child. Rather than as a delinquent foreigner, Eluhanla could now be understood as an Irish schoolboy entitled to an education and a sense of himself in the world. Instead of a fraudulent refugee who abused asylum law, Eluhanla was discursively framed as a child with the rights guaranteed by the Irish state. The ambiguity of Eluhanla as 1.5er, neither adult immigrant nor citizen-child of immigrants, enabled his supporters to negotiate these representations.

THE RESPONSE

In response to this public outcry, the embattled minister for justice, Minster McDowell, asserted that the state had fulfilled its ethical duty by educating Eluhanla (whether or not he had attained his degree), that Eluhanla was now an adult subject to the rule of law, and that it was time for that law to be enforced in this case. In a televised interview, the minister accepted Eluhanla's status as a "schoolboy" entitled to an education. However, Minister McDowell claimed that the state had fulfilled its duty to educate Eluhanla while he remained a minor and, that as he was an adult and a failed asylum seeker, it was now necessary to deport him in order to uphold the integrity of Irish immigration law. The minister said,

I want to say this: . . . [Eluhanla] came here as an unaccompanied minor at the age of seventeen years old—his independent claim for asylum before that age was independently considered by the Refugees Application body. He then appealed it to the independent Refugees Tribunal; he had the assistance of lawyers at all times. The Irish government has a policy of giving the highest standards of protection to people who seek asylum—asylum protection here in Ireland—and the particular facts of the case show that he was given very generous educational facilities by the Irish state. So, I don't want to get involved in individual cases, but I do want to say this: if you have a system of law—a system of immigration law—in a country, there are circumstances in which you have to deport people, *even* people at the age of nineteen. (RTE Morning Ireland 2005b)

When a journalist inquired about Eluhanla's humanitarian need as an orphan and as a schoolboy who had been deported while still in his school uniform, the minister cut him off with a curt reply that betrayed his consternation.

I don't accept the point about the school uniform, firstly. The second point is that I don't accept that he has no relatives, and thirdly, he came to Ireland as an unaccompanied minor—he didn't bring his relatives here to Ireland with him! . . . It is not the law of Ireland that orphans can come to Ireland or people who have lost both their parents can come to Ireland. If I made that the law, our immigration law would be in a shambles! I can't do that. People have to understand these decisions are difficult, but they are decisions which have to be made in the best interest of all the Irish people. (RTE Morning Ireland 2005b)

Countering the protester's call for humanitarian compassion, the minister asserted his authority and the rectitude of enforcing immigration law on a legal adult and a failed asylum seeker, suggesting that the very integrity of Ireland's immigration law was at stake in this decision.

Within a modern civil-legal framework, states take on the responsibility for protecting children and national boundaries within a discourse of rights that assumes a Western liberal understanding of the body, sovereignty, and space, values themselves that in the Irish context are prefigured by a Catholic morality. That is, "bodies in need of protection" (national and individual) emerge from a discourse of space that is defined by an essentially Western understanding of the body as a self-contained, autonomous unit. Protecting individual and national bodies (spaces) often complement one another, one serving as the proxy for the other; for example, nationalist narratives evoke kinship metaphors (Grewal 2006). However, the protection of national and individual bodies is at odds when it comes to child migrants, since the merit of protecting one body must be weighed against the merit of protecting the other. Since it is the state that ultimately decides the question of merit in an asylum case, the state must adjudicate between its basic function of protecting itself and its mandate to protect vulnerable individuals.

Caitríona Ni Laoire (2011) argues that policy makers view migrant children in terms of vulnerability and difference, causing some to perceive migrant children's presence in Ireland as problematic in and of itself because migrant children are thought of as being temporary and, therefore, less deserving of state investments and resources (including education). In this context, educating immigrant children could be viewed as an act of generosity (an act that can be revoked), rather than an obligation. For Minister McDowell, effective, coherent governance meant the exercise of sovereign power through the broad application of Irish immigration law and in the consistent execution of deportations, regardless of the emotional difficulty of denying a child an education. Thus, he reasoned, individual humanitarian concerns could not be considered reason enough to undercut the integrity of the immigration law.

In the proceeding days, however, the minister was bombarded with calls, letters, and complaints. Sensing the tide of public opinion turning against him, it took just two days for Minister McDowell to reverse this position. Conceding that his decision had been "a little bit harsh," the minister allowed Eluhanla to return on a six-month student visa. In his retraction statement, Minister McDowell said,

> Upon reflection, I should have given him a chance to finish his leaving cert. So I have decided that the best thing to do is to stop digging in and to do the right thing by letting him come back. . . . I think in the circumstances, and to maintain public confidence in the deportation system, it was correct to give him the time to finish his leaving certificate, and I want to thank those who brought this to my attention. . . . I always try to be fair in the decisions I make, but in this case I came to the conclusion that it wasn't publicly perceived as a fair decision, and that was uncomfortable. . . . I think that it's very important that the public confidence in the fairness of the procedures be maintained. (News at One March 24, 2005)

Anthropologists have noted that European immigrant regimes often treat migrant youth as immigrants first, and children second; however, public opinion may alter these priorities (Crawley 2006). In his rather dramatic and unusual reversal, the minister drew two key conclusions. First, he asserted that the public made clear to him that the individual facts of this case merited further consideration. Rather than the inflexible application of the law to a legal adult, Minister McDowell conceded that there *are* certain cases in which the regular application of the law could be considered inhumane; as he was a schoolboy, Eluhanla's deportation was tantamount to exiling a child. Secondly, the minister agreed that, together with the consistent application of the law, the integrity of the immigration system *also* requires public consent for the way in which the law is applied.

The minister's reaction suggests that the protesters successfully recast Eluhanla's case as a humanitarian issue. In essence, the protestors reframed the debate from one of state sovereignty over space to one of the moral rectitude of protecting the child. Minister McDowell's reversal suggests that he was aware that the hard line he had taken had put his moral authority into question. Consequently, the minister's demonstration of compassion was required to maintain state legitimacy, and Eluhanla was allowed to return to Ireland in March of 2005 to complete his leaving certificate and earn his high school diploma.

Political struggles like Eluhanla's highlight the real impact that debates over the moral and legal limits of belonging can have on the life opportunities and sense of belonging for migrant youth of the 1.5 generation. As symbols in a critical debate over the legitimacy of the state and the limits of belonging in Ireland, immigrant children within the legal space of the state highlights the state's dual roles as enforcer and protector and call attention to an underlying tension that these paradoxical functions evoke for the Irish public. State officials, public protestors, and individuals trace battle lines around childhood in their efforts to assert belonging (or nonbelonging) at the intersection of moral and legal spaces of the modern nation state.

CONCLUSION

Several months after he completed his exams and graduated from secondary school, Eluhanla was ticketed for driving without car insurance. This made him vulnerable to deportation as a "threat to the common good" (RTE News, January 25 2006). Having completed his education, Eluhanla was no longer a "child" by any legal definition, and the moral and legal conflicts that had beset Eluhanla's case had dissipated. Consequently, the Department of Justice acted by again deporting Eluhanla back to Nigeria.

The complicated debate over Eluhanla highlights the ongoing moral and political challenge that 1.5-generation children, particularly those who are failed asylum seekers, pose to intersecting spaces of legal and moral authority. As a particularly powerful object of governance, the rights of the child emerged as a symbol at the nexus of this debate over sovereign power and state humanitarianism. Both the protestors and the minister pushed the very legal limits of the definition of a child in order to contest Eluhanla's deportation. Ultimately, both sides agreed to temporarily gerrymander the definition of the child in order to resolve the crisis of state legitimacy that the case had provoked.

Moments of public conflict, like this, offer insights into the ways communities demarcate boundaries and negotiate belonging. In places, such as Ireland, where dramatic demographic shifts are challenging deeply held beliefs about national identity, social conflicts are expressed through debates over the role of the state, the purpose of government, and modes of governance. Exploring moments of tension, such as that provoked by the Eluhanla case, highlights ongoing struggles over belonging within local contexts and raises important questions about the way that states and publics exercise power. Likewise, these struggles highlight questions about the place of migrant youth within the legal and moral spaces of states. For migrant youth of the 1.5 generation, who exist both inside and outside the reach of state power, belonging is complex and has real repercussions for these children's life chances and sense of personhood. As states strive to resolve the legal questions newcomers present, the physical presence of immigrant children within the state present new moral quandaries that can be neither easily anticipated nor easily resolved, but which have far reaching consequences for individual belonging within a nation.

REFERENCES

Bernard, H. Russell. 2008. *Research Methods in Anthropology: Qualitative and Quantitative.* Plymouth, UK: Altamira Press.

Central Statistics Office (CSO). 2006. *Census 2006: Preliminary Report.* Dublin: Stationary Office, July.

———. 2009. *Statistical Yearbook of Ireland 2009.* Dublin: Stationary Office, November.

———. 2012. *Statistical Yearbook of Ireland 2011.* Dublin: Stationary Office, November.

Chatterjee, Partha. 1993. *The Nation and Its Fragments: Colonial and Postcolonial Histories.* Princeton, NJ: Princeton University Press.

Children's Rights Alliance. 2006. *From Rhetoric to Rights: Second Shadow Report to the United Nations Committee on the Rights of the Child.* March.

Coe, Cati. 2008. The Structuring of Feeling in Ghanaian Transnational Families. *City and Society* 20 (2): 222–50.

Cole, Jennifer, and Deborah Durham. 2008. Introduction. In *Figuring the Future: Globalization and the Temporalities of Children and Youth*, Jennifer Cole and Deborah Durham, eds., pp. 3–23. Santa Fe: School for Advanced Research Press.

Coolahan, John, et al. 2012. Forum on Patronage and Pluralism in the Primary Sector: Report of the Forum's Advisory Group. Irish Department of Education.

Crawley, Heaven. 2006. *Child First, Migrant Second: Ensuring That Every Child Matters.* London: Immigration Law Practitioners' Association.

———. 2010. "No One Gives You a Chance to Say What You Are Thinking": Finding Space for Children's Agency in the UK Asylum System. *Area* 42 (2): 162–69.

Eastmond, Marita, and Henry Ascher. 2011. In the Best Interest of the Child? The Politics of Vulnerability and Negotiations for Asylum in Sweden. *Journal of Ethnic and Migration Studies* 37 (8): 1185–200.

Giner, Clotilde. 2007. The Politics of Childhood and Asylum in the UK. *Children and Society* 21 (4): 249–60.

Grewal, Inderpal. 2006. "Security Moms" in the Early Twentieth Century United States: The Gender of Security in Neoliberalism. *Women's Studies Quarterly* 34 (1/2): 25–39.

Helleiner, Jane. 1998. Contested Childhood: The Discourse and Politics of Minority Childhood in Ireland. *Childhood: A Global Journal of Child Research* 5 (3): 303–24.

Irish Naturalization and Immigration Service. 2005. *Asylum Brief: Asylum–Some Key Facts Emerging from Our Determination Process.*

Jenks, Chris. 1996. *Childhood.* London: Open University, Milton Keynes.

Laoire, Caitríona Ni. 2011. Introduction. In *Childhood and Migration in Europe: Portraits of Mobility, Identity and Belonging in Contemporary Ireland*, Caitríona Ni Laoire, ed., 17–18. Surrey, England: Ashgate.

Office of the Refugee Applications Commissioner (ORAC). 2009. *Annual Report 2009.* Dublin: Stationary Office.

Quinn, Emma, et al. 2008. *Handbook on Immigration and Asylum in Ireland 2007.* Research Series 5, October, Dublin, Economic and Social Research Institute.

Rosen, David. M. 2007. Child Soldiers, International Humanitarian Law, and the Globalization of Childhood. *American Anthropologist* 109 (2): 296–306.

RTE Morning Ireland. 2005a. Dr Diarmuid Martin, the Archbishop of Dublin, Says Olunkunle Eluhanla Should Not Have Been Deported before Sitting His Leaving Certificate. March 24.

———. 2005b. Joe Higgins, Socialist Party TD, Says the Manner in Which Olunkunle Eluhanla's Deportation Was Carried Out Is Scandalous. March 22.

RTE News at One. 2005a. Olunkunle Eluhanla Expresses His Relief at Being Allowed to Return to Sit His Leaving Certificate. March 24.

———. 2005b. Martina Fitzgerald Speaks to Students Who Protested outside the Dáil This Morning in Support of Olunkunle Eluhanla. March 23.

RTE Nine News. 2006. John Kilraine Reports on the Plight of Olunkunle Eluhanla. January 25.

Scheper-Hughes, Nancy, and Carolyn Sargent (eds.). 1998. *Small Wars: The Cultural Politics of Childhood.* Berkeley: University of California Press.

Sheppard, Ann. 2000. Child Soldiers: Is the Optional Protocol Evidence of an Emerging "Straight-18" Consensus? *International Journal of Children's Rights* 8 (1): 37–70.

Stephens, Sharon (ed.). 1995. *Children and the Politics of Culture.* Princeton, NJ: Princeton University Press.

Udombana, Nsongurua. 2006. War Is Not Child's Play! International Law and the Prohibition of Children's Involvement in Armed Conflicts. *Temple International and Comparative Law Journal* 20 (1): 57.

UN General Assembly. 1989. *Convention on the Rights of the Child.* Document A/RES/44/25. December 12.

Watters, Charles. 2008. *Refugee Children: Towards the Next Horizon.* Routledge London.

AFTERWORD:
SPACES OF IDENTITY

Rejecting the Hegemony of Assimilation

Louise Lamphere

These nine chapters give us new insights into the ways young 1.5- and second-generation immigrants are forging identities that preserve and rework cultural meanings from their parents' homelands yet simultaneously incorporate the values and behaviors of the nations to which their parents immigrated. As the editors of this volume (Faith Nibbs and Caroline Brettell) point out, the earlier literature on the second generation of "new immigrants" (roughly the children of those who left their homelands in the last fifty years) was focused largely on assimilation. This literature was preoccupied with the possibility that the second generation would not fully integrate into the societies to which the parents had migrated. In the United States, studies often utilized macro-level data on education, the acquisition of English, occupational mobility, and intermarriage with established residents as indicators of assimilation and integration (Portes 1996; Zhou 1997; Portes and Rumbaut 2001; Alba and Nee 2003).[1]

In Europe, early studies more typically analyzed barriers to assimilation such the rise of anti-immigrant political parties, and national ideologies that blocked citizenship or prevented the maintenance of cultural traditions. For example, in Germany until 2000, children of Turkish immigrants could not claim citizenship since they were not German by heritage, while in France beginning in 2004, the hijab could not be worn by young Muslim women in schools since this betrayed French adherence to the value of *laïcité* or secularism (Bowen 2007; Mandel 2008).

This collection picks up on a more recent, but still not dominant, strand in both first- and second-generation studies, one that foregoes the emphasis on assimilation. Here a number of researchers stress the transnational ties of the new immigrant communities and focus on the attachments that contemporary populations maintain with their homelands leading to cultural retention, often helped through the continuous replenishment of immigrants between 1980 and 2000 (Levitt and Waters 2002: 2; Waters and Jimenez 2005). First-generation immigrants sustained economic, political, and religious links to their countries of origin through remittances, frequent visits, and participation in hometown associations or fiestas. Their children often accompanied them on homeland visits, and as this volume shows, these children have developed transnational ties but in different ways than their parents. But even for those who do not visit their parents' homeland, the resources, discourses, and social contacts of their parents' country of origin strongly shape their lives, as Nina Glick Schiller (1999) has pointed out. Thus more authors are emphasizing the ways in which second-generation youth draw from both the cultures of their parents' homeland and the country of their own birth or childhood. Influenced by the work of Homi Bhabha (1994), Lisa Lowe (1996), and Pnina Werbner and Tariq Modood (1997), several anthropologists have suggested the terms "cultural hybridity" and "lived hybridity" (Shankhar 2008; Brettell and Nibbs 2009) to characterize the second-generation experience. In a similar vein, Vertovec (2009) introduced the term "transnational habitus" to describe the transnational aspects of second-generation lives.

Expanding on the social processes that generate lived hybridity and a transnational habitus, the authors in this volume examine second-generation youth through the lens of identity outlining the way individuals as parts of kin and friend networks forge repertoires of "self-making." As anthropologists they utilize participant observation, interviewing, and individually written textual materials. Emphasizing identity allows them to explore the variability among individuals in the populations they are studying and more easily characterize the variety of different social contexts through which youth move. Yet, because these chapters represent cases from several different nations and one analyzes second-generation experience at two points in the twentieth century, there is still attention to historical and national contexts and ideologies as they impact second-generation immigrants.

In this Afterword, I focus on several themes that are shared across groups of chapters: the creation of transnational identities in shifting spaces, the impact of new social media, and the significance of historical and social context. I then end with comments on what is left out and thus where research on the children of immigrants might move next as well as on the policy implications of research like that encompassed by this volume.

FLEXIBLE SPACES: CREATING TRANSNATIONAL IDENTITIES IN SHIFTING CONTEXTS

Parallel to the focus on identity is the shift in this collection away from institutions or class locations to "spaces," often discussed as contexts or social fields. As Nibbs and Brettell clearly state in their introduction, "spaces" for them are not bounded and fortified locations or even institutions such as churches, schools, or prisons that are part of religious or state bureaucracies. Rather they are flexible, shifting spaces as the term "social field" also suggests. Several of the authors emphasize the importance of family, kin, and friend networks in creating the spaces and social fields, but the chapters analyzing organizations suggest that they are flexible, loose spaces rather than rigid, fortified ones. The Italian youth associations studied by Bruno Riccio have been created by the young immigrants themselves (mostly students) and very much depend on energetic leadership rather than a formal perpetuating structure. The annual Asian American Leadership and Education Conference (AALEC) described by Brettell is a program of a similar student organization (the Asian Council). In both the Italian and US cases, larger university institutions may have defined much of the lives of these second-generation youth, but these two contexts left room for relatively autonomous organizing by the young immigrants themselves.

There are two exceptions in the collection—the mental care health centers and schools in Stéphanie Larchanché's article and the Irish legal and political institutions that were so important in the asylum case described by Erin Moran. These remind us of the power that institutions with laws, rule, and regulations and the professionals or officials who implement them have in denigrating the lives of immigrant youth and often stigmatizing their behavior.

Transnationalism has been analyzed in a number of different domains (political economic, social, and religious) for first-generation immigrants (Levitt and Jaworsky 2007), but this collection goes into much greater depth than most previous work in describing the extent and variation of transnationalism as practiced across second-generation groups (whom many thought would probably not engage in transnational networks). The actual cases, it turns out, actually represent a range of transnational ties. On the one end are the shin-nisei whom Tsuda calls "fully bicultural." Almost all of Tsuda's shin-nisei interviewees are fluent in Japanese, visit Japan frequently, and are comfortable in monolingual Japanese contexts in both Japan and the United States. Several talk about easily "switching to a Japanese identity" or "being totally accepted as Japanese in Japan." Yet these shin-nisei are likely to see themselves as both Japanese and American and like the idea of a fluid, flexible, and transnational identity.

Next are the Azorean second- and third-generation immigrants who, like the shin-nisei, are fluent in their parents' language (Azorean Portuguese), visit relatives in the Azores during summer vacations, and feel as comfortable in the Azores as in Canada. Within the framework of constructing a transnational habitus (Vertovec 2009), Le Gall and Gherghel characterize these young people as cultivating a nostalgic, emotional transnationalism. This pattern survives into the third generation, perhaps because it is based on childhood years steeped in dense Montreal Portuguese neighborhoods with participation in local church activities, religious festivals, and family life filled with Portuguese food, customs, and daily conversation in Portuguese.

Hmong youth may also be part of tight-knit communities and dense kin networks, but since the Hmong fled from Laos after the Vietnam War, contact with their homeland and return visits are less likely than with other members of the diaspora. Perhaps it is because they share a similar history of expulsion and Western resettlement, or because of an unintended consequence of having more access to technological forms of communication, either of which has resulted in more intense contact with German Hmong as described in Nibbs's chapter. Vietnamese second-generation immigrants are in a similar position since most are from South Vietnamese families or Catholic families who were expelled from North Vietnam in 1954. Although many visit relatives still in the South, others are reluctant to return because of antigovernment sentiments. Yet connections with family members in France, Austria, Australia, and other countries are maintained through visits and e-mail. This makes the pilgrimages of Vietnamese immigrants to former refugee camps in Indonesia all the more interesting. As Linda Ho Peché suggests, these camps are spaces where second- and third-generation young people can learn about family experiences and commemorate those who died in the camps. Participants, Ho Peché suggests, are partaking in a discourse of rebirth and empowerment, reclaiming the label of "boat people" as a positive one and building a "heritage" Through these trips children of immigrants are also forging transnational connections to their ancestral homeland and religious traditions.

In contrast to the chapters emphasizing transnational spaces of identity are those that focus more on how identities are formulated in local contexts. Lisa Haayen describes Mexican teenagers in Pleasant Park in Dallas who turn toward neighborhood, school, and association relationships to create friendships that solidify their identities. At the Dallas university discussed by Brettell, South Asian university students participate in local campus South Asian and Asian associations, while some second-generation Italian immigrants, as described by Bruno Riccio, have joined broad non-ethnic-specific organizations with local chapters in Bologna. These immigrant-run organizations focus on local ties and discrimination rather than on homelands or heritage preservation. Given the focus of these three chapters, it is difficult to gauge whether these second-generation immigrants have strong transnational ties through family, kin, and return visits, but it seems likely that they are present and could be as important as local ties in shaping identities.

Finally, the nisei raised in the United States before and during World War II have very few transnational ties. They consider themselves to be Japanese Americans, speak little Japanese, and have rarely, if ever, visited Japan. This more assimilated stance, Tsuda argues, is directly attributable to their experiences in relocation camps and the concomitant pressure to become Americanized both before and during World War II.

This range and variety in transnational contacts indicates that researchers should pay closer attention to their role in identity formation. There seem to be at least three different models. The shin-nisei and Azorean youth seem to have dual identities being either Japanese or Azorean in some contexts and switching to being American in other settings. In contrast, South Asian students described by Brettell and Nibbs (2009) have embraced "lived hybridity" as exemplified by the student celebration of Diwali festival that combines traditional Hindu elements (dress, regional foods, décor) with more Americanized elements (a fashion show, talent show and after party). Second-generation nisei represent the assimilationist possibility where these older second generation saw themselves as different (i.e., Japanese Americans) but with few transnational ties and little in the way of Japanese language or cultural heritage. Hmong, Vietnamese, Mexican, and second-generation youth in Italy may fit well into these categories or be in the process of forming other kinds of identities. Whether the frequency, strength, or characteristics of transnational ties impact these different models or whether structural factors in the receiving society are more important is a question for future research.

FORGING KIN AND FRIEND NETWORKS: UTILIZING THE INTERNET AND SOCIAL MEDIA

It is both striking and significant that many of these chapters involve identity formation through use of the Internet and social media. This is surely a change from the 1980s and 1990s when the first second-generation immigrants were being studied. In the hands of second-generation immigrants the Internet is a useful took in making connections, especially transnational ones. For Azorean teens in Montreal, bonds with Azorean cousins, friends, and others can deepen contacts made on holiday visits. Their parents and grandparents might have traveled home for an annual vacation, visited their home village for a summer feast day, or invested in a house for retirement. They maintained more frequent contact through letters or, in more recent years, on the phone. However, their children sustain contacts through e-mail, Skype, chat room participation, and Facebook pages. These links reinforce the Azorean rather than the Canadian side of second-generation identities, keep interest in language maintenance alive, and build greater attachment to the Azoreans than might have otherwise been possible. Here the new media are opening and deepening transnational ties and hybrid or multiple identities.

In her chapter "Too White and Didn't Belong," Faith Nibbs also shows that Hmong teenagers forge transnational links with coethnics, in this case between American Hmong and those in Germany. But rather than emphasizing dual identities or hybridity, the Hmong teenagers have used the Internet to police ethnic boundaries. Second-generation youth (especially the males) engage in "intraethnic othering," that is, shunning those whose language skills are not up to par. There is much more emphasis on marrying someone who is Hmong as well. Hence, putting forward one's linguistic and cultural knowledge on one's Facebook page and evaluating those skills in others is partly to weed out potential marriage partners who are not sufficiently "Hmong." Marrying a non-Hmong German or American casts one out of the family and the ethnic group as well. The Internet in this case is a tool for consolidating Hmong identity rather than sanctioning hybridity or assimilation.

A third example comes from Bruno Riccio's analysis of second-generation associations in Italy. They employ websites in a two-pronged way: to create ties among young second-generation immigrants and to change Italian perceptions of immigrants and alter Italian immigration policies. For example, the fifteen-hundred-member AssoCina started as a small online chat group for second-generation Chinese youth that was purely a means of making connections and supporting identity issues. Its later full-blown website has taken on other functions. It has a "news" section where members write their own articles combating stereotypes about the Chinese or articles about citizenship. One member called this offering "counter-information," while another emphasized it was a way of "letting ourselves be known to the Italian audience."

Of course the Dallas Mexican American teenagers who engaged in creating intense and satisfying friendships with other Mexican Americans may also be using cell phones, texting, and Facebook to solidify their networks or particular "best friend" relationships. And South Asian students in Dallas may be just as active in constructing electronic mailing lists and websites as the second-generation immigrants in Bologna. The collection as a whole and other literature on second-generation use of new media (Block and Buckingham 2007; Brinkerhoff 2009; Alonso and Oiarzabal 2010) suggests that future research on immigrant youth will uncover additional ways in which new media are being used both to solidify language and cultural heritage and to forge flexible, transnational identities that can range from more to less focused on their parents' homelands.

HISTORICAL AND NATIONAL CONTEXT

One of the strengths of this collection is that it includes articles that span historical periods and implicitly contrasts second-generation identities as shaped in different national contexts (Canada, the United States, France, Ireland, Italy). Takeyuki Tsuda, by examining two different second generations gives us a sense of how different the 1920s through 1940s were from more recent times as contexts that pressed immigrants to assimilate. This was particularly acute for nisei Japanese because of their experience as children in Japanese internment camps. The shin-nisei interviewees, by contrast, speak fluent Japanese, travel often in Japan, and feel comfortable being Japanese in Japanese-speaking contexts or Americans in English-speaking contexts.

The Tsuda chapter reminds us that it is also important to characterize our own time and how it has shaped the new immigration and the possibilities for identity formation for second-generation youth. Some of these characteristics include the increased flow of capital, the creation of a global economy, and demand of countries in the global north (the United States, Canada, and Europe) for labor in the global south. More recently this need for labor has increased in the growing cities of the oil-rich sector of the Middle East and in the growing cities of a rapidly urbanizing China (which has solved this issue with vast numbers of internal migrants).

Nations have dealt with immigrant labor forces in a variety of ways through birthright and naturalization citizenship policies that impact identities. Both the United States and Canada have birthright citizenship. In the United States, 1.5-generation immigrants whose parents are undocumented and who came to the United States as children (now called Dreamers) face the greatest difficulties since they cannot be legally employed or receive Medicaid benefits or federal financial aid for college tuitions. France, Germany, and Italy are more restrictive but have policies that allow eventual citizenship. Children of immigrant parents born in these countries can become citizens only after they have reached adulthood (France and Italy) or after parents have lived in the country for eight years (Germany). Children who come as immigrants can be naturalized but only after a period of continuous residence, and after submitting a birth certificate, residence certificate, and, in the case of Italy, other certifications.

Perhaps Ireland is the most restrictive of the countries discussed in this collection. Ireland repealed birthright citizenship, and since 2005, a person is entitled to Irish citizenship only if during the four-year period preceding the person's birth one of the parents has been a resident for at least three years. Naturalization is discretionary and only for those who are eighteen years or older and of good character. They also need to swear loyalty to the state and have met a four-year residency requirement. Asylum seekers have none of these possibilities unless the minister of justice and equality waives one or more of these conditions for someone who is recognized as a refugee or stateless person.

Thus we see that European societies have been or have become more reluctant to grant citizenship through birthright or naturalization amid anti-immigrant sentiment. This is clearly discussed by Riccio concerning Italy where he mentions media presentations of immigration as a threat, the stigmatization of non-European immigrants, and a form of cultural racism where being "black" and Italian are seem as mutually exclusive (Andall 2002). The associations he studied are a response to an environment of discrimination. Thus for many of his interviewees legal citizenship is not the primary issue but rather equal treatment. As one of his research participants said, "I think the second generation should go beyond formal citizenship and work on the sense of belonging to a territory and on the meaning participating in its life." This is clearly a reference to what Rosaldo has termed "cultural citizenship." This concept refers to the "right to be different and to belong in a participatory democratic sense." Cultural citizenship entails the "full membership in a group and the ability to influence one's destiny by having significant voice in basic decisions" (Rosaldo 2004: 402).

Aihwa Ong takes a very different approach to the concept of cultural citizenship, aligning it to the idea of subjectification or subject making. "Cultural citizenship is a dual process of self-making and being made within webs of power linked to the nation state and civil society" (Ong 1996: 738). The process of subjectification or subject making is clear in two chapters that deal with state and institutional discourses and the wielding of formal and informal power. In Stéphanie Larchanché's chapter, schools and mental health care centers in France are sites where subtle labeling of second-generation youth is difficult to dislodge. Some "children of immigrants" (itself a stigmatizing category) are classified as those with learning or behavioral "difficulties" often thought to be due to immigrant family structures, lifestyles, and child-rearing practices. The school psychologist often mediated between teachers who insisted that a child be labeled as having a disability and parents who had a very different explanation for their child's behavior. In addition, indicators of class status (dress, appearance, residence in a homeless center) are seen as matters of "culture" rather than connected to economic distress.

Erin Moran offers a glimpse into the power of the state to define and control an immigrant's life chances and definition of self through the heartrending story of a young Nigerian asylum seeker who was deported from Ireland wearing his school uniform just before he was to take his final high school exam. His teachers and classmates helped bring the case to national attention, stressing his vulnerability as a child, his right to complete his secondary school education, and the humanitarian nature of the case. The minister of justice initially refused to allow the student to return to Ireland, but after a barrage of calls and letters, he reversed his decision, indicating that public protest can, in some cases, counter state power.

What is interesting about both of these chapters is the role nonimmigrants (school psychologists, classmates, politicians, journalists) have in attempting to upend state decisions or intervene as they are being made, often calling on other cultural constructs (e.g., the notion of the "child" as vulnerable, in need of care) to build a counterhegemonic logic that is less stigmatizing. These are attempts to bring immigrant children and asylum seekers into a space of belonging, no longer treated as "others" or "second-class" outsiders.

CARRYING THE RESEARCH FORWARD: MORE ATTENTION TO GENDER AND CLASS

In the context of analyzing spaces of identity, second-generation scholarship will be strengthened with additional analysis of the role of class and gender in forging identities and transnational networks. The role of gender in immigration was especially salient in US anthropology through the work of Patricia Pessar (Grasmuck and Pessar 1991; Pessar 1999, 2003, 2007), Maxine Margolis (1994), Yen Le Espiritu (1993, 2003), and Nancy Foner (2008). With some exceptions (Gunewardena and Kingsolver 2007; Boehm 2012), recent studies have been dominated by sociologists, political scientists, and women's studies scholars, especially those researching caregiving occupations (nursing, child care, domestic work, home care workers) and the lives of female immigrants from the global south. And class was crucial to the formulation of segmentary assimilation theory, since many of those in the second-generation populations that were downwardly mobile in the United States were from lower income groups in their homelands (Haitians, Mexicans, Dominicans, Cambodians) while those from a higher socioeconomic status had higher educational aspirations and achievement (Portes and Rumbaut 2001).

This collection focuses on ethnicity and cultural heritage although there are some tantalizing hints about the role of class and gender. In terms of gender, Lisa Haayen shows that young Mexican males make friends as a way to deal with the daily pressure to engage with drugs and alcohol and provide support for decisions to "stay on the right track." In contrast, girls often use their friendships to work out issues about education, motherhood, and pregnancy. Daughters have transformed their mothers' expectations that they will master the traditional skills of cooking, cleaning, and hosting family gatherings into a vision that these skills will be part of being independent women, able to care for themselves, rather than just wives and mothers. They have also been able to convince their mothers that they should participate in school sports and extracurricular activities including those important for college admissions.

Faith Nibbs shows how young Hmong males are more rigorous in imposing standards of "Hmong-ness" including language proficiency on young women. They are often effective in stigmatizing or marginalizing young women, seeing them as "whitewashed" and thus outside of the pool of possible mates. For their part, women seem careful not to post material that would be out of line with their Hmong identities. Nibbs sees this trend as associating females with "whiteness," and indeed at least two women struggled with their decisions to marry outside the Hmong community. Similar incorporation of gender analysis will be an important contribution to future work as well. For example, Le Gall and Gherghel's research may be enhanced by examining gender differences among their Azorean interviewees. Among the ten young women and four young men quoted extensively in the case material, perhaps there are no differences in either the content or type of transnational relationships these young people cultivate; but the Nibbs and Haayen chapters suggest some possibilities that could be examined.

The chapters by Larchanché and Moran give us pictures of what Pierre Bourdieu calls the Left Hand of the neoliberal state (public education, health, social assistance, public housing) and the Right Hand of the state (enforcing economic discipline through budget cuts, fiscal incentives, and deregulation) (Bourdieu et al. 1993). Loic Waquant has argued for the inclusion of judicial and penal institutions (the police, the courts, and the prisons) into the Right Hand side. The Left Hand is dominated by a female labor force (teachers, social workers, school psychologists, welfare workers, nurses, child care workers), while the Right Hand is composed of a predominantly male labor force (police, immigration agents, prison guards, lawyers, and judges). The female-dominated professions are often associated with a care ideology rather than a punitive, legal one that holds sway in the male-dominated penal institutions. More recently under neoliberal state regimes, there has been much blurring of the boundary between these two functions as the social service provisions of the state have been rolled back (welfare rights, social security payments, government-funded health care, housing supplements) and have become more punitive. This is born out in the French case that shows how women teachers, administrators, and advisors can have rigid views of how to apply rules and regulations and can also have stigmatizing views about immigrant families and cultures. This dovetails with the Irish case, where the Right Hand (penal and judicial institutions) plays a conservative role in enforcing a narrow interpretation of immigration law, until public sentiment pushed officials to relent. Nevertheless, more can be done in this field of study by analyzing how these two very different parts of the state operate to block or enhance the possibilities for both legal and cultural citizenship.

Much more is waiting to be said about class, and it will be fruitful to use class as an analytic category for further examining differences in second-generation identities. The Mexican youth of Pleasant Park seem to be working class, since a number of the males work as busboys and waiters, and I suspect that many of the Azorean and Hmong families came to Canada and the United States as working-class or low-income immigrants. The contributors here reference other studies of Azoreans and Hmong indicating that these immigrants entered factory and service jobs (Azoreans) or were refugees who had welfare, food stamps, Medicaid, and rent subsidies for their first years in the United States (Hmong). One of the intriguing questions is how many of these second-generation youth (from the Azores, Laos, and Mexico) have access to educational opportunities that will propel them into lower-middle-class or middle-class occupations. Future work on educational and occupational placement will help locate these young people in the class structure of Montreal, Dallas, and other locations if we knew more about the economy of the cities and the occupations of their parents. Their media savvy suggests a middle-class orientation. On the other hand, cell phones, computers, and Facebook pages are now so widespread that, for example, young Navajo (from rural and low-income families) text each other hourly and have access to face Facebook pages.

In contrast, the students at the Texas college Brettell studied seem to be from much more affluent backgrounds with professional upper-middle-class parents and perhaps private school educations. However, some (e.g., Vietnamese students) may be from more modest backgrounds and have scholarships, loans, and student jobs on campus. The second-generation youth in Bologna are primarily university students it seems, though it is not clear how they fit into the Italian class structure. The shin-nisei are clearly from affluent, business-oriented families and probably contrast with the backgrounds of the nisei who in their young years may have been children of small entrepreneurs, farmers, or even service workers. A careful class analysis of local economies, first-generation immigrant jobs, and educational opportunities will help us better understand the potential for class mobility, frequency of homeland visits, and opportunities to utilize cell phones, computers, and other technologies that ease transnational contacts, language maintenance, and heritage preservation. It may be that working-class communities can provide just as rich an environment to support bicultural and transnational identities as do upper-middle-class and wealthy contexts, though possibly through different strategies. Alternatively, working-class second generation youth maybe restricted in the types of new media they can access unless they are enrolled in colleges or universities or are located in work places that support learning these tools.

It is difficult in any study to keep at the forefront of analysis such varied aspects of intersectionality as ethnicity/race, class, gender, and sexuality, but it will be important to add further background and analysis on each of these if we are to understand the relative impact of national context, state institutions, local economies, educational institutions, and new media in creating different experiences for second-generation immigrants as they continue to mature, form families, and move through different occupational situations.

There is much here that is relevant for immigration policy, especially since there are forces for change as well as retrenchment in both Europe and North American. First and foremost is changing the notion that the integration of immigrant communities, including the second generation, depends on assimilation rather than the possibility that dual or hybrid identities or a transnational habitus can contribute to a vibrant twenty-first-century nation-state. Second, researchers can collaborate with nongovernmental organizations, advocacy groups, and educational institutions to support immigration reforms that can encourage and support equal access to education, housing, and jobs for immigrant youth. Along with this would be work with programs already in existence that foster language and heritage preservation and that incorporate this kind of diversity into school curricula and public events that reach broad audiences. Third, writing and public presentations would help expand notions of citizenship and more flexible approaches to identity beyond monolithic and narrow categories. This would also support and encourage the sort of dual and hybrid identities being created by second-generation youth.

This collection paves the way to an acceptance of the position that does not stress assimilation, but shows how second-generation immigrant youth are forging transnational relationships and strategies that perpetuate language and cultural retention. It is no longer adequate to see second-generation immigrants as "caught between two worlds" or facing downward rather than "successful" assimilation. There is not one or two, but a variety of patterns across and within ethnic groups and national contexts. Identities may be appropriately called bicultural, dual, and hybrid. This collection is an excellent prelude to future research that will continue to explore how second- and third-generation immigrants carve out new terrain as they create ways to retain their cultural heritage and yet find acceptance in the societies where they will continue to reside.

NOTE

1. Both Alba and Nee's revision of traditional assimilation theory (2003) and Portes and Zhou's (1993) emphasis on segmented assimilation leave room for ethnic neighborhoods, economic enclaves, and language and cultural maintenance. But they argue that these will be less relevant for the second and especially the third generation, as children and grandchildren move into other sectors of the economy, acquire more education, and speak only English at home.

REFERENCES

Alba, Richard, and Victor Nee. 2003. *Remaking the American Mainstream: Assimilation and Contemporary Immigration*. Cambridge, MA: Harvard University Press.

Alonso, Andoni, and Pedro Oiarzabal. 2010. *Diasporas in the New Media Age: Identity, Politics, and Community*. Reno: Nevada University Press.

Andall, Jaqueline. 2002. Second Generation Attitude? African-Italians in Milan. *Journal of Ethnic and Migration Studies* 28 (3): 389–407.

Bhabha, Homi K. 1994. *The Location of Culture*. New York: Routledge.

Bhabha, Homi K. 1996. Cultures in Between. In *Questions of Cultural Identity*, Stuart Hall and Paul du Gay eds., pp. 53–60. London: Sage.

Block, Liesbeth de, and David Buckingham. 2007. *Global Children, Global Media: Migration, Media and Childhood*. New York: Palgrave.

Boehm, Deborah A. 2012. *Intimate Migrations: Gender, Family, and Illegality among Transnational Mexicans*. New York: New York University Press.

Bourdieu, Pierre et al. 1993. *Weight of the World: Social Suffering in Contemporary Society*. Stanford, CA: Stanford University Press.

Bowen, John. 2007. *Why the French Don't Like Headscarves: Islam, the State and Public Spaces*. Princeton, NJ: Princeton University Press.

Brettell, Caroline B., and Faith G. Nibbs. 2009. Lived Hybridity: Second-Generation Identity Construction through College Festival. *Identities: Global Studies in Culture and Power* 16 (6): 678–99.

Brinkerhoff, Jennifer. 2009. *Digital Diasporas: Identity and Transnational Engagement*. New York: Cambridge University Press.

Espiritu, Yen Le. 1999. Gender and Labor in Asian Immigrant Families. *American Behavioral Scientist* 42 (4): 628–47.

———. 2003. *Home Bound: Filipino American Lives across Cultures, Communities, and Countries*. Berkeley: University of California Press, 2003.

Foner, Nancy. 2008. Gender and Migration: West Indians in Comparative Perspective. *International Migration* 47 (1): 3–29.

Glick Schiller, Nina. 1999. Transmigrants and Nation-States: Something Old and Something New in the US Immigrant Experience. In *The Handbook of International*

Migration: The American Experience, Charles Hirschman, Philip Kasinitz, and Josh De Wind eds., pp. 94–119. New York: Russell Sage Foundation.

Grasmuck, Sherri, and Patricia R. Pessar. 1991. *Between Two Islands: Dominican International Migration*. Berkeley: University of California Press.

Gunewardena, Nandini, and Ann Kingsolver. 2007. *The Gender of Globalization: Women Navigating Cultural and Economic Marginalities*. Santa Fe, NM: School of Advanced Research Press.

Levitt, Peggy, and B. Nadya Jaworsky. 2007. Transnational Migration Studies: Past Developments and Future Trends. *Annual Review of Sociology* 33: 129–56.

Levitt, Peggy, and Mary C. Waters. 2002. *The Changing Face of Home: The Transnational Lives of the Second Generation*. New York: Russell Sage Foundation.

Lowe, Lisa. 1996. *Immigrant Acts: On Asian American Cultural Politics*. Durham, NC: Duke University Press.

Mandel, Ruth. 2008. *Cosmopolitan Anxieties: Turkish Challenges to Citizenship and Belonging in Germany*. Durham, NC: Duke University Press.

Margolis, Maxine. 1994. *Little Brazil: An Ethnography of Brazilian Immigrants in New York City*. Princeton, NJ: Princeton University Press.

Ong, Aihwa. 1996. Cultural Citizenship as Subject-Making: Immigrants Negotiate Racial and Cultural Boundaries in the US. *Current Anthropology* 37 (5): 737–62.

Pessar, Patricia. 1999. Engendering Migration Studies: The Case of New Immigrants in the United States. *American Behavioral Scientist* 42 (4): 577–600.

———. 2003. Anthropology and the Engendering of Migration Studies. In *American Arrivals: Anthropology Engages the New Immigration*, Nancy Foner, ed., pp. 75–98. Santa Fe, NM: School of American Research Press.

———. 2007. Gender and Family. In *The New Americans: A Guide to Immigration since 1965*, Mary C. Waters and Reed Ueda, eds., pp. 258–69. Cambridge, MA: Harvard University Press.

Portes, Alejandro (ed.). 1996. *The New Second Generation*. New York: Russell Sage Foundation.

Portes, Alejandro, and Rubén G. Rumbaut. 2001. *Legacies: The Story of the Immigrant Second Generation*. Berkeley: University of California Press; New York: Russell Sage Foundation.

Portes, Alejandro and Min Zhou. 1993 The New Second Generation: Segmented Assimilation and Its Variants. *Annals of the American Academy of Political and Social Science* 530: 74–96.

Rosaldo, Renato. 2004. Cultural Citizenship and Educational Democracy. *Cultural Anthropology* 9 (3): 402–11.

Shankhar, Shalini. 2008. *Desi Land: Teen Culture, Class, and Success in Silicon Valley*. Durham, NC: Duke University Press.

Vertovec, Steven. 2009 *Transnationalism*. Oxford: Routledge.

Waquant, Loic. 2009. *Punishing the Poor: The Neoliberal Government of Social Insecurity.* Durham, NC: Duke University Press.

Waters, Mary C., and Tomas R. Jimenez. 2005. Assessing Immigrant Assimilation: New Empirical and Theoretical Challenges. *Annual Review of Sociology* 31: 105–25.

Werbner, Pnina, and Tariq Modood. 1997. *Debating Cultural Hybridity: Multi-cultural Identities and the Politics of Anti-racism.* London: Zed Books.

Zhou, Min. 1997. Segmented Assimilation: Issues, Controversies and Recent Research. *International Migration Review* 31 (4): 975–1008.

CONTRIBUTORS

Caroline B. Brettell is University Distinguished Professor at Southern Methodist University and a member of the faculty of the Department of Anthropology. She has served as director of Women's Studies (1989–1994), chair of the Department of Anthropology (1994–2004), and interim dean of Dedman College (2006–2008). She has written extensively on problems of international migration in general, and on aspects of US and Portuguese emigration in particular. Her most recent books are *Civic Engagements: The Citizenship Practices of Indian and Vietnamese Immigrants* (with Deborah Reed-Danahay); *Gender in Cross-Cultural Perspective* (sixth edition; coedited with Carolyn Sargent); *Citizenship, Immigration and Belonging: Immigrants in Europe and the United States* (coedited with Deborah Reed-Danahay); and *Twenty-First Century Gateways: Immigrant Incorporation in Suburban America* (coedited with Audrey Singer and Susan W. Hardwick).

Ana Gherghel is a researcher at the Centre for Research on Community Services, the Centre for Research on the Adaptation of Youth and Families at Risk at Laval University, in Montreal, Quebec. She received her PhD in sociology and post-doctoral research experience in migration studies. Her research focuses on migrant families, life course, family transitions, and family solidarities at distance.

Lisa Haayen received her PhD in the Department of Anthropology at Southern Methodist University, in Dallas, Texas. Her research interests include migration, the second-generation children of immigrants, and the ways these youth and their immigrant parents engage with schools and other civic organizations in their receiving communities. She is currently the Director of Marketing and Community Relations for CitizenD, a nonprofit organization in Dallas, Texas. She has worked as a visiting professor at the University of North Texas, and she is an active teacher of English as a second language within the largely immigrant neighborhood of Vickery Meadow, where her current research is being conducted.

Linda Ho Peché received her PhD in anthropology at the University of Texas at Austin in 2013. Her research interests include diaspora, transnationalism, migration, cultural citizenship, race, gender, heritage politics, cultural memory, and material religion. She teaches courses on cultural anthropology, ethnography, and Asian American studies, most recently for the Center for Asian Studies at Rice University.

Her recent publications have focused on issues among the second generation, including "I'd Pay Homage, Not Go 'All Bling': Race, Religion and Vietnamese American Youth" in an anthology titled *Sustaining Faith Traditions: Race, Ethnicity, and Religion among the Latino and Asian American Second Generation* (2012).

Louise Lamphere has been Distinguished Professor of anthropology at the University of New Mexico since 2001. She was a faculty member at UNM from 1976 to 1979 and again from 1986 to 2009, when she became a professor emeritus. Lamphere received her PhD from Harvard in 1968. She has published extensively throughout her career on subjects as diverse as children of migrants; the Navajo and their medicinal practices; and deindustrialization and urban anthropology. She is possibly best known for her work on feminist anthropology and gender issues. Lamphere was the coeditor, with Michele Zimbalist Rosaldo, of *Woman, Culture, and Society*, the first volume to address the anthropological study of gender and women's status.

Stéphanie Larchanché is a medical anthropologist whose work focuses on immigrant health. More specifically, her research examines the interaction between immigration politics, social representations of immigrants, and the management of West African families in health care institutions in France. She currently holds a postdoctoral position at IRIS-EHESS, and coordinates the research and training department of a mental health care institution catering to immigrants and refugees in Paris.

Josiane Le Gall holds a doctoral degree in anthropology and is currently a researcher with the Health and Social Services Centre (CSSS) of de la Montagne and an associate professor with the Social Services School of the University of Montreal. Her research focuses on family relationships (local and transnational) in the migratory context and on issues related to the interface between immigrant families and the health network. She currently serves as a member on several University of Montreal research groups, including Urban Diversity and Migration and Ethnicity in Health Interventions and Social Services, and at the Centre for Ethnic Studies.

Erin Moran is an assistant professor of anthropology and geographical sciences at Pierce College. She received her PhD in cultural anthropology from the University of California, Irvine in 2012. Her doctoral dissertation, entitled "Geographies of Belonging: Mapping Migrant Imaginaries in Ireland's Ailing Celtic Tiger," was the result of over fifteen months of fieldwork in Dublin, Ireland (supported by the National Science Foundation). Her research explores the way that legal categories (particularly citizenship) shape the subjectivity, the everyday practices, and the ongoing contests over social and political belonging between natives and nonnatives.

Faith G. Nibbs is the founding director of the Forced Migration Upward Mobility Project in Arlington, Texas. Her research focuses on the anthropological understanding of diasporic refugee communities, livelihood innovations, and how long-term transnational involvement and incorporation into local host societies coexist. She has published on US and European immigrant issues (*International Migration, Identities, Hmong Studies Journal*); is the author of the monograph *Belonging: The Social Dynamics of Fitting In as Experienced by Hong Refugees in Germany and Texas* (Carolina Academic Press); and has done public and academic speaking on topics of immigrant integration in the United States, Germany, the Netherlands, Belgium, China, and elsewhere.

Bruno Riccio holds a doctoral degree in social anthropology (Sussex) and is associate professor of cultural anthropology at the University of Bologna, where he teaches cultural anthropology and anthropology of migration. He is on the editorial boards of *Afriche e Orienti, Mondi Migranti,* and the *Anthropological Journal of European Cultures.* He has published extensively in edited books and scientific journals (*Modern Italy; Journal of Ethnic and Migration Studies; Population Space and Place; Stichproben/ViennaJournal of African Studies; Cahiers d'Études Africaines; African Diaspora;* and *Journal of Modern Italian Studies*), and he is the editor of books and special issues on the broad areas of West African transnational migration, hometown associations and codevelopment, citizenship, politics and policies of multiculturalism, translocal and multisited ethnography, urban everyday racisms and cosmopolitanisms. He has recently coedited *Transnational Migration and Dislocated Borders* (2010) and *Disasters, Development and Humanitarian Aid* (2011).

Takeyuki (Gaku) Tsuda is a professor of anthropology in the School of Human Evolution and Social Change at Arizona State University. After receiving his PhD in anthropology in 1997 from the University of California at Berkeley, he was a collegiate assistant professor at the University of Chicago and then served as associate director of the Center for Comparative Immigration Studies at the University of California at San Diego. His primary academic interests include international migration, diasporas, ethnic minorities, ethnic and national identity, transnationalism and globalization, ethnic return migrants, and the Japanese diaspora in the Americas. He is the author of *Strangers in the Ethnic Homeland: Japanese Brazilian Return Migration in Transnational Perspective* (2003). He is also the editor of *Diasporic Homecomings: Ethnic Return Migration in Comparative Perspective* (2009) and *Local Citizenship in Recent Countries of Immigration: Japan in Comparative Perspective* (2006) and coeditor of *Controlling Immigration: A Global Perspective* (second edition, 2004).

INDEX

www.ingramcontent.com/pod-product-compliance
Lightning Source LLC
Chambersburg PA
CBHW080418270326
41929CB00018B/3074